Books by Thom S. Rainer

Simple Life (coauthor)
Essential Church (coauthor)
Vibrant Church (coauthor)
Raising Dad (coauthor)
Simple Church (coauthor)
The Unexpected Journey
Breakout Churches
The Unchurched Next Door
Surprising Insights from the Unchurched
Eating the Elephant (revised edition) (coauthor)
High Expectations
The EveryChurch Guide to Growth (coauthor)
The Bridger Generation
Effective Evangelistic Churches
The Church Growth Encyclopedia (coeditor)
Experiencing Personal Revival (coauthor)
Giant Awakenings
Biblical Standards for Evangelists (coauthor)
Eating the Elephant
The Book of Church Growth
Evangelism in the Twenty-first Century (editor)

Books by Art Rainer

Simple Life (coauthor)
Raising Dad (coauthor)

TIME

RELATIONSHIPS

MONEY

GOD

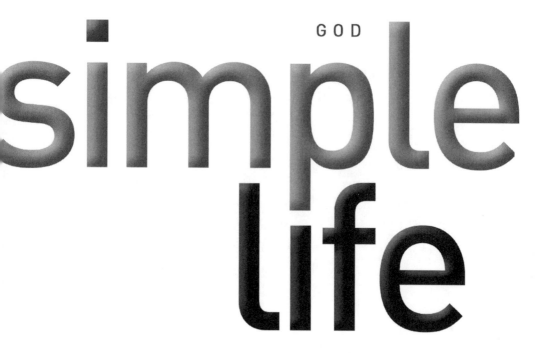

simple
life

THOM S. RAINER & ART RAINER

B&H
PUBLISHING GROUP
Nashville, Tennessee

978-0-8054-4886-3

Published by B&H Publishing Group and
LifeWay Research, Nashville, Tennessee

Dewey Decimal Classification: 248.4
Subject Heading: QUALITY OF LIFE \ STRESS
MANAGEMENT \ LIFE SKILLS

Persons depicted in this book were part of a survey of
1,077 people and other interviews by the authors. In some
cases several responses were combined to create composite
accounts based on the data of the study. No actual names of
the respondents are used in this book in order to protect their
identities and confidential life circumstances.

1 2 3 4 5 6 7 8 9 10 • 13 12 11 10 09

Dedication

From Thom

To Nellie Jo, my bride of thirty-two years. Your life and love have always been focused on those things that really matter. I yearn to emulate your God-given passion for the simple life. I love you so very much.

To my grandson who will be born one month after this book is released. I don't yet know your name, but I do know I love you with all my heart.

From Art

To A. C. King, the man for whom I am named, the man I call Granddaddy. The influence of your simple life stretches well beyond the farms of rural Alabama. Thank you. I love you.

To Sarah, my beautiful wife. Thank you for loving a work-in-progress husband like me. I need you. I love you.

Contents

Part 3: Simple Life: How to Simplify and Build Healthy Finances

Part 4: Simple Life: How to Get Closer to God

Acknowledgments

From Thom

Grace is an amazing thing.

I speak first, of course, of the love of God given to me through His Son Jesus Christ. But grace continues to flow into my life.

There is the immeasurable love that I have for my bride of thirty-two years, Nellie Jo. And then there is the act of grace where she loves me as well. I don't deserve it. I didn't earn it. Her love for me is truly an amazing thing.

Then came my three sons. There is Art, the coauthor of this book, then Sam and Jess. I love those boys so much. And now to have the opportunity to be a part of their lives as grown men is an incredible measure of grace. I never take it for granted. These boys gave me three wonderful daughters-in-law. Sarah, Erin, and Rachel have added so much to my life. Grace yet again.

It is another measure of grace that I am able to do speaking engagements with my sons and to write books with them. This book is yet another example of the underserved blessings I have received. As I read Art's words and wrote my own for *Simple Life*, I realized what an incredible opportunity this is. I am continuing to be invested in my sons' lives. I continue to have almost daily conversations with them. I continue to partner with them in other endeavors. I do not deserve this, but I treasure it greatly.

I must thank those men and women who were a part of this study. There are more than one thousand of you, and each of you contributed significantly to the research and the book. We heard you. We heard your cries. We heard your expressions of pain. And we heard your dreams and hope. Thank you for your time, your transparency, and your forthrightness. Art and I learned much from you.

Though Art and I expressed our thanks jointly to LifeWay and the B&H team, I must say a personal word as well. LifeWay is an incredible place. The joy, commitment, and sacrifice of the LifeWay family are something to behold. I am humbled to be the leader of LifeWay. And I am honored to work alongside some of the finest men and women I have ever known. Stacy Edwards deserves many accolades for her help in this book, specifically, and for her wonderful service as executive assistant to the president. Now, with a third child on the way, Stacy has made the decision to be fully employed as a stay-at-home mom. I understand your decision Stacy; I even admire it. But that doesn't mean I have to like it! You will be missed.

Finally, to the readers of *Simple Life*: thank you for your investment in reading this book. Some of you told me that you have read every book I have written. That is hard for me to imagine. I pray that this book will be used of God to make a difference, to help you simplify, to move you even more to focus on that which really matters. You are a blessing to me. And your willingness to read this book is yet another measure of the grace I receive but don't deserve.

Yes, grace is an amazing thing.

May you experience blessings and grace as you move toward the simple life.

From Art

A married man cannot write without the full support of his wife. Writing is an enjoyable feat that can take precious time away from loved ones. To write well, a man's wife must demonstrate what the Bible calls the fruit of the Spirit: love, joy, peace, patience, kindness, goodness, faith, gentleness, and self-control. Fortunately God gave me such a woman. Sarah is an amazing person who daily rocks my world. She is smart, beautiful, and loves Jesus. Sarah is a constant encouragement. She believes in me, which in turn, helps me to believe in myself. After a day of writing, I close my laptop and know that she is there, waiting for me, loving me. Within three years of marriage, Sarah has seen me through two books. Neither one would have been possible without a wife like her.

Even more important than the combined genetic makeup, I am blessed to be under the influence of my parents, Thom and Nellie Jo. I say this in present tense on purpose. Their roles in my life are in a constant evolution that gets more meaningful with each passing year. I value my dad's wisdom and constant support in my career and life. I cherish my mom's consistent encouragement. She has been a fan of mine all my life. And I am a fan of her. Both have played the role of parent well. Both have now become much more than a parent.

I have good in-laws. Really. From the moment I first walked into their kitchen beside their treasured daughter, Tom and Dale treated me like family. I am grateful for their love of my wife Sarah. I am grateful for their trust in me to take care of their precious girl. I enjoy seeing them. I enjoy spending time with them. I wish all could be blessed to have in-laws like Tom and Dale.

The journey that became *Simple Life* is embedded with influence. So many people, both the known and the unknown, played critical roles in the development of this book. Their participation, stories, encouragement, and love remain an inspiration, even until this day. We can only hope that this book, and its place in the lives of our readers, will be enough to say, "Thank you."

From Thom and Art

We cannot express adequately our gratitude to the B&H team. Beginning with the superb leadership and vision of our editor, Tom Walters, to the incredible team that made this book a reality: thank you. Those words seem so small. But we mean it with all of our hearts. LifeWay Christian Resources in general and B&H Publishing Group specifically represent some of the most incredible people on the planet.

The two of us sometimes refer to this book as a "God thing." We don't mean to be irreverent. We are simply recognizing that all credit and glory goes to our God for this book becoming a reality. We pray that readers' lives will be changed and blessed as a result. And when that happens, we know that it will be a work of His hands and not our own.

Thank you to all the readers for joining us on the journey toward simplicity. We do not know you by name, but we have already prayed for you.

And now, welcome to *Simple Life*.

Simple Life

You're probably too busy to read this book.

Yet for some reason you now have it in your hand. Perhaps the title intrigued you. Perhaps you've read other books we've written. Or perhaps you know that your life is not exactly the way you would like it to be. You are over-committed, overstressed, and underfunded.

You are looking for a better life: the simple life. You are not alone.

We have had the incredible opportunity to listen to more than one thousand people across America. They come from every geographic area, represent a diversity of races and ethnic groups, cross the age spectrum, and are nearly equally divided by gender.

Their stories are different, but at the same time they have similar concerns. Life is stressful. Life is busy. They don't have enough time for the things that really matter. And, most of the time, they feel financially stressed.

Jesus said, "I have come that they may have life and have it in abundance" (John 10:10). Yeah, right. Some of you may feel like you're barely hanging on. You would settle for just a mediocre life if you could get matters in some semblance of order. The abundant life seems to be a fantasy.

The apostle Paul said, "Rejoice in the Lord always. I will say it again: Rejoice!" (Phil. 4:4). You may roll your eyes at that verse. We heard from hundreds of people for whom joy had no reality in their lives. One of the respondents, a single mom who was forty-two years old, made her point powerfully: "I wish I knew how to have joy in my life. I am just trying to survive each day."

You probably have noticed that we are using Scripture quotations early in this book. We need to state our biases up front. We are both evangelical Christians. We believe that Jesus is the only way (John 14:6). We believe the Bible is the Word of God.

But, in this massive national study of how people saw and assessed their own lives, we heard from both Christians and non-Christians. Slightly more than one of five respondents is not a Christian, and even more are not evangelical Christians. We wanted to see if the perspectives on life were significantly different for the groups. We think you will be surprised at some of the responses. We were.

Our thesis is simple. We were not created to have miserable and joyless lives. We were created to have abundant and joyful lives. But for most of us, such a life is elusive at best and seemingly impossible at worst. The two of us have listened to thousands of hours of interviews. We have heard the cries and, sometimes, the desperation.

For those who struggle we present the simple life. But first, let us hear from someone for whom life is anything but simple.

The Not-So-Simple Life

Maryanne is thirty-seven years old. She is married to Jeff, whom she met in college. They have two children at home: Franklin is eleven and Beth is nine. They live in one of the many suburbs of the Dallas/Fort Worth metroplex.

"I don't guess I should complain," Maryanne began. "I am blessed with a great family, and we do have our basic needs met. But, I have to admit, life is not very happy these days."

"Why?" we asked.

"You know the old cliché, 'You need to stop and smell the roses,'" she said. We nodded in affirmation. "Well, I am so busy and so worried I don't even know where the roses are," she laughed hesitatingly. "I have a decent job, a middle management HR position for a large company. The pay is steady but not great." Maryanne paused for a moment. She was measuring her words carefully.

"Jeff," she began slowly, "has not had the steady income that I have. He is a salesman for a local auto dealership. He's a good salesman, but the commissions are unpredictable. And the economy has not been that good for sales lately. We've had some pretty tough arguments over our finances lately. And I admit that I've been the one who has started most of the arguments."

We listened as she continued a familiar story.

"I also carry a tremendous amount of guilt about my role as a mom and a wife. I have to commute an hour and a half each day. When I get home, I am exhausted. I really don't give the kids the time they need. And Jeff complains that I have no time for him for . . . well, you know."

We understood.

Tears began to well in Maryanne's eyes. "I can't believe I'm telling you guys this. It just seems that life is such a mess. It's a blur. I wish I could snap my fingers and everything would slow down."

At this point we were hesitant to ask further questions at the risk that we were piling on. So we asked the question with a bit of reservation, "Are you a Christian?"

"Wow, you guys are really sending me on a guilt trip." Her comment was terse, but she didn't seem angry. "Yes, I am a Christian. In fact, when Jeff and I first married, we were active in church. And I know that I should be taking Franklin and Beth to church. I know how important it was for me to be in church when I was a child."

Maryanne paused for a moment. "I guess if I just face reality, I have to say that I don't have time for God. I don't go to church. I don't encourage my family to be in church. My prayer life hardly exists, and I can't remember the last time I read the Bible."

We changed the topic to avoid further discomfort. But when we turned to the topic of finances, Maryanne's demeanor was no better.

"I told you that was a sore subject in my marriage." There was tension in her voice. "I get paid twice a month, and almost one whole paycheck goes to pay our mortgage. Jeff convinces me that we can put other expenses on credit cards until he gets a commission check. Well, those checks are slow in coming, and they are never enough to cover the full balance. It keeps growing, and the interest charges keep mounting."

We obviously had opened a can of worms. Maryanne continued to talk with the decibels increasing.

"Jeff has no concept of saving. We have nothing set aside for the kids' college education, nothing set aside for future purchases, and nothing set aside for unexpected expenses. Nothing. Absolutely nothing. And he is considered self-employed but puts nothing aside for retirement. I don't put the maximum in my 401(k) because we need every penny just to pay our normal expenses. If we continue down this path, we will be paupers when we retire. Or we may never get to retire."

The interview was exhausting both for Maryanne and for us. We tried to wrap things up. But she had one last comment, a comment that was barely audible.

"I just wish my life would slow down. I just wish that somehow I could make my life simpler."

Maryanne's wish is what this book is about: a simpler life.

The Simple Revolution

Americans are rediscovering simple. At least they are aware that they need to rediscover simple. People are hungry for simple because the world has become so complex. The technology revolution has really become an overwhelming information revolution. We have access to more information, more products, more research, and more ideas than at any point in history.

We can plan an entire trip to another country with the punch of a few buttons. We can research the most complex topic without leaving our laptop. But the information revolution and the material abundance of Americans have made life more complex.

Thom Rainer and Eric Geiger wrote *Simple Church* a few years ago. They were amazed at the response. The book became one of the biggest best sellers ever in its genre. Why? Church leaders wanted simple. Church members wanted simple.

The more we saw the phenomenon of simple grow, the more we realized that the desire for simple is widespread. This book is being written on a MacBook Air instead of a PC. Why? Because Apple has discovered simple. We do all our Internet searches on Google. Why? Because it is so simple. We fly Southwest Airlines frequently. Why? Because booking, pricing, and travel are all so simple. And all of the wives in the Rainer family (four of them) received gift subscriptions to a single magazine. Its name? *Real Simple.*

But there is an overarching theme beyond the types of laptops we use, beyond the Internet search engines, beyond our travel plans, and beyond our reading preferences. We are searching for simple in our lives.

In the midst of the harried world of complexity, in the midst of uncontrollably complex lives, people want to find simple for their lives. They long for it, seek it, pay for it, and even dream of it. The simple-life revolution has begun.

As Christians, we are amazed at Jesus' earthly life. Despite the demands of the entire world on His life and time, Jesus found time to spend with His closest friends, His disciples. He found time to greet and hug little children. He found time to give one-on-one attention to those in need. And He found time to listen patiently to those who desperately needed someone to hear their deepest longings.

We know that we cannot replicate all that Jesus did, but we can pattern our lives after His. His life was many things, but it was clearly simple. He kept His focus and managed His time on what really mattered. And so should we.

The Study

We are not going to bore you here with all the details of the research we did for this book. At this point, however, we want to give you the framework for our study.

Our survey had forty-one questions that dealt with a plethora of life issues. The total number of respondents was 1,077. With a survey of this size, the margin of error is plus or minus 2.8 percentage points at the 95-percent confidence level. Okay, unless you are a statistical nerd, those numbers are meaningless. In simple terms it means that our survey is very accurate.

We focused our research on those who still had children living at home, but the overall research applies to almost any life situation. We learned that many, if not most, Americans are looking for the simple life.

The respondents were fairly equally divided by gender, 57 percent female and 43 percent male. The age, racial and ethnic backgrounds, family income, and geographic diversity were pretty much a snapshot of United States demographics.

While eight out of ten of those surveyed said they were Christians, there was a wide range of religious or church involvement and denominational affiliation. We asked certain qualifying questions to classify a person as an evangelical and a born-again Christian. Only 35 percent of the respondents were born-again Christians, and even fewer, 11 percent, were evangelical Christians. We will dig into the responses of each of these subgroups later in the book.

What did these people say needed to happen in their lives for greater fulfillment? Simple. They needed simple.

When we concluded our study of these 1,077 individuals, we learned that they needed simple in four areas:

1. **Time:** They wanted simple so they could have time for areas of their lives that really mattered.
2. **Relationships:** Without a doubt many of the respondents struggled with balance in relationships. The simple life for them meant having better and closer relationships with others.
3. **Money:** Financial strains were pervasive with many in this study. They longed for a simple life free of past-due bills, limited income, deficient savings, and increasing debt.
4. **God:** These people, above all, saw a big void in their relationship to God. They saw clearly that they were too busy for God. They needed a simpler life in order to get closer to God.

We realize that many readers may have a greater concern with one or two of the areas above rather than all four of them. Feel free to turn to the section where you see your greatest need. In this book you will see four words again and again: Clarity, Movement, Alignment, and Focus. You will see the words in this chapter and in the introduction of each section. We think these concepts are important, so let us be clear what we mean.

Clarity

Clarity means that you know where you are going.

Before you move closer to a simpler life, you need a blue-print of where you are going. Many of you may not know where to turn because you have not made a plan to go any-where. You need clarity.

We will challenge you in the first part of each section to develop a clear plan toward the simple life. We will call that the "Clarity Chapter."

- How do you plan on spending time on things that really matter?
- What is your plan for developing healthier relationships?
- How do you plan to get your finances in order?
- What is your plan for getting closer to God?

Clarity means that you have a plan and that the plan clearly states where you want to go. We will encourage you to write your own mission statement for each of the four areas: time, relationships, money, God. But don't leave those mission statements as inactive files on your computer. Make them the blueprint for the simple life.

We all know that we need clarity in these four areas, but most of the time we will not make a plan. Listen to the heartfelt cries of those we surveyed. You can hear their need for clarity.

- "I want to be able to spend more time with my child instead of working all the time and having him go to day care."
- "I would just love for kids to get along and quit fighting so we could have some peace in the house."
- "We really need a bigger apartment because we're very cramped here."

- "I wish we could manage our time better so we could spend weekends together."
- "I spend too much time taking everyone where they need to go when they need to be there."
- "I want a job that will satisfy all of our financial needs without taking time away from our family time."
- "We are constantly on the go due to our children's sporting events. Whether it's for practice, scrimmages, or games of multiple sports, we literally are gone from home almost every night of the week."
- "I wish we could pay off all our debt. It would take a lot of the stress off at home and allow us to spend more time together."
- "We all really need to be on the same page spiritually. Our relationship with God is an afterthought in our family."

We begin each of the sections with clarity. Simply stated, we help you see the path you need to travel. Many of those surveyed did not know where to begin. They need clarity, but there must be movement as well.

Movement

Congestion is rarely good. The word can take on different meanings, but few, if any, of them are good. *Congestion* means to be blocked up or to be too full of something. Congestion in the sinuses means you could have a headache or trouble breathing through your nostrils or you have a fever. None of those are good.

Congestion in traffic means that you aren't moving. Unless you planned well ahead, you are likely to be late. You get frustrated because too many automobiles are crammed into too few lanes on the highway.

Congestion is bad.

Congestion in life means you aren't making progress. You can have a clear plan of where you want to go, clarity, but you aren't moving toward the goal.

I (Thom) was forty pounds overweight for four years. The pounds crept on at the pace of about half a pound a month. It took almost seven years for the total weight gain of forty pounds to move me toward obesity, but it happened. Then I decided one day that I was going to lose the weight. I had clarity: lose forty pounds for greater health, stamina, and confidence.

But I stayed forty pounds overweight for four years. Why? Because I had no movement toward my goal. Wishing and hoping didn't get the job done.

Then one day I visited my youngest son, Jess, and his wife. He looked so slim and healthy, the best he had looked in years. I was both amazed and convicted. What had he done?

His response was simple. "Dad, Rachel (his wife) is cooking for me so I will eat healthier, and I am exercising regularly."

Hmmm. Eating healthy and exercise. What a novel idea!

Jess inspired me. I made commitments to eat better and exercise more. I removed the congestion. I had movement toward my goal. Today I am forty pounds lighter and feeling great.

In each of the "big four" areas of Time, Relationships, Money, and God, we will look at movement, how we remove the congestion to get where we need to go. But, for now, let us see some common elements in movement.

The first element is *intentionality*. We are sometimes asked how we write a book. We hate to admit it, but it is really simple. We decide that we are going to write a book, and then we begin researching and writing.

"No, wait a minute! We want to know the secret to book writing. Between the two of you, you have authored more than twenty books. Tell us the secret!"

Sorry, there is no rocket science here. We are just intentional. We act on our plan. Like Nike, we just do it.

After you have decided that you will make better use of your time, you act on your decision. You are intentional.

After you have decided that you have a purpose of better relationships, you act upon it. You are intentional.

You get the picture, don't you? The same is true for finances. And the same is true for getting closer to God. You are intentional.

Another key word is *incremental*. You don't try to conquer the world in a day. To add metaphor upon metaphor, how do you eat an elephant? One bite at a time. You create short-term steps. You have the clarity of where you want to go, but you don't try to arrive at your destination all at once.

We love the concept of Real Age. It started out as a book by a physician named Michael F. Roizen. Now it is a movement. The concept is simple (that word again!). Your biological age can be increased or decreased by many different factors. Those factors change your biological age to a real age.

For example, a thirty-five-year-old overweight man who smokes, never exercises, eats poorly, and has a family history of heart problems may have a real age of fifty-two. But a fifty-five-year-old man who takes care of himself physically and has no history of medical problems could have a real age of forty-eight. So the fifty-five-year-old man is physically younger than the thirty-five-year-old man.

Here is what we like about Real Age. You can go to the Web site www.RealAge.com and answer an hour's worth of questions, and it will give you your real age. Then it lets you know different steps you can take to become "younger."

Dr. Roizen is clear that you couldn't and shouldn't try to do everything at once. He advocates that you progress in steps. You may start with a mild exercise program. You may take a multivitamin. Or you may start eating healthier foods. You have literally dozens of choices, but you only take one or a few steps at a time.

You see, the Real Age experts know that if you try to do everything at once, you will become frustrated and give up.

That's the way it is with the simple life. Movement means you are intentional and you take incremental steps. You won't give up. You eat that elephant one bite at a time.

Now we have the clarity, our clear purpose toward simple. And then we have movement, how we will move from the complex life to the simple life. The next goal is alignment.

Alignment

You know the feeling. You are driving seventy miles per hour down the interstate. The road is flat and the surface is smooth. There are few curves; most of the interstate looks at you straight ahead. You can relax your hands from the steering wheel and the vehicle should handle fine.

So you let go for just a second. The car begins to veer to the right. You grab the steering wheel again.

In a few days your car is so badly out of alignment that you find yourself fighting to hold the vehicle steady. You can't put it off any longer. The wheels need alignment.

Since you are reading this book, there is a likelihood that your life is not in alignment. You are fighting the road. Something's wrong.

As we delve into the tough issues of moving toward the simple life, we look at areas where we go wrong, where our lives are out of line. And, most of the time, it only takes one small misstep to evolve into a major problem. Do you remember Thom's story of his forty-pound weight gain? He only gained half a pound a month. But in seven years he was obese.

According to the math of calories, he only overate the equivalent of one small piece of bread a day. But that small amount became a large amount over seven years.

Most people don't develop debt problems overnight.

Most Christians don't stop attending church suddenly.

Most relationships don't fail over one incident.

Most people don't become workaholics in one day.

Instead, their lives get out of alignment. It usually begins small. But it doesn't remain small.

We will share with you why the best of intentions get thwarted. In fact, we will let you listen collectively to more than one thousand people who shared their stories with us.

So you state clearly where you want to go (clarity). You begin to make incremental steps in the right direction (movement). You look at bad habits and problems that are interfering with your progress (alignment). Then you eliminate some good stuff.

Huh?

Yep, you read right. You eliminate some good stuff.

You see, it is one thing to get those bad habits and problems out of the way. But it is another thing to stop doing some good things. We call this last phase *focus*.

Focus

The year was 1985. I (Thom) was a student in seminary. My three sons were preschool age. Art, the coauthor of this book, was three years old.

My studies at seminary consumed about forty hours each week, including fifteen hours in the classroom. I also served as the pastor of a small church and gave that church at least twenty hours a week.

Oh, the church paid me $50 a week. My wife, who was a stay-at-home mom, suggested that I find additional income. I listened to my wife.

I took a job at a bank where I had to work a minimum of thirty hours a week. And I almost lost my family and my sanity.

Can you name the bad things I was doing? Studying for the ministry? Serving as pastor of a rural church? Working at a bank to provide for my family?

But I almost lost my family and my sanity.

Many of the problems we heard in this study were not always the result of people doing bad things. Instead they were doing too many things, none of which by themselves were bad.

We looked at the lives of those who graciously participated in the study, and we saw many good intentions. We saw too many good intentions. We saw families take on activity after activity. We saw work lives that became workaholism. We saw the good become the bad because there was just too much of the good.

The simple life demands that we focus.

The apostle Paul said in Philippians 3:13–14, "But one thing I do: forgetting what is behind and reaching forward to what is ahead, I pursue as my goal the prize promised by God's heavenly call in Christ Jesus." One thing was Paul's focus: The goal of Christlikeness compelled him to move forward in his spiritual journey. In fact, for Paul, everything else was filth compared to this one thing (Phil. 3:8).

The simple life means that we eliminate some things in our life. It means that we have to make some tough decisions. In fact, focus may well be the toughest step toward the simple life. But it is absolutely necessary.

The intuitive sense of the MacBook Air is incredible. We are truly fans of Apple and the company it has become. Apple excels in simplicity because they are focused. Steve Jobs, the leader of the company, said he is "as proud of the things they have not done as he is of the things they have done."

Did you catch that?

He is excited because Apple said no. The company has made some tough choices, and they are better for it. They have focus.

Clarity. Movement. Alignment. Focus.

With these four you head toward the simple life.

Our Prayer for the Simple Life

This book was a tough project. Not because the research was daunting. Not because the writing was laborious, but because we heard so much pain. Because we heard about so many lives out of control. Because we heard cries of despair and voices of hopelessness.

Still we believe there is hope. We believe that the messed-up and complex life can become the simple life. We do not despair. And we want you to join us as we win and celebrate victories toward the simple life.

To that end we have prayed for you, the reader. We don't know you by name, but we know that the God to whom we pray knows everything about you. And by His power you can see despair become hope and confusion become simple.

Join us for the journey.

Join us for the victory.

Welcome to the simple life.

PART 1

Simple Life: How to Make Your Time Really Count

CHAPTER 1

I Want to Spend More Time Doing Things That Matter

CLARITY → Movement → Alignment → Focus

(Art) read grave markers:

"Automatic Angel"

"Beloved Wife, Mother, Grandmother, and Great-Grandmother"

"Our Sweetheart"

"The music may be stilled, but the memory remains"

"Forever in our hearts"

"All things come and go yet you remain in our hearts"

Undoubtedly the engravings provide some comfort to those still living. Maybe it just helped give closure. Maybe they felt like their dead could somehow sense that they were missed. Maybe it was one last act to show love. Maybe they wanted others, like me, to see that underneath the sod lay a body that was once breathing, moving, and talking. Beneath the headstone was a body that was once alive, and when it was alive, it was something special to them.

Some markers still have blank spots, anticipating another's death. A wife who passed away was waiting for her husband's body to be laid next to her. Her time line was already engraved in the rock, but her husband was still increasing the number next to his dash. So her physical body waited.

I walked around for a little while, looking, thinking. I passed marker after marker. Each one represented a life that had come and gone. Each one placed there in memory of a human being that once walked this earth, an earth that you and I now walk.

I soon came across a granite marker with a bronze plate screwed into the stone. On the plate was molded the name "Arthur."

That's my name.

I stared at it for a while. This name represented another Arthur, but one day that same name on a stone will represent me. It will represent my body. It will represent my life, a life that will be over. I was looking at my physical end.

I had no relatives, no friends who were buried at this site. I knew of nobody beneath the ground on which I walked, and yet I had a connection with each one. They were my physical future; I was their physical past. This thing called life that I am experiencing, they have already experienced.

I came to this cemetery to gain perspective. When facing the topic of time, I could not think of a more inspirational location than to be surrounded by those whose earthly story had come to an end. If they could, what would they tell us? Now that their lives are over, what wisdom would they want to pass on? What were their regrets? Where did they get it right? Though the sands of time in my life's hourglass are still running for me, with every breath I breathe, I am moving toward my physical closure.

My body will become like theirs.

On each grave marker is a dash between two years. The dash is time, and that is where we are, in our dash. And before there is some year placed on the other end, we need to figure this whole time thing out. And it all starts with one day.

Humans at Risk

The value of time is not lost on our culture. We spend massive amounts of money developing new ways to increase the efficiency of our breathing moments on earth.

With each passing day our culture becomes more and more proficient in the ways that we can maximize time in our lives. We often joke that when we purchase a computer, the software is obsolete by the time we leave the store's doors. Because of the time-saving technology that has defined our generation, we are able to do more, learn more, and experience more in a lifetime than any of the generations that preceded us. And this is good. God created us with intellects to explore His world and do great things with it.

But we do have a problem. Our obsession with time has become unhealthy. It has permeated into areas of our lives that it should never have entered.

With good intentions we have gotten into the mind-set of "making the most out of our time." No one ever thought,

I am going to fill up my life with so many things that I feel like I can't even breathe. No, the thought probably sounded more like, *I think it would benefit my life if I did this.* And if it stopped there, it might be fine. But then we want something else, something more. We don't let go of the former and still pursue the other. After a few more "enrichments," our life is out of control.

Busyness has consumed us.

In our survey we were amazed to see that approximately 44 percent of respondents agreed that if their daily life continued at the current pace, they would probably have health problems. That number is alarming. And as frightening as it may sound, they are probably right. The stress of a go-go-go lifestyle has been linked to some of the following:

- heart disease
- obesity
- depression
- memory problems
- sleep disorders
- anxiety
- high blood pressure

Our obsession with time has come at a high cost. We are literally putting our lives at risk for the pursuit of personal gain.

Of course, not just our physical health is suffering. Our families are also impacted by the fallout of this problem. Some 57 percent of married survey respondents admitted that they rarely are able to go on a date with their spouses. Another 84 percent of the married respondents said they need to spend more time with their spouse.

Our children are inundated with activities. Little Billy is an athlete. Rarely does he have a season without practice after practice. Little Mary Lynn is a classroom superstar. Her free time is filled with math camps, band practice, and French club. By the way, she is also class president. Though we may not realize it, we are training our kids to be busy, to follow in our shortcomings. During the earliest stages of life, we are already molding their minds to sense that free time is wasted time.

If our children are most easily influenced during their childhood, and the most influential people in a child's life are their parents, what does that say about the impact of our lifestyle on our children?

Proverbs 22:6 says, "Teach a youth about the way he should go; even when he is old he will not depart from it." But what if our influence, our training, is wrong? Will they depart from it?

Somehow God, the giver of time, is being ignored. We are too busy for Him. Our children are too busy for Him.

We are hurting ourselves, our children, and others.

How long can this continue? How fast are we able to go until something gives, something falls apart? What will be the breaking point?

The faster an object goes, the more difficult it is to stop and the greater impact it will have when it hits something. As we become more and more inundated with activities, we will find it increasingly difficult to break away from the life we now live. And when something does finally give, the outcome can be disastrous. We've seen it on the highway: a car mangled on the side of the road. Before the wreck this car was moving at incredible speeds, getting to where it needed to be. But something happened; something made the driver lose control. Maybe something unexpected came in his path. Maybe he overcorrected. Whatever happened, the result is a mangled piece of metal. The speed of the car exaggerated the outcome. It was fast and powerful. So was the crash.

We are at risk. The frantic way in which we do life cannot be sustained. Something will come in our paths, something unexpected. And that something will cause a dramatic crash in our lives.

You already know this. You sense that you are at risk. You see that the ability to "have time" is dwindling in your life. Your day has become way too full.

And you don't want it that way. You want something different. Something more. And yet, something less. The simple life.

When More Becomes Less

One of the most powerful stories in the Bible about the allocation of time takes up five verses in Luke 10:38–42.

The story involves two sisters, Mary and Martha. Lazarus, Jesus' friend whom He will later raise from the dead, was their brother. Both sisters loved Jesus, but each demonstrated her love in her own way.

Jesus and His disciples had arrived in Bethany, Mary and Martha's town, and had decided to visit with them for a while. They willingly opened their home to Jesus and His disciples.

But the house wasn't ready for guests. They had not anticipated Jesus' arrival and were not prepared for company. There was much to be done, and it had to be done quickly while their guests waited.

The Bible tells us that Jesus was in the house conversing. As He spoke, Martha was frantically running around the house making preparations. The desire to please her unexpected company was causing her much stress. She wanted everything to be right.

This is an easy picture for me (Art) to imagine. Any time that we have guests, whether family or friends, my wife declares war on anything that remotely resembles dirtiness. The floor must be mopped, the carpet vacuumed, the counters scrubbed; the toilets must sparkle.

While Martha was busy trying to get the house prepared for their company, she looked and saw her sister just sitting at the feet of Jesus, listening to His words. She naturally became upset. How could Mary just sit there while she poured her all into making these guests feel welcome? How could she be so selfish? Did she not care about all that had to be done?

Heated, Martha approached Jesus and asked why He didn't care that Mary left her to do all of the work. "Lord, don't You care that my sister has left me to serve alone? So tell her to give me a hand" (v. 40).

Jesus saw Martha hard at work while Mary just sat and listened. But after she said this, I imagine Jesus looking at her with love in His eyes, a slight smile on His face, and shaking His head ever so gently. The Lord answered her, "Martha, Martha, you are worried and upset about many things, but one thing is necessary. Mary has made the right choice, and it will not be taken away from her" (vv. 41–42).

Martha was so busy that she missed what was most important. Her desires were good, but the outcome fell short. While she was frantically preparing for the feast of men, she was missing a feast for the heart.

Martha's more became less. Mary's less became more.

As Christians, we are to look at time differently. This life is literally a blip on the eternal time line. In fact, no example is sufficient to appropriately describe the brevity of our life. Because we live in a world in which time exists, we struggle to wrap our minds around the infinite. But we still know it's there, waiting on us.

If we could somehow grasp the concept of never-ending, then our time on this planet would be different. But we can't. We find it difficult to move beyond the day, much less the eternal. Ever since we took our first breath of air, we spend our energy figuring out how best to put together a day as if this is our eternity. We make choices based on the only time span that seems important, the blip.

We do know that our time, no matter how brief it may be, is highly important. We know that our life and what we do with it matters. We know that God set this whole thing in motion with a quick spin of the globe and He passionately watches over this place called Earth. He cares what happens to me and to you. He cares about what we do with the days and moments He has given us.

He cares about today. He cares about tomorrow. He cares about every single day. He doesn't want us to fret about today or tomorrow.

So here we are, temporarily fixed by time. We want to make the most of the day, but somehow that good desire has turned into a monster. We built our lives trying to accomplish much, trying to help our family succeed, but this grand structure of a life that we envisioned now suddenly seems somehow more like a prison. We are stressed, overwhelmed, and we want out.

Figuring Out Time

Evelyn sat on the other side of the desk and let out a deep sigh. "Jared and I are completely overwhelmed."

Evelyn, thirty-four, was married and had three children. Jared, her husband, was not there. It was tough for him to get out of work by this time.

Evelyn had recently taken a new job with the city's newspaper. It was a great opportunity that she felt couldn't be missed. She liked that it was viewed as more prestigious than her previous job, and the bump in salary definitely helped their financial situation. The job did require more hours during the week, but she figured that it would be okay. It was nothing compared to Jared's job.

"Every day we are swamped. From the time we try to get our kids ready for school until the time they finally fall asleep, life is nonstop. Our youngest just started his first year of T-ball, so now we have three children in three separate leagues. It is a logistical nightmare. I don't even want to think about when the baseball season starts overlapping with soccer. My youngest will, of course, be starting that as well. I don't know how we're going to do it."

Evelyn's children were active. Their appetite for sports was insatiable. If there was a ball involved, they wanted to play. Jared and Evelyn tried to hide hockey from them. There was a local league, but none of the neighborhood kids played in it so their children didn't know about it.

Jared and Evelyn hoped that it stayed that way.

"And, of course, it's not just the kids. They take after us. Jared and I are really dedicated to our careers. We have worked hard to get where we are today. The opportunities that have presented themselves are in large part due to the fact that we just outworked everyone else. We put in the time, and we get to reap the rewards. Thank God for day care!"

In a way she was joking. In a way she was not.

Evelyn had always tried to put a positive spin on their busy lives. The kids were developing, getting opportunities. Their own careers were progressing. But these good things had come at a cost. They were losing control.

She spoke with some seriousness: "I just need more time in a day. This whole twenty-four hours thing is not working out for me. There is no way I can get done all that I need to in one day and keep my sanity. You know those guys who are able to spin multiple plates on sticks without letting any of the plates fall. That's how I feel. For me life is a delicate balancing act. One wrong move and the plates come crashing down. You've just got to keep things spinning."

Evelyn was looking down, playing with her fingers. She seemed to be deep in thought, maybe reflecting on the life that she and her family lived. Maybe trying to figure out if there was another way to do things, a way to give her more freedom from her time vacuum.

"We do a lot, but we don't get to do all that we want to do. Honestly, outside of taking our kids to and from their activities, Jared and I don't really spend that much time with our children. And I miss the times when Jared and I would go out together, just the two of us. I miss dates. I couldn't tell you the last time we did something like that together."

She paused for a couple of seconds, and then said, "I'm getting kind of depressed thinking about this."

Her ability to make eye contact was gone. With her head slightly lowered, she gazed at the desk's surface in front of her.

"Everybody else seems to have it together. They seem happy. I often wonder if they feel as overwhelmed as me, like there is not enough time. I try to make sure that every day counts for me, for my family. I want to make the best use of my time, but this life is not right."

A slight, saddened smile came to her face. "I don't even know if I am making sense anymore. I'm sorry if I don't." She looked at her watch. "I've got to go. I'm sorry. I knew I would only be able to stay a few minutes. I have to pick up my oldest child from practice. Jared should be on his way to pick up the youngest."

She got up. "Thanks for listening. I hope you can figure out some way to help people like me. Good luck." And with a half-smile and a head nod, she was gone.

It's tough to figure out what we need to do with our time. Like Evelyn, we find ourselves wishing that God had created twenty-five-hour days instead of twenty-four just so we could get done what we feel is important. Of course, most of us would easily fill that extra hour and start desiring another after the first day. We are offered so many different options on what to do with our time.

Will we spend it on our career?

Will we spend it on our kids?

Will we spend it trying to better ourselves?

Will we spend it at church?

What about our relationships?

The only way to figure out what to do with your time is to get a grasp on your priorities in life. Of course, the current way you spend your time is a present reflection of your priorities.

Let's try an exercise. Reflect on a typical day. Maybe it was today. Maybe it was last week. Whatever day you choose, make sure it is representative of a normal day in your life.

Once you have picked that day, take a sheet of paper and make a list that represents a twenty-four-hour day. By each hour write down how you spent that hour. Was it getting ready for the day? Was it working? Was it taking the kids to their recital? You may need to give yourself enough space within each hour as many tasks probably didn't take a full hour. Maybe it will look something like this:

6:00 a.m.	Get ready for work (30 minutes)
6:30 a.m.	Get kids ready for school (30 minutes)
7:00 a.m.	Drop off kids and fight traffic (1.5 hours)
8:30 a.m.	Work (8 hours)
12:00	Lunch (1 hour)
5:30 p.m.	Overtime work (1 hour)
6:30 p.m.	Fight traffic, kids picked up by spouse, get fast food for dinner (1 hour)
7:30 p.m.	Eat dinner (15 minutes)
7:45 p.m.	Help with homework (1 hour)
8:45 p.m.	Put kids to bed (30 minutes)
9:15 p.m.	Set out clothes for next day (15 minutes)
9:30 p.m.	Watch news (30 minutes)
10:00 p.m.	Go to bed

After you have done this, go back and look at your list. If you have a job, cross out eight hours of work. Now what does that day reveal about your priorities in life? Where are you spending most of your time? What defines your day?

If you are like most, your priorities aren't where you desire them to be. Your heart yearns for that day to read differently. And that's good.

We were created to live differently. That yearning is your desire to live your life as you were meant to live it, to have your life reflect its proper priorities.

Grab another sheet of paper. Jot down what you consider, even if your day does not reflect it, to be the priorities in your life. What do you think deserves the most attention in your day? It might look something like this:

1. God
2. Family
3. Health
4. Friends
5. Work

You now have in front of you two lists: one that shows your typical day, the other that tells you what you want the priorities in your life to be.

This is how we figure out time. We try to rearrange our daily life in a way that reflects the priorities of our heart. When you compare your day to the list of priorities, there should be a similarity between the two. Your typical day should be an outflow of that which is beating inside of you.

Of course, we all know that it is much easier to say than to do.

Creating the Mark

When we look at our typical day and compare our heart's priorities, more than likely we will see a difference. Though our heart longs to have its priorities lived out in our lives, we somehow mentally justify other activities as, for the time being, more important and push aside our heart's desires.

During each of the clarity chapters, we ask you to create mission statements that will guide you in your journey to a more simple life. This mission statement will allow you to gauge and understand the decisions you must make in order to progress from clarity to movement to alignment to focus, and, ultimately, to a more simple life.

Unlike our days the mission statement must be clear and concise. This is to add clarity, not add to the already complex day.

Remember, this statement must come with the intention to see it in action. If your heart is not behind it, then change in this area of your life will become stymied. You will ultimately write down the priorities you desire your day to reflect. Your mission statement should be an expression of those priorities.

Keep the plans real. If the mission statement contains abstract aspirations, measurement becomes difficult, success becomes subjective, and true change may not occur. Sliding back into your former ways of handling your day becomes far too easy. Tangibility is important.

Let's say that Evelyn decided to sit down and record her typical day. She then reflected on what she thought should be her priorities in life. She wrote those down and ranked them. Because Evelyn was in a rush, she only came up with three:

1. God
2. Family
3. Health

Hopefully yours will have greater depth.

She compared the two lists. They were not the same. Her day told a different story from her heart. Like many of us, Evelyn realized that the life she was living was causing dissatisfaction in her heart. So she decided that she needed to make some modifications. She wrote down her statement of change:

In order to make the day reflect my priorities, I will only work a maximum of two hours overtime per week, spend thirty minutes daily reading the Bible and praying, only allow my children to play two sports per year, and have one date with my husband per week.

Evelyn was willing to make some pretty large commitments in order to transform her daily life. And this will probably be common for most of us. Evelyn figured that if she worked a little less and cut back on her children's activities, she might be able to spend more time gaining a deeper, genuine relationship with both God and her family. She might be able to live life beyond the constant hustle that surrounded her.

Note: Hold on to your written schedule, priorities, and mission statement since they will be used later.

You First

Simplifying time is about adjusting the way you do life. It is about understanding what is most important to you and then allowing your actions to flesh it out. In the upcoming chapters we will look at areas in your life that might need some tweaking. And almost inevitably you are not going to be the only one affected by your decisions. When you adjust your life, others will be impacted.

Normally those who are impacted most are those who are closest. Sometimes an agreement by another is needed to allow this change to occur. Going back to Evelyn, two of her commitments will require her husband's involvement. Both parents should be on the same page when determining their children's level of participation in activities and, of course, without Jared's agreeing to set aside time for a weekly date, there is no date. If you do have people who will be impacted by your new way of doing life, it's best to sit down and talk it over. Have the other person do his own personal statement. Make sure that as you both try to live out your mission statement, the other's statement will be a catalyst and not a deterrent for both of you to succeed.

Hopefully Jared concurs with Evelyn that some modifications are needed, but there is always a chance he won't. And there is a chance that someone may hinder you from being able to live out your mission statement.

Don't get frustrated. Just do what you can do first. In life, some circumstances are always beyond our control. Some people don't share your feelings. Some people do not share your values.

We cannot change hearts. We cannot make our values their values. However, God is in control of all things, including hearts. When confronted with a situation that pauses your progress, do what you can do and pray.

For Evelyn, this means that no matter what Jared's response is, she can at least spend the thirty minutes reading the Bible and praying and still work no more that two hours overtime. The rest is left in prayer. She will still work hard at pursuing the other goals but at the same time realize that her plans are in God's hands.

The Launch

Pastor Larry Thompson of First Baptist Church, Fort Lauderdale, Florida, told about the time he visited the Kennedy Space Center. He had a friend who had previously worked for NASA and had given him a personal tour. On his visit to the space center, he noticed the massive fuel tanks on the shuttles. When he asked about them, his friend said that almost 80 percent of the fuel held in those tanks was used in the first couple of minutes during launch. Once the shuttle was in orbit, much less fuel was required as the shuttle became easier to control and direct.

Pastor Thompson made a quick connection to any difficult task to which we decide to commit ourselves. Most of the energy is used at launch. Getting over that initial struggle prevents most people from ever accomplishing their goals. We get frustrated and discouraged. We question why we are doing this, and we give up before we even get off the ground. Expect resistance. Expect difficulty. But also expect God.

As you develop clarity for your time, realize that God wants the best for you and wants to see you succeed in making this part of your life simpler. Time was meant to be a blessing, not a burden. Each breath we are given is a gift from God. Reliance on Him is essential to moving you beyond the launch and into orbit where everything begins to operate a little more easily.

Redoing how you appropriate your time will be difficult. For many, massive changes need to be made. These changes will impact you, your family, and your friends. But we cannot let go of our mission. The end result is too sweet. A happier, more fulfilling, and less hectic life lies ahead. We replace an eventual burnout with newfound richness. As we turn to the next chapter, let's move forward with determination to change our living days so that the dash on our gravestone will not be in vain.

APPLICATION
SIMPLE LIFE: CLARITY
A MISSION STATEMENT ABOUT TIME

Take a moment to think about a mission statement on time. Before you write it below, look at the mission statement written by Evelyn in this chapter. Rewrite it here:

Now think about your own priorities and write your mission statement here:

_____

_____

_____

_____

_____

_____

_____

_____

_____

Read Luke 10:38–42. Are you more like Mary or Martha? Would your mission statement be more like Mary's or Martha's? Why?

_____

_____

_____

_____

_____

_____

_____

CHAPTER 2

The Barriers of Time

Clarity → MOVEMENT → Alignment → Focus

He carefully walked into the office. His steps were short, clearly trying to avoid the pain that had accumulated in his aging, eighty-three-year-old body. As he took his seat, his trembling arms braced the slow decent into the chair. Once he had settled himself, he let out a soft sigh followed by a short pause. Then he spoke, "How are you doing today, son?"

I (Art) couldn't help but think that I should be asking him the same question.

"I'm fine, Mr. Bellevue. Thank you."

Though I knew his name, it was the first time I had spoken to him. He would come in and out of the office on a semiregular basis just to say "hi" to those whom he had previously met. He never actually came in to do any business. Of course, at his age, maybe this *was* his business.

"They told me that I would like you," smiled Mr. Bellevue.

I took this as a compliment since Mr. Bellevue clearly seemed to be a likable guy himself.

"Well, Mr. Bellevue, tell me about yourself," I said with a grin.

He chuckled and smiled in a way that made me think there was a kid inside that had never left. Though his head now only sprouted a few wild, sporadic gray hairs, I could tell that the mind underneath was still vigorously sharp.

"Well, where should I start?" he said, trying to rummage through eighty-three years of stories.

"Wherever you want," I replied.

He looked at me. "Are you a Christian?" he said with his finger lightly pointed at me. He obviously did not care whether this was or wasn't a proper question upon meeting someone in this era. I liked that.

"Yes, sir, I am," I said in acknowledgment.

"Good," he affirmed.

And with that an epic conversation began. As he told of his life's stories, I played the part of the quiet listener. My only interjection would include an occasional "man" or "wow."

Mr. Bellevue was not shy; he loved to talk. As a man who had been through the Great Depression and, of course, everything thereafter, he had much material from which to draw his memories. Each story he told vividly, as if it had happened just the other day.

"Let me tell you about the time when I had to play my guitar and sing on the street corner for tips. There were no jobs, and I needed money for milk and bread. I had to take care of my wife and new son. For some reason God allowed us to make it, even though I couldn't sing a lick."

Each story would be followed by a pause and a quick look down, obviously trying to think of which story to tell next.

As he moved through the time line of his life, he soon revealed that he had been a missionary for the majority of his life. He had felt God drawing him to Africa when he was in his twenties, and so he went. He had traveled that continent several times over, establishing churches, telling people about Jesus.

While listening to Mr. Bellevue, I began to recognize a common theme. The stories he told were not ones of great accomplishments, at least not on this planet. They were stories of deep, real struggles. His life had not been easy. But after every story he would smile and give credit to God for allowing him to survive and to have part in such an amazing journey.

Toward the end of our conversation, he disclosed that he was dying. He had contracted a common illness that, because of his age, his body was no longer able to fight.

I wanted to be sad for him, but I couldn't. He seemed to look forward to it.

In almost the same breath that he had told me about his impending death, he said, "I have been faithful to my God, and I wouldn't take it back for anything."

There was such passion in his eyes when he told me this.

He feebly shook my hand and left the office. He still had other people to meet, other people to whom he could tell his stories. His mission did not end when he left Africa and came back to the States. His mission would continue until he closed his eyes for the final time.

I wondered what he would have said had I not been a follower of Jesus.

As I sat there, a proverb came to mind: "Gray hair is a glorious crown; it is found in the way of righteousness" (Prov. 16:31).

That was Mr. Bellevue's verse. Through everything he said in our time together, that described him so well.

In our culture the potential contribution of the elderly is often sadly missed. Though we have much to learn from them, society often views older age as a liability, something we are supposed to avoid. But no matter how hard we try to circumvent the idea of growing old, we are left with the fact that time does not stop.

Whether we want it to speed up, slow down, or remain still, the clock does not give in. It only does what it is supposed to do: it keeps ticking.

If God allows, we will eventually get old. At some point our bodies and minds will begin to fail, and we will no longer be able to do the things we once did. All that we will have are our stories.

What will you talk about when you're eighty-three? What stories will you tell? What adventures will you want to share with those who are willing to sit down and listen? At that point in your life, you will have undoubtedly amassed a series of narratives. But what will they be about?

Something powerful happens when an eighty-three-year-old man says that he has been faithful and would not take back the years of his life. He is saying, "I don't regret the way I did life. I like the stories I am able to tell." What an intensely happy position to be in when you are knowingly nearing death and are satisfied with the priorities you chose to live out in your life.

Some things in our life make us lose perspective. Things get in the way and prevent us from creating the stories we would want to tell when we turn eighty-three. We sometimes hail them as necessary evils, knowing that they are not part of the life we want to live, but are a means by which we can achieve that life. But far too often, those evils never leave and to justify our continued involvement with these actions, we just start calling them necessary.

And life's congestion builds.

Moving Forward

Somewhere along our life's time line, our day became too congested. We filled up our days, weeks, and years with plans and commitments. Our lives now consist of a bunch of to-dos. We schedule everything out so that we can meet the demands of our busy lives, so that we do not lose one second and then think of ourselves as failures.

So we get to the point where so many, 44 percent of those in our survey, say that their current pace of life will likely lead to health problems. Or we join the 84 percent of the married persons surveyed who admit they spend too little time with their spouse.

When we created our mission statement in the previous chapter, we knew that we would encounter problems living it. We knew that "life" was going to get in the way. We knew that what we desired to do would not be easy to accomplish. But so goes every good thing worth pursuing.

Without giving it a second thought, you know that there are barriers preventing you from living out your mission statement. They probably came to mind almost instantaneously after the pen came up from the paper. The goals were dreams, and now we face reality. Staring at the goals, you might have even felt a little bit of uneasiness. You might have looked at your statement and thought that there was no way it could happen. And you might have already thought about giving up and giving in to the life you do not want.

Don't throw in the towel early. Expect hindrances in your path. Hindrances are what brought us to this point. The accumulation of those hindrances has caused us to want something different for ourselves, to pursue a different way of doing life.

When we decide to make the next step, to move beyond staring at our mission statement and actually putting it into action, we need to start clearing out any obstruction that might encumber our movement to a simple life.

Have you ever seen a stream that has been dammed up because of beavers or an accumulation of sediment? The stream's natural course gets altered. The water pools up before the dam and starts overflowing into the surrounding areas. The natural flow of the stream becomes chaotic. The water gets lost to areas where it was never meant to go and sometimes never finds its way back to the original course.

Like the dam of a stream, hindrances can cause us to get lost in the natural flow of our life's time. We become people that we never wanted to become, often unable to figure out how to get back to the life we desire. How did we get there? Only we know. But the removal of these obstructions is necessary to allow us to return to a course that allows us to accomplish our ambitions and become who we want to be.

Choices

Our lives are the culmination of our choices. We made them decades ago; we are still making them today. We weigh our different options and pursue the ones that, at the time, seem to be the better alternatives. Sometimes we look back on our decisions with satisfaction, and other times we view them with regret.

Some of us have the benefit of living in a nation that places the freedom of choice on the highest of pedestals. We are encouraged to make decisions for ourselves, to push the limits of our right to select. For those who enjoy this liberty, we are grateful. We know the power of choice, and it is a gift to be able to use that power freely.

You can't choose between chocolate, vanilla, or strawberry ice cream? Why not take all three and call it Neapolitan?

You don't like the cold winters of New York? Move down to Florida.

Getting tired of your job? Try something new; shift careers.

We treasure our choices.

For most of us, we are where we are in life by choice, and by choice we change. There's no magical wand we can wave to eliminate our hectic day. A run-in with a unicorn or a chance finding of a four-leaf clover will do us no good. We have to be willing to come face-to-face with what stands in the way of our mission statement and make the decision to eliminate it.

The Bible has numerous examples of those who made the right decision. Noah decided to build a boat. Daniel chose not to eat the king's food but to stick it out with vegetables. Esther approached the king. The disciples chose to forget about the fish, drop their nets, and follow Jesus. Paul decided to turn his hatred for Christians into an unyielding passion for Christ. Their decisions allowed God to do incredible things through them.

Of course, we can also find the opposite in the Bible. Adam and Eve decided to eat the fruit. Cain chose to murder Abel out of jealousy. David slept with Bathsheba. Judas betrayed Jesus. Their decisions messed up their lives badly.

Now we hope that all of you can relate mostly to the first group and not to the second. We hope that your lives have been characterized by many great decisions that you have made. But we also know that, like us, you have probably made some choices that weren't the best, some from which you are now suffering.

We all make mistakes. They are some of life's greatest teachers. And one of the great things about choice is that, by choice, you can reverse a previous decision.

Are you working too much? You can cut back.

Are you overly committed to your social life? You can say, "Not this time."

Does your life consist of meeting your kids' every demand? You can say "no."

The course of your day hinges on your decisions. More than two-thirds (68%) of our survey respondents said that they would change their day if they could.

Most of you can. With courage and wisdom you can make the decisions that eliminate your time's burdens.

Self-consuming Congestion

When we invite guests over to our house, it is typically to have a meal together. We work and spend hours preparing because we know that something special happens around the dinner table. Conversations take place; bonds are forged. It's an event that plays an important role in almost any culture.

It's a time when those who are typically separated come together, enjoy some food, and commune. Cultures have, and still do, embrace the idea of sharing a meal together to enjoy the sustenance of life.

Recall the story of Martha, Mary, and Jesus in Luke 10:38–42. Martha busied herself with the preparations for Jesus and His disciples. Being caught off guard, there was much work to be done. The original dinner plan was just for a few. Now food was required for a houseful of guests. The day had suddenly become a frenzy of throw-it-together preparations. Though she was excited to have this company, there was no doubt that she felt an intense amount of stress. The house and the meal needed to be put together in a way that was worthy of her guests. She could not let Christ and His followers down. Just pulling something out of the freezer and popping it into the microwave was not an option. This was to be an important time of communing for all of them.

The author of this story makes it clear that Martha was working hard to make a good presentation for everyone. I am sure that many women can relate to the feelings Martha had at that moment. Often women feel that the house is a direct reflection of who they are; it is seen as an extension of their personalities. If the house is organized, others will see them as organized. If the house is clean, others will see them as clean. Creating a welcoming environment is also important since they want others to feel welcome.

So Martha fretted over the presentation of her house, wanting to be a good host. But what might not seem like a bad characteristic, the desire to be a good hostess, quickly became a hindrance in seeing what was really needed of her. Martha busied herself so that she might appear as she wanted to be seen, not as Jesus wanted to see her.

In two sentences Martha revealed that her work was about more than just meeting the needs of her guests; it was about a focus on herself: "Lord, don't You care that my sister has left me to serve alone? So tell her to give me a hand" (v. 40). It was about her.

As humans, it is often our self-absorption that hinders our moving into a simple life. We are convinced that this life is about us and our appearance to the world. Much of our time is spent trying to create a persona that says, "I have it all together." And we go to great lengths to make sure that no one finds us lacking in any facet of our life.

From our looks, to our careers, to our lifestyle, to our children, we want to be the whole package. We want to be the ones that others look to and say, "How do they pull it off?" We want to be the ones others want to be. And our time becomes full with things that help us reach that elusive goal.

Don't you hate looking at your motivations for the actions and decisions you make? When we dig down deep and start asking ourselves probing questions about the time we spend on our activities, it sometimes gets ugly. We begin to realize that we treat ourselves like the center of our universe. Asking ourselves "why?" and truthfully answering that question helps us uncover the underlying purpose behind many of our actions.

Why do I work so many hours?

Why are my children involved in so many activities?

Why do I spend so much time at the gym?

Why am I on so many councils?

Why do I volunteer so much?

Martha, why are you so concerned about the preparations?

Our drive to become the perfect human with the perfect family and the perfect career erects barriers that stop us from enjoying the simple life. We must figure out what is truly necessary and what is just an outflow of our ego. Those who are able to keep their egos in check will find it easier to achieve and live a simple life. They will be the ones who will be able to break through the dams that block the life stream flowing to simplicity.

Dealing with the Past, Fretting about the Future, and Forgetting the Present

Barriers to achieving simplicity in our daily lives may have been erected to protect ourselves from our own insecurities. Many of us fill our days with time-consuming activities so that we don't have to face who we really are.

For example, Mark worked for a large, well-known commercial insurance brokerage. Immediately out of college, he threw himself into the workforce, spending most of his time and energy developing his career. The work had paid off. Now he was the youngest executive at the company. He was highly successful, but that wasn't enough.

You see, Mark grew up with a hypercritical father. Nothing was ever good enough. His dad never made it past middle management, and that bothered him. Mark's dad took out his frustration and personal disappointment on Mark. He never heard his dad say, "I am proud of you, Son." Mark's dad didn't find joy in his own accomplishments so he resented any of Mark's successes. Mark did everything to try to win his dad's approval, to the point of becoming a workaholic. But that approval never came.

Mark's dad passed away last year. Now Mark is left still trying to prove himself to a father who has passed on. He just wants to be good enough.

Or what about Ruby? Ruby is concerned that her children will not be successful in life, a concern of many parents.

To "ensure" their success she constantly places her children in extracurricular activities. Their schedule is borderline insanity. They are constantly jumping in and out of the minivan to make it to and from their scheduled commitments. She jokes that she drives the "family taxi." She is not a mom but an underpaid chauffeur.

Though Ruby herself feels that she is pushing the limit of her own physical and mental health, she knows that her children will one day benefit from all of these great experiences. Of course, she would never consider that the busyness to which she has allowed her children to grow accustomed may one day be their own physical and mental downfall. So she pushes on, seeking their success.

Is it wrong for us to be concerned with the future and reflect on the past? Absolutely not.

However, for many of us the past and the future are something more. They are our competition. They drive us beyond healthy limits.

For some of us, much of our daily schedule, the rigors we put ourselves through, is a result of fear. We fear the future. We fear the past. And while we concern ourselves with one or both, we forget about the present, the only moment where we have some real control.

The past and the future are important, but their importance has its place. When we become overly concerned about the future, we concern ourselves with the unknown. When we try to overcompensate for the past, we are trying to break away from something that can't be changed. Those who do not find some type of compromise in their schedule will create obstacles for a simple life. They will fill their day with too much activity, trying to achieve the unachievable.

Don't let the concerns of the past or the future swallow up your time. Find perspective and give appropriate attention to them. Remove what may hinder a simple life. Move forward in the present.

The past is done.

The future is not guaranteed.

The present matters.

Your day matters.

Letting Go

By now you've probably started trying to figure out the areas in your life that may be impeding the movement of simplifying your time. You know that there are some things you need to remove from your life but are unsure which ones. You also know that whatever you decide to eliminate, it's going to be a battle to get those barriers removed.

Let's review Evelyn's mission statement from the last chapter:

In order to make the day reflect my priorities, I will only work a maximum of two hours overtime per week, spend thirty minutes daily reading the Bible and praying, only allow my children to play two sports per year, and have one date with my husband per week.

Remember, our mission statement is our guide through this journey. We developed the mission statement by trying to match our typical day with the priorities we believe have the utmost importance.

The statement was created for action, and the removal of impediments will be a reflection of your mission statement. Their removal should bring you that much closer to developing a simpler day that is more in line with your priorities.

Let's say that Evelyn looked at her mission statement and glanced over her priorities:

1. God
2. Family
3. Health

She then studied her hectic day.

We already know that the day did not reflect Evelyn's heart's desires. Many things were missing; many things were added.

Evelyn looked for those activities that did not line up with her heart's desires. She had to find areas that were not reflecting her priorities.

She immediately started crossing out her work's overtime until only twenty-four minutes of overtime remained each day. For her, this one was obvious. This would result in her only having two hours of overtime per week. She would start leaving work a little bit earlier to give her more time during the afternoon.

Next, she would have to talk to the children. She wanted them to be able to pick which sports they most enjoyed. Evelyn hoped this would at least free up parts of the year when they did not have multiple practices and games.

For Evelyn that was enough. She wanted to do this gradually. And that is what you should do.

More than likely, you'll find several areas in your life that you could envision eliminating. Though we love the ambition, sometimes it is best to take things slowly, especially when you are completely rearranging your life. Once you get a few victories under your belt, the less likely you will stop the movement, and the more likely you will thrive at your new way of doing life.

We recommend that you pick just a few barriers to start. Pick one that will be easy and one that might be a little challenging. Don't become overwhelmed with deconstructing the day you used to experience. Allow yourself and your family time to adjust to each obstruction that is removed.

As you adjust, start looking for other obstructions that are preventing movement during your day. Continue to get rid of these until you are free of all that inhibits you from realizing your goals. You will soon be moving closer to the simple life.

Before You Rock Your Day

Toward the end of the book of Deuteronomy, the leadership baton passes for the Hebrew nation. Moses had led the Israelites out of Egypt, crossed the Red Sea, followed a fiery cloud, and presented the Ten Commandments. He had been led by God into a fantastic career that was finally coming to an end.

Next up was Joshua, one of the two who were willing to enter the Promised Land despite seemingly insurmountable odds. Joshua had a deep faith that God would deliver the land to the Israelites as promised. He was a man of deep beliefs and conviction.

I wish I could have been there at the coronation.

Moses had just finished an epic speech about the Israelites' need to passionately follow God and His ways, and at the end he calls Joshua to the stage. I imagine Joshua, with Moses by his side, looking out among the massive crowds that had gathered for this grand occasion, observing with confidence the people he would soon lead. It had to be a proud and weighty moment for the new leader as the burden of a nation was about to be placed on his shoulders.

Then Moses charged Joshua:

> Be strong and courageous, for you will go with this
> people into the land that the LORD swore to give to
> their fathers. You will enable them to take possession
> of it. The LORD is the One who will go before you.
> He will be with you; He will never leave you
> or forsake you. Do not be afraid or discouraged.
> (Deut. 31:7–8)

Joshua was a courageous guy, but Moses just laid out some huge expectations for the new leader. This charge wasn't something Joshua could shirk; it was given before a nation. The crowd heard what Moses said. He had to follow through. He had to be strong. He had to be courageous. He had to lead the Israelites, no matter the cost, into the promised land. All eyes were on this man.

A nation was watching. It was accountability at its extreme.

Everywhere he went he heard, "Hey, Josh, how's that whole strong and courageous thing going? And what about that promised land? You're in charge, right?"

Maybe it didn't go just like that, but we do know that all eyes were on this new leader.

Now we don't think that you necessarily have to get up in front of a nation and be charged by Moses to be held accountable for your commitments. But we do feel that the burden of accountability is vital for the removing of your barriers.

Meet with your family and friends. Tell them what you are going to do and how you are going to do it. You can even let them know when you are going to do it. Ask them to watch you, to ensure that you are following through with your commitments. In the next chapter we will discuss the necessity of an accountability partner, but for right now just make the announcement. Draw the line in the sand.

Movement is a tough but crucial part of simplifying your time, and you will need others to encourage you when there is the inevitable temptation to fill your day with activities that don't match your priorities.

Gaze at your own crowd with confidence, knowing that today is a turning point. Let those eyes follow you in your actions. Today you are going to change how your twenty-four hours operate. Today you will take the next step to making time a matter of simplicity.

Do not be afraid. Move with courage.

Start living the stories you want to tell on your eighty-third birthday.

APPLICATION
SIMPLE LIFE: MOVEMENT
FINDING TIME

You have one mission statement by this point. Review it closely. Does it say all you want it to say? If you knew that you didn't have much time to live, would this statement move you to where you want to be?

Remember, the mission statement itself must be an action plan. There must be intentional movement inherent in it. Look at where you are now in the use of your time and where you want to be. What barriers prevent you from simplifying your life? Note some of them below:

Now see if your mission statement addresses some of those barriers, either implicitly or explicitly. No one is suggesting that removing or minimizing barriers is easy. At this point, take time to pray that God will give you the wisdom to know which barriers to address and the strength to move toward their elimination.

CHAPTER 3

When the Priorities of Time Match Who We Are

Clarity → Movement → ALIGNMENT → Focus

Once every four years the machismo of a man takes a brief summer twist. For just a couple of weeks, he no longer sits in front of the television to watch tackles and mud-laden dives. Instead, he goes to the television looking for balance and grace. His lips no longer form the familiar words, "Hit him! Hit him!" Instead a new, peculiar verbiage emerges as he bellows, "Beautiful landing!" He no longer raises his hands to mimic the celebration of a man who had just hit a home run. Instead, his hands are hoisted high in impersonation of a little girl who just completed the routine of a lifetime. Conversations with his buddies are diverted from a game that requires shoulder pads and helmets to a sport where the only equipment is a skimpy, tight-fitting suit. And crying is permissible as long as it is your nation's flag that is waving in victory.

The Olympics are truly an amazing spectacle. It's the pageantry. It's the flags of the nations. It's the passion of the athletes. It's the excitement of your nation going up against the rest of the world. And though most of us are merely spectators, it's you against them.

The 2008 Olympic Games rolled into Beijing, China, with much fanfare. From the opening to the closing ceremonies, China put on a show unlike any other previous Olympics. It was big, controversial, and exciting.

For a handful of weeks in the summer of 2008, my wife and I (Art) were mesmerized by the games. From the moment the torch was lit over the large stadium until the flame was passed to England for the 2012 Olympic Games, we could not get enough of the "Olympic spirit." We watched the television to view the developments in Beijing. We turned our attention to the games whenever we got a free moment.

One night my wife stayed up until 1:00 a.m. cheering on the American gymnasts. I had to get up early the next morning so I shut the bedroom door and tried to go to sleep. Admittedly, I was jealous of my wife. I wanted to be sitting beside her, holding my breath until every somersault was complete and "my girls" had gold medals hanging around their necks.

Looking back, I should've stayed up. They didn't get gold, and I sometimes blame myself. I was not there for them when they needed me most.

But it was not gymnasts who received the most attention throughout the weeks. The Beijing Olympic Games were headlined with a chase for history, and a man by the name of Michael Phelps took center stage.

Michael Phelps is a United States swimmer. He approached the games with the possibility of breaking a record previously held by fellow countryman Mark Spitz. In 1972 Spitz won seven gold medals in the Olympic Games, a record that many thought could never be broken.

And as we kept our eyes glued to the television, we witnessed Phelps win one gold medal after another until he finally stood on the top platform and listened to his national anthem play for the eighth time.

The record had been broken. In one Olympic game, Michael Phelps had won eight gold medals.

As Phelps began his march into Olympic history, the media began peering into the life of the great swimmer. What made Michael Phelps become Michael Phelps?

A reporter told the story of a typical day in the life of Phelps. At his training grounds in Ann Arbor, Michigan, they followed the future record-holder to observe his daily regimen. Many were surprised to find his day was extremely monotonous. His day could be summarized into three words: *eat, swim,* and *sleep.* That's it. Over and over again: eat, swim, and sleep.

Of course, these were done in an extraordinarily untypical manner. He ate as if he were four men. He swam as if he were amphibious. And he slept, well, maybe he slept like the rest of us.

Needless to say, his entire regimen revolved around becoming one of the greatest swimmers the world had ever known. He developed his lifestyle so that he would be able to maximize his potential as an athlete. All of his activities were lined up for a specific goal. And in 2008, he reached that goal.

As we watched the ten-minute piece on the daily routine of Michael Phelps, I couldn't help but think that images we were viewing somehow softened the life that Phelps lived day in and day out. We saw the Olympian smiling wherever he went: as he ate, as he went to the pool for a swim. There was no way that a ten-minute spot could capture the reality of his daily experiences. Every day was not filled with smiles and laughter. Undoubtedly we missed the struggles and the sacrifices that came with such a disciplined life.

This is alignment: when we structure our life's activities and priorities so that the process of the simple life can be accomplished. It is lining up our schedule so that it runs parallel to our heart's yearning.

In this section we have been discussing ways we can simplify our time. We have already started eliminating activities that were not part of our declared priorities. And like Michael Phelps, our next step is going to be figuring out how we can align our daily activities that remain so they move us toward the realization of our mission statement. Alignment takes dedication; it takes sacrifice. But it is necessary for the simple life.

We have clarified.

We have moved.

Now we align.

So how well have we aligned our lives? Our research indicates that the answer is likely "poorly." Seven out of ten (69%) indicated they need to change how they use their time each day. In yet another example, we might expect born-again Christians to align their time for priorities that reflect their beliefs. But, among that group in our study, only 40 percent pray regularly with their children. Only 35 percent of the married respondents pray regularly with their spouses. And only 30 percent read the Bible together at least once a week.

Not very good alignment.

Do You Have the Time for an Honest Assessment?

> The Lord answered her, "Martha, Martha, you are worried and upset about many things, but one thing is necessary. Mary has made the right choice, and it will not be taken away from her." (Luke 10:41–42)

Jesus said this to Martha after she publicly questioned Mary's "irresponsibility." After these lines the story ends. We don't get to see Martha's reaction to these words. Maybe she set down the cleaning and cooking paraphernalia, asked Mary to scoot over, and listened to the words of Christ. Maybe she persisted with her preparations, still frantic over what she felt needed to be done.

We don't know the response, but we do know that she was confronted with an assessment of herself. Jesus told her that, though she had many concerns, they were not correct concerns. For that moment her heart and mind were in the wrong place.

With this assessment she had to either acknowledge its truth or consider it a fallacy. Pretty simple, we guess. We know that Jesus, being God, was able to know the thoughts of Martha as she stood there in her frustration. It would be difficult for us to consider the words anything but accurate. So in all actuality these words probably cut her to the core.

It's like being in grade school. You go up to the friend of the one you like to ask the friend if *his* friend would ever like you. His friend tells you no because you are not athletic or popular enough. You hate hearing the words, but you know it's true. You're not athletic or popular. And then he pours salt in the wound.

He breaks your grade-school heart even more as he tells you that you need to try to be more like your brother who is more athletic or maybe more popular than you. But you know that you will never be like him. It stings.

Martha might have felt that sting as well because Jesus gave an honest assessment of who she was in that moment. She was compared with her sister Mary and came up short.

There is a wonderful upside to this honest assessment: she was placed in a position to do something about it. There were no more smoke screens; the truth was there in front of her. She could either start listening to Jesus or go back to the preparations. She found herself in a place to make a real, life-impacting decision.

The same thing happens with us when we decide to evaluate our current ability to simplify our time. If we truly evaluate ourselves, we will find ourselves in a better place to make decisions that propel us to our goals.

Don't be afraid to find faults. In fact, get excited about finding your faults.

Sound odd? It's not.

Our life consists of a series of imperfections so it's not unusual that you find deficiencies in your daily stewardship of time. Of course, this is not to excuse any area in which we find ourselves lacking; but it is an opportunity to use those faults to bring change to our lives.

When we find ourselves at odds with our heart's desires, we create a potential turning point. We see things we don't like in our lives, and we can draw a line in the sand. On one side is the old way; on the other is the new, desired way.

Take some time for yourself so that you can make an honest assessment of your situation. It may take an hour; it may take a day. Find the surrounding that best makes you think. For some, this could be a walk outdoors. For others, it may be sitting in a lounge chair with a fresh-brewed cup of Starbucks coffee.

Whenever and wherever that moment and place may be, ask yourself: Are the activities that fill my day aligned with my stated goals? Are they fostering the process, or are they hindering it? We've clarified our goal. We've moved some stubborn obstacles. But does everything else line up?

We've already given you some statistics about our respondents: 44 percent said that their life's current pace would eventually result in health problems, and 40 percent admitted to being on an emotional edge because of their schedules.

You're not alone in this mess. Be honest with yourself, and let your faults show clearly. You're on the brink of change.

A Time to Count on Others

Jon was a middle-aged owner/operator of a local New York-style deli. He originally moved down to Florida from New York City because of a job relocation. After a few years he began missing the sandwich shops he had frequented while in New York. His new city's delis just didn't hit the spot. So he quit his job and started his own deli. After four years of running it, he still loved every minute of the work. It was his baby.

"I actually don't call it 'my baby' anymore. My wife, Angela, started getting offended that I called the shop 'my baby' instead of her or my real baby, Andy. He's three years old now."

When Jon decided to open up the deli, he and his wife knew that it would be a lot of work. They knew that much time would have to be dedicated to the business to ensure its and their survival.

But after a couple of years, Angela was getting frustrated about the amount of time Jon spent at work. She was getting tired of his not spending time with her, and with Andy as well. She wanted her husband back. Jon knew that a change was necessary.

"I just don't want to look back with regret on all of this time that I spent working. I have a great wife and a great kid. I don't want to miss my moments with them."

Jon's heart was in the right place, but every time he tried to make changes in his life, he would go back to his old ways.

"The problem with enjoying the work you do is that you enjoy the work you do. I have fun with it. It's not that I don't like my family. I love them. I try to change; I try to work less. But after about a month I am back to the same, time-consuming schedule."

When we asked him about accountability, he gave a predictable response.

"Well, not really. Of course, I told my wife that I would try to spend more time with the family, but when she confronts me about the lack of follow-through, it seems more nagging than anything else. Not that I am innocent. I would never say that. I guess I can't really blame her. Most of the time she is right on."

Jon is like many people who try to make changes in their lives. They approach the adjustment with good intentions. They see a need to reprioritize their lives and are willing to make some major modifications in their lifestyles. But as time progresses, they slowly slide back into their old rut and find themselves living just as they did before.

Each of us knows how easy it is to rationalize our way out of self-imposed promises. We swear that things are going to be different, and for a little while they are. But then things happen, one here and one there, and we slowly veer away from our original intent.

In everything we are first accountable to God. Romans 14:12 says, "So then, each of us will give an account of himself to God."

But the Bible also teaches us that it is important to be accountable to the men and women who help us on our Christian journey.

"And let us be concerned about one another in order
to promote love and good works." (Heb. 10:24)

God knows our wiring. He knows that we need someone to encourage us in our personal development. Human existence was never meant to be played in solitude. It is intentionally relational.

If we are serious about changing the way we do time, then we need others who are there, watching our progress. We need a set of eyes that can recognize and verbalize the good and the bad, the aligned and the unaligned.

When choosing that person who will hold you responsible for your actions, be picky. Steer away from family members. It can just get too messy; seek an outsider.

Next, search for someone with similar goals that you are trying to accomplish. If your accountability partner is pursuing similar goals, good. If he has already accomplished what you are moving toward, perfect. Don't get your workaholic friend to hold you accountable while his own life is totally out of whack.

Finally, make sure the person you choose holds the same values and will not hesitate calling you out when your actions are no longer paralleling your goals. If he doesn't have the same values, he likely can't understand your goals. If he is quick to congratulate you but reluctant to verbalize concerns, then you need to seek someone else.

Set specific time intervals in which you will meet or speak: weekly or every other week. And be sure to stay in contact. This is a must.

God has put certain people in your life for this specific purpose. Find them. Approach them. Uncover how a single, open relationship can keep you heading where you desire to go.

Uniquely You

Can activities that align with your goal be the wrong activities? Absolutely.

Let's quickly catch up with Evelyn. She had written the mission statement:

In order to make the day reflect my priorities, I will only work a maximum of two hours overtime per week, spend thirty minutes daily reading the Bible and praying, only allow my children to play two sports per year, and have one date with my husband per week.

"Well, I have made some major changes in my life. I definitely seem to be progressing more toward a life that lines up with my priorities. The only part that I don't like about this whole thing is that sometimes things just don't seem to fit. I don't know if I can explain this real well, but even though I am lining up my day with my priorities, parts just don't feel right."

When we probed a little more, we learned that some of Evelyn's plans were not in line with the person God created her to be. Evelyn had always been a somewhat spontaneous person. She liked life on the fly. Whenever she found herself constricted, she became slightly depressed. Even though her previous days were hectic, she felt that she could do what she wanted if something ever came up.

During this process she felt as if she had been stripped of her spontaneity. To make sure she remained on track, Evelyn scheduled everything. While this is good for some, it was not for her. As she looked at her calendar, she just saw a bunch of to-dos. Her simple time had become her constricted time, at least in her mind. Even with all of her previous obligations, she felt that she was in control. But not anymore.

Evelyn's situation is not unusual. When we start aligning our day to fit our mission statement and ultimately our heart's priorities, we will run into areas that run against our personality. It's a conflict that should be avoided.

God made us all the same but all different. Each one of us was made in the image of God, but this does not mean that we will have identical personalities, gifts, strengths, and weaknesses. The fact that each human, past, present, and future, is unique has to be one of the most mind-boggling aspects of creation. Both physically and mentally, we are not duplicates of any other human who has or will walk this planet.

So with this in mind, how can we expect people to proceed aligning their life in an identical manner? We can't. We don't.

To avoid such a situation from happening, take a step back and look at what you have already done. Does it fit with who you are? Is this you?

This whole simple-life process should excite you. You are starting over. The canvas is blank, and you get to paint your own picture. This is your life's art.

If you find yourself unmotivated or, like Evelyn, feeling that something is just not right, ask yourself why. More than likely, it will all be a matter of taste. You may be more of an abstract, but you're painting something that looks more impressionistic. It's not your style.

A key element of alignment is the proper fit. Embrace who God has made you, and use it to mold your simple life.

A Time to Stretch: Flexibility

By definition alignment requires a clear relationship between two objects or, in our case, between our mission statement and our activities. They run side by side, buddies through thick and thin. But as we have seen, sometimes we find ourselves in need of change. Sometimes buddies start going their separate ways.

Adjustments may arise out of a need to play to your strengths. They may occur when you realize that your actions in this process were just a little too aggressive. They may come from life changes, small or large. Going from a wife and a dog to a wife, two kids, and now an aging dog will require some understandable alterations in the way you do life. In fact, it's almost a certainty that at some point you will need to make some changes.

Whether it is within the next week or a few years down the road, changing your alignment presents a challenge.

Have you ever noticed that your life seems to be one big habit? You get up about the same time, alternate between the same two sugar-laden cereals for breakfast, take a quick shower, check the weather on the usual station, pick out your clothes for the day, and head to work, listening to the same talk radio as you ride in your car.

This is just the start of your day. You'll proceed with the rest of your day, doing about the same things, carrying on about the same way as you normally do. We're not trying to depress you. There is a rhythm to each of our lives, a beat that guides us throughout our day. But when the beat takes on a different rhythm, our day's dance becomes disrupted. We feel uncomfortable. Our life's waltz suddenly becomes the funky chicken. We are out of sync and awkward.

These uncomfortable feelings are what often push us to keep the rhythm, to do as we have always done. And like most things in life, this desire to avoid the disruption can be a double-edged sword.

The simple life requires flexibility. Life is not static. Therefore, your day will demand that changes are made to continue this pursuit of yours. The activities or nonactivities will need adjustments as you continue to experience this journey of life. This may happen tomorrow; it may happen next year. Who knows where or what God may do with you?

Do not limit yourself.

Adopt an attitude of flexibility.

What will happen if you stick with your ways, even when change is demanded?

Nothing and everything.

Life will continue to change with or without your permission. Standing ready for the adjustment will help you capture the adventure of what a simple day can be.

Relishing the Blemish

Behind every scar lies a story.

Have you ever gotten into one of those competitive scar-storytelling matches? Someone, maybe you, notices an acquaintance's scar. You ask the acquaintance about the origin of the scar, and he willingly responds with a pride-filled story about his piece of embattled body.

Of course, you have a better scar with a better story. So does someone else in your group, and this provides everyone with the perfect opportunity to share their stories.

A game of "who's got the better scar story?" ensues. This can continue until either opponent runs out of marks or the marks become a little too personal to be unveiled. At this point, all agree with a simultaneous grimace that it would be best to bring the game to its conclusion.

Why do we enjoy talking about our scars?

For many of us, our scars are reminders of dramatic moments in our lives that involved struggle, fear, opposition, or tough times we overcame. Like any landmark, they are points of reference placed on our body to let us know that something happened and our bodies will never fully restore to their original state.

We are still here, but we are not the same.

The story behind the scar may be lighthearted. It might be from the time when you realized that gymnastics was never meant to take place in the family garage. It may be from that high school football game, the one against your cross-town rival, which you won with a lot of sweat and a little blood. Or it could be from the moment you realized that wearing socks while running around on a wood floor can result in a quick slip and a nasty face-plant.

The stories can also become serious. They may remind you of life-saving surgery. It could be from that car wreck where you somehow walked away with only a few cuts; they said you never should have survived. Or it may be from that war in which you fought. You still find yourself wondering at night why you made it home and your buddy did not.

The blemish is a thing of marvel. Much like our physical bodies, our life is often filled with scars, some from the decisions we made, some from the ones we didn't make.

For those of us who have not lived the perfect life and who bear the marks left by past errors, we understand the importance of those marks. One of the beautiful things about a scar is that it is a demonstration that healing took place. It represents an old wound from which we are no longer suffering. So when we see these imperfections, we look at them with joy of what was but is no longer.

As we align our activities to move toward the simple life with our time, we should not expect perfection. As with most areas in our life, we will probably find ourselves making mistakes, creating a few scars. Our response to those mistakes can be more important than the mistake itself. Will we allow it to become a source of frustration or inspiration? Will it be a story to share or a problem that continues to torment us?

Much like our physical scars, alignment can become a remarkable story of overcoming something that we may not have anticipated. Within every struggle lies an opportunity; it is the diamond found hiding in the blackness of coal.

Maybe you found yourself leaning too much on your own strength and not on God's. Maybe you never even sought out God in the first place. Maybe you realized that your "perfect" plan wasn't really all that perfect.

Because time has so many outside variables, mistakes can easily occur; alignment can easily become misalignment. We can't become so focused on the imperfections in this process that they hinder our advancement.

Allow your wounds, your mistakes, to heal. They heal when we step away from them and make a change. If you're lucky, a scar will remain. Use those scars as learning experiences, as markers of personal growth, lessons learned and survived. Don't expect perfectionism in this process because you will only become frustrated with it all. Don't be disappointed if things don't go right the first time.

Use the flaw.

Make it better.

Be proud of the result.

Show off your scars. Tell your story.

Rounding Third

One of the most exciting parts of a baseball game is when a player rounds third base and starts heading home. Dirt kicks up behind him with every lift of the cleat during his mad sprint. The crowd stands and screams with hands flailing in the air, "Go! Go!" knowing that another score is only ninety feet and a touch of the plate away. The adrenaline fills the stadium. It is something special.

We are about to enter the final quartile of this section; we have hit third and are now making our way home. The goal is in front of us and within reach. We have clarified, moved, and aligned. Now we will focus.

And as you run down the line, we applaud you. You declared that you wanted to simplify your time and have committed to action. We're sure it has not been easy. Change never is. We encourage you not to slow down but to keep passionately pursuing what your heart is telling you.

In the end it will be something special.

APPLICATION
SIMPLE LIFE: ALIGNMENT
MATCHING TIME AND PERSONALITY

When we speak about our personalities, we are referring to the total mix of who we are: our disposition, our background, our temperament, our talents, our spiritual gifts, and our personal history.

The mission statement you wrote to prioritize time in your life should align with who you are. It should come close to matching your personality. For example, look at the words on the following page. Circle the ones that best fit who you are. There are no rights or wrongs on the list. It is simply an exercise to remind ourselves to look carefully in the mirror.

Steady	Fast
Structured	Spontaneous
Focused	Scattered
Morning productive	Evening productive
Tense	Relaxed
Hyper	Calm
Talkative	Quiet
Patient	Impatient
Fun	Serious
Compulsive	Thoughtful
Competitive	Noncompetitive
Worried	Hopeful

Now look at each of the words you circled. Does your mission statement fit the personality you just described? Does it align with who you are? If not, what changes should you make in the statement?

_____

_____

_____

_____

_____

CHAPTER 4

A Matter of Time

Clarity → Movement → Alignment → FOCUS

One of the most frustrating parts about writing is trying to formulate an idea when your mind is wandering in a thousand different directions. You know that you have to write. A deadline is approaching, but your thoughts are on everything else but putting something on the page. You sit down and stare at the white on your screen. It is waiting for you to place some words on it, to make some coherent sentences. But you have nothing.

So you sit as the blankness on the computer taunts you and challenges you to write something meaningful, something about which someone, somewhere will care.

It's not that you are doing anything wrong. In fact, your heart is really in the project. It's just that a little focus could help.

Have you ever gone to one of the cheap movie theaters, the ones we call "dollar theaters" but always seem to cost more than a buck?

You skip the concessions because purchasing a pack of Twizzlers that costs more than the movie ticket seems to make little sense. You came to this place to save, not to buy candy for three times more than you can get it at the gas station on the next street corner.

As you take your seat, you brush aside some spilled popcorn from the last showing. Ticket prices don't quite cover cleaning costs. Then the movie starts.

It is somewhat low quality. You can tell that the film has been used many times and is fighting its last battle. The image on the screen isn't nearly as crisp as it used to be. In fact, it's a little blurry.

Everything else is fine. Cheap but bearable. You will make it through the movie. It's just that a little focus could help.

There is a child with great potential. Each day he goes to school and is easily able to grasp the teachings that are tossed his way. His mind is like a sponge, soaking up knowledge with fervor.

But he wants other things. He wants to spend time with friends and not homework. His attention drifts more toward "hanging out" than books.

He still has the ability; that has not been taken away. But his grades aren't where they could be if he gave them more priority. A little focus could help.

This last step in simplifying our time is focus. A lot of people could benefit from it. At this point in your process of simplification, you have done much to make sure your calendar matches your heart's desire. Each day's activities should be a reflection of your priorities.

But we must ask the question: Are the activities that reflect your priorities weakening your ability to fulfill your mission statement?

It's an interesting question.

Let's rephrase it in a more commonly asked manner: Is there ever too much of a good thing?

We know you've heard this question asked before. And for many of you, you know that the answer is yes. There is a point where your good intention can transform into a burden.

While a vacation is great, too much will make you broke and unemployed. While spending time with your spouse should be a main priority, too much time will leave you lacking in your time with God and other important aspects of your life.

Exactly 50 percent of the respondents in our study agreed with this statement: "I want to slow down, but I don't know how." We wondered how many would have agreed if we simply said, "I want to slow down." In other words, they knew what they needed to do, how they needed to do it, but they just didn't make the change. We wonder if intentionality was lacking among many in our study.

By creating an intentional focus, we are allowing our actions to be even more purposeful, more potent, and more direct.

Focus's Fallout

In the story of Mary and Martha, we once again imagine the frustration that Martha must have felt as Jesus told her that her efforts were concentrated on something that meant little for the moment and that Mary was found in an act that meant everything.

Here was Martha, hard at work, trying to prepare a house and meal for Jesus and His disciples. And Mary just sat and listened.

Martha had taken on all of the responsibility and stress that was expected for such a guest's arrival. And Mary just sat and listened.

Martha busied herself in service. And Mary just sat and listened.

Throughout Scripture, we are told to be servants: "Whoever wants to become great among you must be your servant, and whoever wants to be first among you must be your slave" (Matt. 20:26–27).

So why then was Martha's effort, her servant-like desire, not appropriate for the situation? Why would Mary be considered right in her ways and not Martha? Wasn't Martha more like a servant than Mary? She was the one who did the cooking and the cleaning. She was the one with a racing pulse from working so hard.

Maybe another factor was in play here. Maybe, for that moment, there was something that took precedence over a good action.

During His time on the earth, Jesus was constantly aware of the brevity of His time living among us. With each passing day, with each step, and with each breath, Jesus was drawing closer to the cross. Like all of us, His life on Earth was a constant march toward death. Unlike us He knew the final hour, minute, and second.

So maybe it was not that Martha's desire to serve was in itself wrong, but there was something greater to be done in that moment. Times with Jesus were fleeting, and He wanted her to be with Him, to spend time with Him.

Mary had good actions, but there was something greater. She needed to relinquish her serving to participate in something far greater and far more important.

In the book of Acts, Paul had planned to go to Bithynia to share the news about Christ, but God prevented them from entering and directed them to Macedonia. No one faults Paul for wanting to preach in Bithynia; God just had other plans. Sometimes even the best of intentions may come up lacking in comparison if God is not in them.

Taylor is a single man in his mid-forties. He had been employed with a small office supply company for most of his working years. The job did not require much. In fact, most of the time he found himself struggling to stretch his responsibilities into a forty-hour workweek.

Most of Taylor's time outside the office was spent at Graceview Christian Church, a strong church with a great reputation. He gave many hours as a volunteer. It was a fairly large church so he had plenty of opportunities to get involved. But Taylor had taken those opportunities to an unhealthy extreme, hurting other parts of his life.

"I finally realized that I had to step back. I was overcommitted. I had work and church; that's it. If I didn't work with them or didn't go to church with them, I didn't know them."

Taylor took some giant strides in simplifying his day so that he could become more balanced.

"You know, I had to let go of a lot of good things. Let's face it, I was volunteering at the church. How much better could you get?"

As Taylor began to focus on meeting his goal, he found that it was not only the bad that had to go, but sometimes the good had to go as well.

"Honestly," he said with a boyish grin, "it took me a while to realize that it was okay to let go of some of the service I did. But if I was truly focused on the goal, this was inevitably going to happen. It had to happen."

This same thing can happen to us as we pursue a more simplified approach to managing our time.

As we focus our efforts to the mission and the mission alone, we must be willing to allow good things to fall to the wayside. Sometimes the best thing we can do is say no—and not just to that which goes against our priorities but also to those activities that, while aligning with our priorities, are actually pushing us farther away from fulfilling our mission statement.

This leads us to a two-step process to increase your focus and speed at which you can reach your goal: Be willing to let go and discover your imbalance.

Step 1: Be Willing to Let Go

"What will happen if . . . ?"

"Is it okay if I . . . ?"

"What will people think if I . . . ?"

These types of questions often lead to paralysis in our ability to make decisions that will lead to a greater focus.

In the movement chapter we eliminated those bad areas in our life that did not line up with our priorities. They were blocking the flow and hindered us from reaching the potential of our mission statement.

In the alignment chapter we tried to be sure that our activities matched the uniqueness of who we are.

This is different. It has a different feel. It is more difficult to let go of that which truly does line up with our priorities but still may limit us in reaching our goal.

It is a lot different to tell others that you are limiting your overtime at work to free up more time to spend with your family than it is to announce your plans to decrease your family time, even if it is to increase your time with God.

We have been following the story of Evelyn in this section. Remember her mission statement:

> *In order to make the day reflect my priorities, I will only work a maximum of two hours overtime per week, spend thirty minutes daily reading the Bible and praying, only allow my children to play two sports per year, and have one date with my husband per week.*

"You know, one of the most difficult decisions came when I realized that some volunteer work I was doing was causing problems. It was one of those areas in my life that I had not even considered when I started this journey."

Evelyn helped out at a homeless center located on the outskirts of the city about once or twice a week. She usually did this around midday on Saturday or Sunday.

"It was only an hour or so each time. But each time I was there, I found myself troubled with the fact that I had not yet accomplished the goals, but here I was spending time on something that was outside of the goal. It was a struggle of my heart and mind to figure out whether or not I should let this go." She slightly lowered her head. She was in deep thought.

One of the main factors preventing Evelyn from setting aside this volunteer work was that the commitment to do it also came from another source besides her own commitment. Her Bible study volunteered as a group as a way to make service a priority in each of their lives.

"I am just worried about what they will think of me. I don't want them to view my faith as weak. I have a feeling that they just won't understand."

Focusing is about completely purifying your actions so that nothing is preventing you from simplifying your time. And we know that many of you who are reading this book need to hear that it's okay to step away from an activity, even if it is a good thing you are doing.

Don't get us wrong; doing good things is important to the Christian faith. The book of James makes this clear. But evil can find a foothold in our lives when we are too busy with good works. As Peter tells us, the devil is like a prowling lion, looking for someone to devour.

Seek God in these decisions. Spend time in prayer asking God to reveal to you whether or not you should let go of these activities, at least for a time. Ask for peace that transcends your human understanding to guide you in your decision.

Many of our respondents said that they desired to have one meal a day with their family. For most of them, the only possible meal for everyone to be together is dinner. Maybe you are like them. Maybe you see a family meal as an outcome of simplifying your time, placing family as a priority. If you have placed this as a way to fulfill one of your priorities, allow it to become just that, a priority.

Of those who claimed to be Christians, 45 percent said they rarely or never attended worship together as a family. If this is one of your goals, make it a priority. Maybe switching to another Bible study will allow your family to worship together. Maybe serving in the nursery during the first service will open up a way to worship together. Seek other options.

Understand that there is a big difference between activities you want to do and those you have to do. Focus on what has to be done in order to simplify your time.

Step 2: Discover Imbalance

The book of Genesis tells of a man named Noah who decided to obey God and build a massive wooden ship that could house two of every kind of animal. Undoubtedly many thought he was crazy, spending so many of his years building a large boat. Noah probably seemed unbalanced.

The book of Matthew tells of a man named John. He lived out in the desert, ate locust and wild honey, and wore clothes made of camel hair. No, he was not trying to protest clothes made from cotton or promote the latest fad diet. He was trying to prepare a nation for Christ. But he probably seemed unbalanced.

There was also a man named Paul. He said that his life was worth nothing to him. When he preached in the Roman colony of Lystra, some of the Jews did not agree with his words. They stoned him and dragged him out of the city thinking that he was dead, but he got up and went back into the city. Some probably said that he was unbalanced.

We often hear from our culture that the best way to do life is to live a balanced one. Honestly, we're not sure what this means. Ask a few people what a balanced life would actually look like, and you would probably get the same number of different responses as the number of people you questioned.

Many of our Bible heroes were unbalanced. They lived life in extremes. Yet because of their extremes we talk about them today.

Focus is unbalanced. It is narrowing your field of vision so that you block out the unnecessary.

Focus is powerful. When harnessing your energy into one or a few goals, your impact will be multiplied. Why is a laser so powerful? It is focused energy.

As you let go, understand that you may be losing some balance in your life. But also understand that balance is not always the best pursuit. It can sometimes spread you too thin with activities and make life more complex than it needs to be. It can also mean your life will have less of an impact.

In basketball you often hear of a player being "in the zone." This happens when every shot he takes seems to go in, and every move he makes on the court seems to be the right move. Though thousands of rabid fans may be screaming at him from the stands, he hears nothing. Outside factors are kept on the outside. And so he plays the game with total skill and precision.

Take hold of your priorities. Narrow your vision, be focused, and be in the zone. Sure, you might become a little unbalanced, but you are in good company.

Be Patient

Do you remember the first time you were told that a magnifying glass, if aligned with the sun, could burn a hole through a leaf or even set fire to an ant? If you were like me (Art), you ran home to find the closest thing that resembled a magnifying glass, took it outside, found an unsuspecting ant, and tried to harness the power of the sun.

Admittedly, the combustion of the ant never happened. They never told us kids how long it would take for this thrill to occur. So I waited. And I waited. And I waited. I think the ant might have taken a nap while waiting for its impending death.

So I gave up. I brought the instrument of supposed destruction into the house. I lost my patience trying to make it happen.

Of course, the futility of the project was exacerbated because of my instrument of choice. I couldn't find a magnifying glass in our house, so I opted for what my curious mind thought would be the next best thing . . . a plastic Coke bottle.

But some did burn a hole in a leaf. Some had the endurance and the right instrument to capture the sun's energy. They watched in awe as they created fire from what appeared to be nothing.

If you were one of those children, I commend you.

Our culture doesn't have much patience with patience. When we were young, time seemed to creep at a snail's pace. Every day, every year lived was such a large percentage of our life. When we were eight, getting to sixteen and a driver's license required doubling our life's time line. It seemed like we would never get there.

And now that we are older, we lack patience for another reason. We realize how short life is. For some, eight years can be just a blip on the time line. In a blink, eight years will have come and gone. We want life to slow down, but it never does. Every year becomes less and less of a portion of our life. And so we want to wait for nothing that eats up our precious time.

If we want to harness this energy created by our focus, we must have patience. We need to be willing to let the clock tick a little. Like the magnifying glass and the leaf (or ant), we need to be committed to maintaining our focus, even when it seems like nothing is happening.

We must realize that something is really going on. There is an unseen force at work. Momentum is building. And as we continue with our commitment, we will soon see smoke and then, maybe, a little fire.

From a place where there seemed to be no change, something dramatic happened. And out of less came more.

The Ultimate Story of Focus

There is no greater demonstration of focus than that which Jesus gave us while He trod the dirt of this world. And even though His eternal stakes were more important than anything we can offer, the story needs to be told.

We cannot compare, but we can learn.

For thirty-three years Christ was placed on the planet Earth with one goal: save the human race from sin.

In His sight was the cross. That was His focus.

While on this earth Jesus healed many, exorcized evil spirits, and raised some from the dead. But for all that He did for others, the majority went without. He traveled only one small part of this sphere. He saw only a small portion of the world's population. He only lived into His early thirties.

Many were not healed.

Many demons remained within.

Many still died.

Even as Jesus entered each city, He did not always take care of all the needs in the town. It's easy to sit back and wonder why. With all His power, all His authority, why would Jesus not reverse every sickness, every death, and every trouble?

He was on a divine schedule. From the moment of birth, His countdown began. Christ knew His main purpose was not to heal physical needs because those healings would only provide temporal relief. He was sent to conquer the spiritual realm, a battle where the implications were eternal.

So He set aside some healings and allowed some to die. He had greater work to do, work that was grossly misunderstood in His time on Earth. And we are left with an undeniable result.

It worked.

Jesus overcame that which He was sent to overcome. He kept a laser-like focus on the battle between good and evil, death and life.

And He won.

Some things are just more important than others. One good thing might be better than another good thing. It is okay to choose one over the other. In fact, it is critical.

Stay focused; reach the goal.

Time to End

We started off this section on simplifying your time in a graveyard.

Where we want to leave you now is not a physical place. It has no markers, no inscriptions on a stone, no flowers left by loved ones, no concrete statues, and no gate by which to enter or leave.

We want to leave you with a greater awareness of the brevity of time. Your time is important. This you already know.

Every day we walk a path on which we do not know its end. The next step may be one of many or the very last. Each moment that we have is precious.

God has wired us with priorities of the heart. Make sure you do not leave this little, round rock called Earth without living out what God has placed on your heart.

Let your last breath be one of satisfaction, not regret. It's all a matter of time.

APPLICATION
SIMPLE LIFE: FOCUS
ELIMINATING SOME OF THE GOOD TIME

Focus is tough. We've made that clear. When you begin to focus on time, you are looking to eliminate some of those good activities that consume your day. In this case you are not dealing with eliminating those time wasters like television and the Internet. You're faced with the stark reality that your life may have too many good things.

The simple life demands focus. That means we have to eliminate some of the good things we do. This section on time, in many ways, really overlaps with the other sections: God, relationships, and money. If we're not focused on the simple life of time, we will not do well in the other areas.

On this day take a few moments to think about one or two, probably no more than three, areas where you can say no even though you are saying yes today. It won't be easy because we're challenging you to consider eliminating some of the good things you do.

Now write one to three sentences about your plan to eliminate some of your good activities:

1. _____

_____

_____

_____

_____

2. _____

_____

_____

_____

_____

3. _____

_____

_____

_____

_____

_____

If you look at those areas where you can eliminate some of the good things, you may be a bit overwhelmed or fearful. It's not easy to say no to good things.

So pause for a moment. Pray for God's wisdom for discernment, for the pace you eliminate things, and for His strength.

> But Jesus looked at them and said, "With men this is impossible, but with God all things are possible." (Matt. 19:26)

PART 2

Simple Life: How to Create and Keep Healthy Relationships

CHAPTER 5

I Want to Have Healthier Relationships with Family and Friends

CLARITY → Movement → Alignment → Focus

I am a terrible friend."

Those words didn't come from a terrible person. To the contrary, in our interview with Samantha, we perceived her to be caring and compassionate. We didn't see a terrible person.

The Vermont native is a single twenty-seven-year-old living in Worcester, Massachusetts. Samantha has many friends, and she comes from a healthy family situation. But her view of her own relationships is not healthy.

At least the last time we checked, "terrible" is not healthy.

We asked the obvious, "Why do you consider yourself a terrible friend?"

She didn't hesitate to respond. "I have four friends that I am extremely close to. Two of them I have known since high school, and two of them I first met in college. Somehow, I guess through me, all five of us became really connected. We don't live that far from one another, but it would be at least a half-day drive for any of us. The point is that all of the others write one another and me. They are all good about calling. Most of them even make a point of visiting and getting together."

She paused. "All of them but me."

"Is your schedule so busy that you don't have time to stay connected to your friends?"

"Well," she said pensively. "My schedule is incredibly busy. I don't know many people who have a lot of free time. I don't think I'm that much busier than my friends. But somehow they make time to call me, send me e-mails, and even to come see me. My best friend, Laura, sends me a handwritten note about once a month. She thinks she is encouraging me. If she only knew how guilty she is making me feel."

Then Samantha said it again. "I am a terrible friend."

Who Are These People?

Just who among us is looking for healthier relationships? If our surveys of more than one thousand people are any indication, the answer is "most of us." One bit of anecdotal information supports this thesis.

In 2008 the low-budget movie *Fireproof* was released. Like its production predecessor, *Facing the Giants*, the movie touched many lives. The central characters in the movie were firefighter Caleb Holt and his wife, Catherine. Caleb's rally cry each time he fought the dangerous fires was, "Never leave your partner behind." He practiced that principle with fidelity on the job.

The problem was his failure to live that principle in his marriage. The argumentative and strained relationship resulted in the couple moving toward divorce. Catherine had enough, and Caleb was unwilling to fight for his marriage.

In a last-minute intervention, Caleb's father challenged his son to fight for his marital partner with even more zeal than he would fight for his firefighting partner. His marriage and his wife were worth it, his dad exclaimed. In the movie the challenge is called "the love dare."

An amazing consequence of the movie's positive impact was the sale of a corollary book, *The Love Dare*. Shortly after the movie's release, the book began to climb in sales. In just a few days *The Love Dare* was a national best seller.

The book is a forty-day challenge for husbands and wives to practice unconditional love toward each other. If sales were any indication, the need was great. Relationships needed improvement at the least, and total rehabilitation at most.

The respondents in our study told us the same thing. There is a hunger, as we will share later, for a healthy relationship with God. We could call that the vertical hunger. But there is also a hunger horizontally, a desire to be in healthier relationships with husbands, wives, fathers, mothers, sons, daughters, friends, coworkers, and a list too long to enumerate here.

We heard this longing from different family structures. Of our respondents, 53 percent were in traditional families,

16 percent were in blended families, and 31 percent were in single-parent families. But the responses were similar.

The responses were close regardless of age. They included 27 percent under the age of thirty-five, 44 percent ages thirty-five to forty-nine, and 29 percent age fifty and older.

The patterns were similar among whites who accounted for 66 percent of the respondents, for African-Americans (14%), Hispanics (14%), and Asians (4%). And there were no significant differences among the varying household incomes.

The responses showed no variation among those in different geographical locales, including the Northeast (20%), Midwest (24%), South (24%), and West (33%).

And we heard the same longings regardless of marital status. Including those presently married (69%), previously married (20%), and never married (11%). And among those presently married, 68 percent were in their first marriage, 25 percent were in their second marriage, and 7 percent were in their third or more marriage.

But the responses were the same.

There was a longing for relationships and for more healthy relationships. Look at some of the comments from our survey:

- "I would love for our family to spend more time together instead of needing to work so much and sending our son to day care."
- "I would just love for my kids to get along and quit fighting so we could have some peace in the house."
- "I wish we could manage our time so we can spend more weekends together."
- "I don't feel like I know my husband anymore. With our schedules we hardly even have time to talk."

- "I wish I could have just one friend I could talk to anytime."
- "We are constantly on the go due to our children's sporting events and hardly have any quality time together. Whether it's for practice, scrimmages, or games of multiple sports, we literally are gone from our home almost every night of the week."
- "I need better relationships with my stepchildren. They really resent me."
- "I have lots of people and family around me, but I am so lonely."

Clarity and Relationships

In this chapter we look at the second of the "big four" needs we heard across our nation. The respondents said that they needed to simplify their lives by having significant and healthy relationships.

As you recall, the first step in the simple life is the determination to move forward with a few clear and concrete action items. We have called this step "clarity" because you state clearly what you plan to do. We also recommend you put your action items into a mission statement. That statement should have the following characteristics.

First, it should be easy to understand. Whether you or someone else is reading the statement, there must be no doubt about what you plan to do.

Second, the mission statement should also be a process. It is not only a declaration of your intentions; it includes the steps to fulfill the intentions.

Third, this statement should be doable immediately. It should not be some lofty set of wishes you know you can't fulfill in the near future. Set your sights on something realistic and achievable.

What types of relationships need improving? The responses were all over the place, but we could put them in three broad categories: parents to children, spouses to each other, and then a catchall "other." Before we begin looking at devising a mission statement for relationships, let's see where the breakdown is taking place.

Once again we saw in the survey results an interesting trend when the responses called for one of four choices: agree strongly, agree somewhat, disagree somewhat, and disagree strongly. In follow-up interviews, we found that many who answered, "agree somewhat," could have just as easily given one of the more negative responses. How is this so? Listen to Jackie from Minneapolis.

"When I read the statement, 'I am a good parent,' I answered 'agree somewhat,' but I could have just as easily said 'disagree somewhat.' Look, you're not going to find a lot of parents who think they are perfect. Most of us really want to improve. But you won't find many of us saying we're bad parents either."

We thus looked at all the responses but "agree strongly" as indications of need for improvement, sometimes even significant improvement. This pattern was continued in the three categories of relationships we examined: parenting, marriage, and other.

Seeking Healthier Relationships between Parents and Children

The simple life will never be simple unless parents and children have a reasonably healthy relationship. Fortunately a majority of the respondents did think they had a pretty good relationship with their children:

> **I am a good parent.**
> Agree strongly: 56%
> Agree somewhat: 41%
> Disagree somewhat: 3%
> Disagree strongly: 0%

The good news is that most parents think they are doing okay. The bad news is that about four of ten parents really see the need for healthier relationship with their children. Not surprisingly, when we asked the question of the parents from the child's point of view ("My kids consider me to be a good parent."), the responses were identical to the question above. The majority of parents think they are doing a good job, and they believe that their children would give the same assessment. But four of ten parents really want to improve.

In fact, when we changed the question to see how many parents were worried about how their children will turn out, the numbers indicate even more concern. Of course, these higher numbers reflect the reality that our children are free-will creatures, and even the best of parents can have children who disappoint them.

> **I am worried about how my kids will turn out.**
> Agree strongly: 29%
> Agree somewhat: 38%

Disagree somewhat: 22%
Disagree strongly: 10%

When the question is rephrased to ask how parenting ultimately affects the lives of the children, the concerns are obviously higher. More than two-thirds of parents worry about their kids, not really a surprising conclusion.

But the comments and the interviews revealed some of the reasons for the concerns. One prominent issue, for example, was the common concern of lack of time. We discussed this issue in the previous section, but let's also hear from Rebecca about time and relationships.

"I wouldn't call myself a bad parent," she began. Rebecca is a thirty-three-year-old mother of two from Abilene, Texas. "I didn't answer the survey question that way anyway. But I really feel guilty for not spending quality one-on-one time with either my son or my daughter. My husband and I, as well as the two kids, are so busy with our own activities that we really don't have time for one another. It's kind of ironic. We want the best for our children, but we aren't giving them what they need the most: our time."

Rebecca paused for a moment. We sensed that she had a few more thoughts to express.

"No, I shouldn't say it's ironic. A better word would be *stupid*. We're staying so busy doing things for our kids that we're not giving them one of the things they really need: us. That's really stupid."

When we saw the look on Rebecca's face, we decided not to argue with her just to make her feel better.

Less than one third of parents feel strongly that they give their children enough time. Yet most of these same parents think they are working hard to be good parents. The hectic schedule in which they find themselves leaves them feeling exhausted, confused, and guilty.

And despite the seemingly best efforts of parents, they tell us that they know their children less as the child gets older. Look at some of these disturbing results from our surveys.

> **I feel strongly that I really know my kids.**
> When the oldest child is younger than six: 73%
> When the oldest child is nine to eleven: 58%
> When the oldest child is twelve to eighteen: 48%
> When the oldest child is nineteen and older: 43%

Parents tend to get their children involved in a plethora of activities at very young ages. But that busyness often does not provide the desired results. As the children get older, the parents feel less and less that they know their kids. Activities alone do not seem to provide healthier parent-child relationships. To the contrary, they may be at least partly responsible for doing just the opposite of the parents' dreams and wishes for their children.

Seeking Healthier Relationships between Husbands and Wives

You don't need any more statistics and data. In fact, you are already convinced that marriages are in trouble.

Depending on the source and the method of research, you will hear that as many as one in two marriages will end in divorce. And you will hear that marriages after the first marriage have an even higher rate of failure. We could cite statistics on spouse abuse, on separations in marriage, or on the number of spouses seeking crisis intervention in marriages.

But you don't need to be convinced. Many of you see it right in your own home. Oh, there may be a few of you who are convinced that your marriage is so strong it needs little help. But not most of you. Read on.

The news begins on a positive note. More than half of the respondents (58%) strongly agree that their marriage is strong.

Well, that looks like a positive note. The flip side is that 42 percent of those currently married cannot say strongly that they have a good marriage.

What are the issues? By this point you would expect that the time issue is pervasive. That's why we addressed that in detail in the previous section. A large number (84%) of the respondents indicated that they needed to spend more time together. These feelings were almost universal, cutting across lines of age, race, gender, and religious belief.

Married couples are time starved for each other. Their unusual response is to get busier and have less time for each other. They know what they need to do, but they don't do it.

Such a contradiction is the plight of all of us. The apostle Paul even struggled with knowing what is right, but not doing what is right. In his letter to the Roman church, he wrote: "For I know that nothing good lives in me, that is, in my flesh. For the desire to do what is good is with me, but there is no ability to do it. For I do not do the good that I want to do, but I practice the evil that I do not want to do" (Rom. 7:18–19).

A lot of us married couples are not doing the things we want to do. That's the complex life. That's one reason you might be reading this book about the simple life.

You are not alone. Most of the respondents indicated that they needed help in their marriages. Listen to Shirley's story.

"I guess I should have dated Larry longer before we got married and really gotten to know him. But many of my friends dated for a long time before they got married, and most of them tell me the same thing."

Just what is that same thing?

"We would really like our husbands to demonstrate love to us like they did when we were dating and first married. Why can't there be romance after we've been married a while?" Shirley looked right into our eyes. We felt uncomfortable. "What's wrong with you men?"

We no longer felt uncomfortable. We *were* uncomfortable.

Shirley is both right and wrong. She is right that many spouses (60%) would like their husbands and wives to demonstrate love to them. But she is wrong in assuming that the issue is just a cause for concern for wives.

Men feel that way.

Young married couples feel that way.

Older married couples feel that way.

Both the religious and nonreligious feel that way.

Activities have replaced demonstrations of love. That's not good. But there is more.

Demonstrations of love were not limited to sex between the husbands and wives, but sex is a significant part of it. And the sexual facet of a couple's relationship did not get a good report either. In fact, only 38 percent of the respondents strongly agreed that they were satisfied with the quality of their sex lives.

Let us state the obvious in inverse terms. A large majority, 62 percent to be exact, of married couples can't state
strongly that they are satisfied with the quality of their sex
lives. We see a direct relationship in the previous results with
this dilemma. If romance and demonstrations of love are not
taking place outside the bedroom, it is unlikely that romance
in the bedroom will be satisfying.

We saw similar problems with satisfaction with the
frequency of sex among married couples. Only 33 percent
agreed strongly that they were satisfied with the frequency
of sex in their marriage. And, surprisingly, this result was
pervasive among both the husbands and the wives. Only
38 percent of the wives were satisfied with sexual frequency,
and only 27 percent of the husbands were satisfied with
sexual frequency.

Which subgroup in our study was most satisfied with the
quality of their sex lives? Perhaps the answer is surprising:
evangelical Christians. They were the only subgroup where a
majority (55%) strongly agreed that they were satisfied with
the quality of their sex lives.

Okay, for those who aren't evangelical Christians, we won't
use that statistic to persuade you to join us in our beliefs. But
it is a nice ancillary benefit.

So what is it that spouses seek in each other? What can
help the marriage grow stronger? One of the reasons we
highlighted the book *The Love Dare* is its bold challenge for
husbands and wives to practice unconditional love toward
each other.

As we interviewed more than one thousand people, the
married people were clear in what they would like from
their spouses. The good news is that the requests are not

unreasonable. The bad news is that the needs are largely unmet.

For example, husbands and wives would like their spouses to do little things for them. What are these "little things"? The responses were varied but predictable. Listen to some of them.

- "I wish he would help with just a little of the housework."
- "I would be happier if she showed more interest in my work."
- "Why can't she just try to enjoy watching one football game with me?"
- "I would love a shoulder rub without having to ask him."
- "Flowers. Just once a year. Unexpected. No special occasion."
- "We need to have more grown-up talk. All of our conversations are with the kids or about the kids."
- "He would shock me if he loaded the dishwasher one evening."
- "I wish he would spend as much time with me as he does his computer."

So how are couples faring on the little things? Just fair. About four out of ten married men and women said that their spouse does these little things for them.

We also asked as a separate question the "little thing" of encouragement. Both husbands and wives longed for words of affirmation and encouragement from their spouses. But only about one-third (36%) of all the married people could

strongly agree that their spouses offer words of encouragement for them.

The simple life is really about simple things, and it's those
simple things we neglect the most. To paraphrase the apostle
Paul, we don't do those things we know we should do.

Before we leave the topic of the marital relationship, let
us share with you what we consider to be the most significant
question to married couples. Would you marry the same person again?

At first glance, the results appear encouraging. Nearly
two-thirds (64%) of the married people in our study strongly
agreed that they would marry their current spouse if they had
to do it all over again.

But then the number started bothering us. More than one-
third (36%) of married people can't say with certainty that
they would marry their current spouse again. And though we
don't have the precise numbers, we can presume that more
than half of all marriages have at least one spouse who is not
sure that he or she is married to the right person.

That's scary. The simple life is desperately needed for
healthy marriages.

Back to Clarity

We have looked at some of the responses of our study
dealing with relationships. The discussion has not been
exhaustive. We said nothing about children seeking better
relationships with their parents. Likewise, we didn't address
the issue of relationships between bosses and subordinates, or
employers and employees. In fact, we could have cited many
more examples.

But we think our point about relationships has been made. Most people want better relationships in some aspect of their lives. And most people realize that the improvement of relationships begins with a dependence on God and a commitment to take some small steps.

May we make some suggestions to get you started?

First, decide which relationship you would like to see improve. We realize that some of you may be dealing with multiple relationship issues, but you need to work on just one at a time. Perhaps you can start with the relationship that gives you the most concern. Maybe you need to begin with the person closest to you. The point is you need to choose one now. To work on more than one simultaneously defeats the purpose of the simple life. You instead invite more complexity.

Where is the relationship need the greatest? Your husband? Your wife? Your child? Your parent? Your friend? Your adversary? (We had a tough time saying "enemy.") Your coworker? Your boss? Your subordinate? Your neighbor? Your classmate? Your fiancé? Your in-law (pick one)? The list could go on, but you need to choose one for now.

Second, define your "how" as well as your "what." Make a mission statement on how to improve your relationship. But first let's see what's not effective. Maybe Faye desires to improve her relationship with her husband, William. She then writes her mission statement: "I will strive to be a better wife to William."

Most of the time that kind of statement is doomed for failure. It states the "what" (to have a better relationship with her husband), but it doesn't express the "how" (the process she will take to accomplish her goal of being a better wife).

Instead, she takes a different approach. She lets the mission statement define the "what" and the "how": "I will become a better wife to William by complimenting him at least once a day for the next ten days, and by refraining from criticizing him during that same period."

Now Faye is getting the job done. She not only has a mission statement that seeks to accomplish her goal; she has some steps to accomplish that goal. And speaking from the perspective of the husband, we both know that William is likely to love the change he sees in his wife. But notice that the mission statement is not overpowering or overpromising. That leads to our next suggestion.

Don't overcommit yourself through your mission statement. Faye has made a commitment for ten days. That's manageable. She has committed to pay at least one compliment to William each day. She can probably do that. And she has committed to refrain from criticizing her husband during this ten-day period.

That's tough. We both know how we husbands can irritate wives. And we both know that there will be times when Faye has had enough of something that William has said or done or not said or not done. The key is not to let failure be final. If she slips up on one day, she can commit to getting it right the rest of the ten days.

Seek some type of accountability person. Neither one of us particularly likes having a formal time and/or place to report to someone. Some of you could do fine with the formality of accountability, but we all can be open with someone we trust about our intentions. When we tell someone of our plans, we have inherently created accountability. And that accountability increases our prospects for accomplishing the intent of our mission statement.

So how did Faye respond? She purchased a blank journal and wrote her mission statement on the first page:

I will become a better wife to William by complimenting him at least once a day for the next ten days, and by refraining from criticizing him during that same period.

Faye realized that she might not get it perfect every day, so she noted her progress or lack of progress in her journal daily. And she realized that she couldn't become the perfect wife in ten days. But she had to start somewhere. How did she do?

"The process was amazing. I did give William at least one sincere compliment each day, usually two. I messed up on the criticizing thing two of the days, but I didn't let it stop me from keeping at it. I discovered two amazing things. First, selfless love and giving are so freeing. You don't give expecting anything in return. Second, I noticed a difference in William's attitude toward me after just three days. I think I like this so much I will try something new soon."

Maybe we can help. By now you know we're going from clarity to movement. We'll look deeper at this issue of relationships in the next chapter.

APPLICATION
SIMPLE LIFE: CLARITY
MAKING A SELFLESS COMMITMENT

The analytical part of healthy relationships was easy. Simply stated, relationships become healthier when at least one of the parties has a selfless attitude. Of course, it's a great relationship when all of the parties are selfless.

But you've probably been (are?) in a relationship where one person is obviously selfish. In fact, he or she may be a jerk at times.

We challenge you to be totally (okay, let's say almost) selfless in your relationship with someone for a week to ten days.

Here are some points you may want to remember:

- Make the commitment for a brief time. Don't get too ambitious.
- Don't go overboard on what you'll do. You are likely to fail if you do.
- You may want to tell someone else about your commitment for accountability.
- Stay true to your commitment for a week even if the other person is not responsive.

Do you remember Faye's example from this chapter? Here it is again: "I will become a better wife to William by complimenting him at least once a day for the next ten days, and by refraining from criticizing him during that same period."

Now write your relational mission statement below:

_____

_____

_____

_____

_____

_____

_____

_____

CHAPTER 6

Moving to Healthier Relationships

Clarity → **MOVEMENT** → Alignment → Focus

Shortly after Thom's dad and Art's grandfather, Sam, died, the family sat in the family room with Nan, the grieving widow. The conversation was mostly lighthearted. Several made comments about Sam's quiet and dry wit. Many of the family members were in tears, a strange combination of grief and laughter.

There was a moment of silence. It was not awkward. Everyone in the room seemed to enjoy the brief moments of reflection about this man we all loved dearly.

Soon the conversation began again. We're not sure which one of the family members asked Nan this question, but the memory of the words themselves was unforgettable: "What do you already miss most about him?"

Nan did not hesitate. Her response was quick and certain, "The flowers."

None of us were surprised. We didn't have to ask for clarification. Those two simple words were all we needed to hear. We understood. "The flowers."

You see, during the long warm seasons in south Alabama, Sam was able to keep a healthy flower bed in his yard most months of the year. And each morning he would awaken early, go to the flower bed, and pick the most beautiful flower of the day. That flower was for Nan, the love of his life. It was his simple act of love.

When people describe Sam Rainer as a simple man, they meant nothing but affirmation. He was extremely smart, near the top of his graduating class. He was both a bank president and a mayor in the small town where he lived all of his life.

But Sam just didn't need many "things" to be happy. He declined significant job offers in other towns. Why? He was happy in the small town. Why change just for money or prestige? Some urged him to build a larger home. He declined. Why? The home he owned had plenty of room—all sixteen hundred square feet. And when the town urged him to continue serving as mayor, he declined. Why? It was time for someone else to do the job. There were plenty of gifted people in the town.

After all, he missed his hunting and fishing. With all of his responsibilities, he needed to be on the lake or in the woods more than the two times a week limitation he had while he was both mayor and bank president.

His was a simple life and a good life.

Sam was never stingy with his family. To the contrary, he would give you anything you needed. And he wasn't stingy with his beloved wife. He did buy Nan some of those "things" from time to time. And when Nan expressed a desire to see other countries, he did relent and take her on tours of Europe and South America.

But Nan did not mention the "things" after he died. She said nothing about the magnificent trips they took together. She missed the flowers.

Sam would bring Nan a cup of coffee and a freshly picked flower in a simple vase nearly a hundred times a year. And he would greet her with his simple smile, "Good morning, honey."

Of all the things she could have missed, she missed the flowers.

Sam Rainer practiced and lived the simple life.

Congestion and Relationships

Do you remember our discussion of congestion earlier in the book? Congestion consists of those things that keep us from living the simple life. Congestion includes those activities that keep us too busy to live the simple life. And congestion hinders relationships from developing to their full potential.

Congestion is bad because it blocks the movement we must have to live the simple life. Congestion is bad because it means we are busy in other areas of our lives when we could be spending more time growing healthy relationships.

In the previous clarity chapter, we looked at a simple mission statement. If you recall, Faye wrote a simple mission statement about her relationship with her husband:

I will become a better wife to William by complimenting him at least once a day for the next ten days, and by refraining from criticizing him during that same period.

The mission statement has clarity. It is certainly doable. But what could hinder its progress?

What if Faye was so busy with other activities that she simply forgot her commitment? What if she was so tired by doing so many other things that she had no energy to change her patterns of behavior? What if things got in the way?

Faye would have clarity, but she would experience no movement toward accomplishing her goal. The best of intentions would be thwarted by the busyness of life.

That's congestion. And that's bad.

Movement must follow clarity.

Recognize the Need for Healthy Relationships

This subtitle may seem silly to you. Who doesn't recognize the need for healthy relationships? Our point is that a true recognition of the need means that we will move in that direction. And the direction that seems to be the best for relationships involves the little things.

Sam gave Nan a flower in the morning. Faye committed to compliment William at least once a day for ten days. Little things.

Only one out of three parents strongly agreed that they give their children adequate one-on-one time. Little things.

Nearly three out of four parents desire to do better controlling their tempers with their children. Little things.

Do you notice the conspicuous absence of so many of the things that prevent movement, the things that cause congestion?

You don't see spouses and parents saying that they need to provide more material items for their loved ones. You don't see family members indicating that they need more activities in order to enjoy the good life.

In fact, in our surveys we heard little about nicer cars, getting children more involved in sports, taking on more work hours, or buying bigger homes with bigger mortgage payments. Instead, we typically heard that these items were congestions. They represented the blockage that prevented movement toward the simple life.

We know what we need to do. But we aren't doing it.

Clarity is the intention. Movement is the action.

Healthy relationships depend on less congestion and more movement. And that usually happens best when we focus on the little things.

Recognize the Congestion of Activities

When Thom Rainer and Eric Geiger wrote *Simple Church*, they were amazed at the responses of church leaders. Here is a portion of an e-mail sent to Thom from a senior pastor in the Bakersfield, California, area: "I picked up *Simple Church* first because the title appealed to me. But what I read blew me away. The book talked about activities replacing true disciple making in churches, revealing that many churches were so busy adding things to do that they neglected seeing if lives were really being changed. Well, you nailed our church. We're really just a collection of activities. Things will change though. I am committed to leading our people to become a church that really understands what we're supposed to be doing and why we're supposed to be doing it."

What is true in many churches is true in many lives. Activities are replacing purpose. We are so busy doing activities that we are neglecting what really matters. And most of you don't really need this book to address this reality. You already know it.

One-third of the respondents to our survey indicated that their lives were just too busy. But another 44 percent were unable to state with certainty that they weren't too busy. In all, more than three-fourths of the respondents either stated clearly that they were too busy or were unable to say they weren't too busy.

Often activities replace the important matters that help relationships grow. Nan Rainer didn't talk about the international trips or the material items her husband got her. After his death she said she missed the flowers.

When we asked the respondents the question in another way, the results were similar. We asked if their family members were able to relax and enjoy one another. Only 13 percent agreed strongly that they could. That's a small number, too small.

Victor from Oklahoma City expressed thoughts that were similar to many of those who took the survey. "Two years ago we took a vacation on this secluded beach that had almost no amenities. There were no amusement parks nearby. There was only one small restaurant. The nearest theater was ninety minutes away. In fact, there was nothing to do but enjoy the beach and one another for a week."

"How did your family fare?" We were particularly interested since he and his wife, Jamie, had three sons, all under the age of ten.

"The first two days were miserable," Victor confessed. "I don't know how many times the boys complained that they had nothing to do. But then we started to enjoy the place. We went on some hiking trails during the day. We went hunting for crabs at night. We fished two to three hours a day. We played board games we brought with us. I don't think the boys knew that you could play a game that wasn't on a video screen."

Then Victor paused. "Our entire family remembers that vacation with so much joy. We talked more as a family than we ever have. We learned to relax together. And we just stopped being so busy doing things. You can probably guess where the boys want to go on vacation next year . . . the same place. I think we made memories for a lifetime."

What activities are hindering you from developing deeper relationships? Do you have the best of intentions, but the congestion of so many things to do doesn't let it happen? Is it time to get closer to your spouse? Your kids? Your friends? Is it time to recover the simple life so you can have real relationships?

Moving toward Selflessness

One of the most common types of congestion in the development of relationships is selfishness. Simply stated, you look at the relationship through the lens of what the other person can and should do for you.

But movement toward meaningful relationships will only succeed if you decide that you will seek the best for the other person. Anything else is just an exercise in self-interest.

When the apostle Paul wrote the Corinthian church in his first letter to the congregation, he was dealing with a church that was pretty self-centered. He confronted a plethora of problems in the church. He even had to deal with arguments about the superiority over spiritual gifts.

The so-called "love chapter" of 1 Corinthians 13 is often read at weddings as a testimony of the bride and groom's love for each other. While there is certainly nothing wrong with reading the love chapter at weddings, it is fascinating to understand its original context. Members of the Corinthian church were arguing about which of the spiritual gifts were superior in 1 Corinthians 12. And in 1 Corinthians 14 the issue was the appropriateness of the spiritual gift of tongues.

Sandwiched between these two contentious chapters is the love chapter. Paul was warning the Corinthians to cease their selfish ramblings and to start practicing selfless love toward one another. While we won't take time to do a complete exegetical study of 1 Corinthians 13 here, let's just look at some of the descriptions Paul gives of true and unconditional love. And remember, he is doing so to let church members know how they are to relate to one another. It's simply a biblical lesson on right relationships.

Love is patient (v. 4). Maybe some of us need to look at the inverse of this description: love is not impatient. Do you sometimes lose patience with your spouse? A child? A coworker? A friend? Do you know what you're doing at those moments? You are looking after your own desires and needs before those of others. Patient love is always placing someone else's needs before our own.

Love is kind (v. 4). Kindness implies intentionality, a subject we will look at shortly. When we are kind to someone, we are making an overt effort to do a good deed or to say a positive word about him or her. Kindness typically requires forethought, and that forethought is an effort itself to demonstrate love. The very act of thinking about what we can do for someone else is a selfless act. In many early stages of romantic relationships, kindness is more natural. But true love will demonstrate acts of kindness in all kinds of relationships, and in all stages of relationships.

Love does not envy (v. 4). "I only want the best for my wife." We will leave the speaker of that sentence anonymous. The reason for anonymity is that his wife totally disagreed. "You say that you want the best for me," she told her husband calmly. "But your actions say otherwise. I can't remember the last time you asked me what I would like to do or where I'd like to go. You seem to resent the idea of me enjoying myself."

The husband looked uncomfortable.

What if we looked at relationships through the lens of only wanting the best for the other person? Congestion occurs when we envy others.

Love is not boastful (v. 4). We know someone who has been pretty successful, at least by the world's standards. And we admit, he has some pretty impressive accomplishments. But do you know what else we noticed about him? From our perspective, he has no friends. We could be wrong, but he really doesn't seem to have any friends.

As a matter of fact, we don't enjoy being around him either. Why? He's always talking about himself and what he's accomplished. The only people who are around him these days are eager sycophants, not real friends.

Love does not seek to dominate the conversation with self. Love is eager to hear from others.

Love is not conceited (v. 4). This comment from the apostle Paul is parallel to his comment about boasting. When one boasts, he talks about himself. When one is conceited, she focuses on herself. But love is focused on others. Love is concerned about others.

Love does not act improperly (v. 5). Some translations say, "Love is not rude." At the heart of rudeness or acting improperly is a disregard for others. This lack of love is also a lack of respect for another person.

Love is not selfish (v. 5). "My primary problem with my husband," the California wife told us, "is that he seems always to be thinking about what he needs and what he wants. Our relationship is strained because he never asks what I want. Do you know what he did last year? We had been saving for a down payment on a home, and he took the money and bought himself a new car. He told me that he deserved it. If I hear that one more time from him, I am leaving. Sometimes I think the only thing keeping me in this relationship is the kids."

Admittedly the situation described in that interview is extreme, but our surveys indicate that selfishness is pervasive in many relationships. Rarely did we hear a spouse talk about what he or she should do more for the other spouse. Movement toward the simple life is not taking place in many relationships because so many are only looking out for their own needs.

Love is not provoked (v. 5). Sometimes anger is appropriate. Paul himself became angered when he encountered the idols in Athens (Acts 17:16). Jesus was angry when He saw the hardness of many people's hearts (Mark 3:5) and the money changers in the temple (John 2:14–17).

But this text speaks to those who are easily angered. It is for the hotheaded among us whose temper becomes ignited over the smallest of things. That type of quick anger is again a focus on self and an unwillingness to be patient.

Love does not keep a record of wrongs (v. 5). The story of the prophet Hosea and his wife Gomer is one of the toughest applications in the Bible. The story is about God's mandate to Hosea to take Gomer as his wife, even though she was a promiscuous woman. The story continues as God tells Hosea again and again to take back his wife even though she has been unfaithful.

It helps us understand this book of the Bible when we learn that Hosea received this burden from God to show God's forgiving love to the unfaithful Israelites: "Then the LORD said to me, 'Go again; show love to a woman who is loved by another man and is an adulteress, just as the LORD loves the Israelites though they turn to other gods and love raisin cakes'" (Hos. 3:1).

The strange part of that passage is the raisin cakes. They were made of dried, compressed grapes and were apparently a rare delicacy in the Israelites' diet. But they were also a part of the fertility ritual in the worship of the false god Baal. So the raisin cakes were further demonstration of the nation's unfaithfulness.

This passage describes God's persistent and forgiving love toward the wayward nation. It foreshadows the same type of

forgiving love Christ demonstrated by His death on the cross
(Col. 1:20).

But our challenge comes when we begin to understand
that persistent and forgiving love should be a part of our lives
as well. We often feel more justified when we hold grudges
and refuse to forgive. After all, that person wronged us. Why
should we even think about forgiving him or her?

But the apostle Paul said that love keeps no record of
wrongs.

But sometimes relationships are hindered because we have
an unforgiving spirit, even though we were wronged.

That's tough to remedy. But it's mandatory and it's
biblical.

Movement Away from Selfishness

If one of the greatest hindrances to movement in relationships is selfishness, then 1 Corinthians 13 is a great place to
start. And if we even come close to demonstrating love as
described in that passage, we have come a long way.

It's kind of ironic, isn't it? We are looking at ways for you
to move to the simple life in relationships. We are trying to
help you. We are looking out for your interests.

Then we tell you that you need to give up your own interests and look out for the interests of others. We can almost
hear some readers telling us to get back to their needs.

We are. One of the greatest needs we have in all relationships is to focus on others. It is ironic, but that's the way it
works.

The apostle Paul said again, this time in Philippians 2:3–4,
"Do nothing out of rivalry or conceit, but in humility consider

others as more important than yourselves. Everyone should look out not only for his own interests, but also for the interests of others."

How?

Incremental Movement . . . Again

Let's return to Faye's mission statement:

I will become a better wife to William by complimenting him at least once a day for the next ten days, and by refraining from criticizing him during that same period.

We expressed our concern about Faye's attempting to do too much by committing to refrain from criticizing her husband at all for ten days. It's admirable. It's right. But it's tough.

On the other hand, the goal of complimenting William once a day is doable. And lest you think that such a goal is too meek, think about how many times you compliment your spouse, a friend, a coworker, or a neighbor in the course of a day. Sure, some of you are regular encouragers.

Menda Sue Hatfield is a friend of ours. We got to know her when we lived in Louisville, Kentucky, and Thom worked with her husband. If you are around Menda Sue for ten minutes, you are likely to receive five compliments. Spend an hour with Menda Sue, and you will wonder why millions of Americans have not pleaded with her to run for president of the United States. She really has the gift of encouragement. But not all of us are like Menda Sue.

Make a small commitment, just as Faye did. Hers was one compliment a day for ten days. It's reasonable. It's doable. It's incremental.

We realize that in ten days you won't transform from where you are to where you need to be in relationships. But you will make progress. That's how you have movement toward the simple life. That's how you begin the steps toward healthier relationships.

Those Two Things

Many years ago the two of us went to a hands-on museum in St. Petersburg, Florida. Art was only seven years old then. One of the exhibits was "The Dark Maze," a labyrinthine tunnel that went in multiple directions.

The problem with the challenge of the maze was twofold. First, you had to crawl in the tunnel. At no point was it high enough for even a seven-year-old to stand. Second, once you entered the tunnel, you were in total darkness. You could not see your hand in front of your face.

Art was allowed to enter with me (Thom) with the stipulation that he was required to hold on to his father at all times.

I entered the tunnel with total confidence that I would make it through in record time.

Wrong.

I made one wrong turn after another. Every attempt to find the open path was met with resistance. One dead end. Then another. And then another.

Art was patient at first. He even obliged me when I told him that we would have to back up and try another path. Still, we met obstacles at every point. Finally Art spoke in exasperation, "Dad, we really just need to get out of this place."

So Art, the independent child, found the exit on his own. Unfortunately for my pride, the maximum time allowed to get through the tunnel expired. Someone on the outside opened a hatch and bright light penetrated the darkness. Father and son were free to leave. Actually, we were told to leave.

Art was relieved. I was humiliated.

Sometimes our relationships are much like "The Dark Maze." We start with the best of intentions. We are confident that we will get through the challenge with victory. But we meet one dead end after another.

The simple life is a life toward healthier relationships. We have a mission to have great relationships. That's clarity. And then we begin making progress toward those healthy relationships. That's movement.

But movement is hindered by congestion. And the two most common types of congestion are activities and selfishness.

We heard it from more than one thousand respondents to our surveys. And we wouldn't be surprised if you, the reader, identify with some of these comments:

- "Michelle and I always loved to spend a couple of hours talking each night when we first married. Now we are so busy taking the kids everywhere during the day that we are too tired to have much conversation at night."
- "I work more than sixty hours a week. I don't know where I will find time to connect with my friends. I'm barely connected to my family."

- "When we first married, Mark focused on the little things that meant so much to me. He would write me a note almost every week. Or he would bring home a single flower for me. Now that we've been married three years, he's stopped doing those little things."
- "Sometimes I wish I were a football game so Jeremy would give me that kind of attention."
- "I try to stay in touch with Susan, but she doesn't reciprocate. I'm about to give up on her."
- "What happened to our relationship? Will somebody tell me what happened?"

We began this section by looking at your plan or mission statement for healthier relationships. Then we began to examine how best to act or move on that plan. According to our research, the two greatest hindrances toward movement are activities, the overcommitted life, and selfishness, putting our desires above others.

We pray that you have addressed those two hindrances. We pray that you have made a commitment to begin, even if it's just a small step, to move beyond those obstacles.

It's time to get out of the dark maze. It's time to move toward healthier relationships in the simple life.

Are the values and actions in your life so well aligned that the accomplishment of your goals is possible? That's what we call alignment, and that's the subject of the next chapter.

APPLICATION
SIMPLE LIFE: MOVEMENT
PUTTING RELATIONSHIPS FIRST

We are so busy that we hurt and hinder relationships.

Movement means you get the obstacles out of the way. In the spaces below, list some of the activities that hurt and hinder your ability to spend time with people you care about.

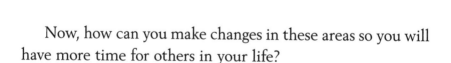

Now, how can you make changes in these areas so you will have more time for others in your life?

CHAPTER 7

The Five Hindrances to Healthy Relationships

Clarity → Movement → **ALIGNMENT** → Focus

Both Art and Thom still laugh about the fight and the telephone call. Art made the call from his home in South Florida to Thom in Nashville. Art and Sarah had been married for a couple of years, and their marriage was growing stronger by the day. But like most married couples they have their moments of disagreement. This time, however, the mild disagreement degenerated into a full-fledged verbal fight.

The marital fight became so heated that Sarah went into the bedroom alone and shut the door. Art was now alone, still reeling with anger but also trying to figure out how to bring the fight to an end and begin reconciliation with his wife.

He had an idea. He would call Thom, his dad. After all, he knew that Thom had experience in the area of marital disagreements.

The phone rang and Thom answered. Art did not waste words. "Dad, Sarah and I are having a fight. This one's pretty bad. You got any recommendations?"

Thom's thirty-two years of marriage and modest level of experience in marital conflict prepared him for the moment. "Art," Thom began, "you need to go to the bedroom, put your arms around your wife, and tell her you're sorry."

A pause in the telephone conversation. "But Dad," Art interjected, "I don't know that I did anything wrong."

"Art," the older and dubiously wiser Thom responded, "you're always wrong!"

So Art followed his father's instructions and called back several minutes later with the exciting news that reconciliation with his wife had been quick and easier than expected. The turning point was when Art told Sarah that he was wrong. She then asked Art why he was wrong. Art responded, "I have no clue; I just know I'm wrong."

Husband and wife thus reconciled in a boisterous fit of laughter.

Alignment and Relationships

We have looked at the concept of clarity in relationships, understanding what your true purposes and goals are. Then we dealt with movement, getting beyond congestion and blockages. Now we are looking at the issue of alignment, making certain that all that we do moves us toward the accomplishment of our purpose.

In our survey we found that many times relationships were solid because people were all on the same page. Husbands and wives saw things from the same perspective. Friends had similar values. Coworkers had common goals. And neighbors saw the same needs in their neighborhoods.

Such was not the situation with Art and Sarah. They simply were not on the same page, and they weren't even sure how it happened.

But goals cannot be accomplished and missions cannot be fulfilled when those in relationships are not aligned with one another. In this section on relationships, we will take a different approach. Instead of looking at how we can best be in alignment, we will look at common reasons alignment doesn't take place.

In relationships the failure to align often does not mean that one party is right and the other party is wrong. Instead, the failure of alignment could mean that people in a relationship see things from a different perspective.

Thom was walking in his neighborhood on a walking path. In front of him were three people, a husband and wife and a female friend of the wife. The man stopped just a brief moment to do some stretching exercises. Much to Thom's horror, he saw a car jumping the curb and headed right toward the man on the walking path.

It was too late to do anything. The man was hit by the front of the car. He was thrown back several feet. Though he survived, he was in bad condition and continues to have medical problems to this day.

There were four witnesses to this accident, other than the victim and the driver of the automobile.

Thom saw the car coming from a north intersection, where the driver ran a stop sign but at a slow speed, probably less than twenty miles per hour. In Thom's view the driver tried to stop once he realized that he ran a stop sign. Thom was only twenty feet behind the victim when he was hit and saw the impact take place on the front of the car.

The two women were engaged in conversation. From their perspective the car was traveling at a much faster speed, maybe forty miles per hour. The only reason the man was not killed, they said, is because the curb slowed the vehicle's speed. They were only about ten feet from the victim. They also said the victim was hit by the front of the car.

A fourth witness was a jogger who had a side view of the accident from sixty feet away. From his angle he said that the car did not run a stop sign but lost control after the vehicle crossed the intersection. And he said that the victim was hit on the left side of his hip, not straight on. He could not judge the speed.

Though Thom gave his statement to the police that reflected his initial impression, he began to doubt his own recollection when he heard about the other perspectives.

For the record the driver was a sixteen-year-old boy. He was not sure if he stopped at the intersection or not. He was text messaging a friend and not paying attention. And he had no idea about his speed or the point of impact.

Perspectives can be different. They can also be funny. But if we don't acknowledge the reality of different perspectives, they can keep relationships out of alignment. Let's look at five of those hindrances.

Men and Women *Are* from Different Planets

Okay, we are not totally different. And some men and women do see eye-to-eye on many issues, if not most issues. But the reality is that many times the perspectives are vastly different. The result is often that both parties know that they are right and the other person is wrong. Yet we found that the issue is more often one of perspective.

Our gender breakdown for our study was 465 males and 612 females. Though the females had an edge in the number of respondents (57% to 43%), the sample size of each gender group was sufficient to give us some pretty fascinating insights into the different perspectives between men and women.

For example, let's look at the relationships between mothers and children and then fathers and children. While few parents believe they are perfect in their parenting skills, mothers are more likely to be confident that they are doing okay. When we asked mothers if they were spending enough one-on-one time with their children, 40 percent agreed strongly that they were.

When we asked men the same question, only 20 percent strongly agreed that they spend enough time with their children. That number, only half the level of the mothers, is statistically significant and relationally staggering.

While a significant number of both fathers and mothers confess that they really do need to do better spending time with their children, the fathers were more likely to struggle with this issue. And while we could surmise that there were more stay-at-home moms in the survey sample than stay-at-home dads (we did not ask that question), the difference is notable in any circumstances.

Joseph is a certified public accountant who was recently promoted to senior partner in his CPA firm. He lives in the Houston, Texas, area and really considers his family to be a priority. But he also acknowledges that his family does not always get sufficient time from him.

"I do okay except for tax season," Joseph told us. "The problem is that tax season does not end with our firm on April 15. With all the extensions requested, our busy season is really more than half the year now. And my family gets shortchanged during that time. But I am the provider for our family, and I have to give priority to my work."

Interestingly many of the working moms did not express that same priority. While they admitted that they were stressed at times balancing family and work, they typically yielded to sacrificing work for family. The men conversely sacrificed family for work.

It is not the place of this study to get into the psychology of gender differences but, suffice it to say, men and women are often different in their perspectives. Let's look at a few more examples related to parenting.

When we asked both parents if they knew their children well, the responses were not surprising. If mothers were more likely to give time to their children, then they were also more likely to know their children well. More than 55 percent of the mothers strongly agreed that they know their children, but only 47 percent of the fathers expressed the same sentiment. Again, the difference is statistically significant.

Women in the study tended to be generally more religious, and more were specifically Christian than men. It is therefore no surprise that the females more than the males in our study were more likely to teach their children how to have a relationship with God. More than 45 percent of the mothers strongly agreed that such teaching was important, compared to less than 31 percent of the men. Again, the difference between the two is significant both statistically and relationally.

Let's look at one more gender issue related to parenting. More than two-thirds (68%) of the females indicated that they made efforts to be a better parent compared to 59 percent of the men. We could note several more examples, but the point is well made. Men and women have different perspectives about parenting.

But gender differences are not limited to parenting perspectives in relationships. We could cite several examples, but perhaps this one response is most notable. When asked if they had a strong marriage, 62 percent of the wives strongly agreed, compared to 54 percent of the husbands. While the difference is not huge, it does point to other potential differences.

For example, 51 percent of the wives agreed strongly that their husbands were physically affectionate, but only 40 percent of the husbands expressed the same sentiments about their wives. More specifically, 41 percent of the wives state that they are satisfied with the quality of their sex lives compared to 35 percent of the husbands.

Okay, enough statistics. The abundance of numbers can be boring and tedious. But we keep giving you this data to reinforce the obvious. Men and women are different. They have different perspectives and different needs. Sometimes they are on the same page, but oftentimes they are not.

We are not suggesting that relationship alignment means that men and women should become relational clones. To the contrary, we celebrate our differences. But we are suggesting that men and women should be aware of their potential differences in dating relationships, in marriages, and in sibling relationships.

Relationship alignment between genders is important. And the alignment works best not when men and women become like each other, but when they have an awareness and appreciation for their differences.

Faith Misalignment

We stated our biases at the onset. We are both Christians—evangelical Christians who have a high view of Scripture. We can't speak about faith matters with total objectivity, even in a research project such as this one. But we can look at the responses and give you a glimpse of the problems when matters of faith become misaligned. In our survey the number of persons who identified themselves as Christians was higher than those who did not. Approximately 79 percent said they were Christians, while 21 percent said they were not Christians. We realize that self-identification does not necessarily mean that one is truly a follower of Christ, but the differences between the two groups were significant on relationship issues.

Some of the differences were expected. For example, 45 percent of the Christian parents teach their children how to have a relationship with God, but only 14 percent of the non-Christian parents do so. From our perspective the surprise here is not the difference between the two groups but the fact that less than half of self-described Christians feel that it is important to communicate their beliefs to their children.

When the wording is changed to ask if the parents think it is important to teach their children moral values, the positive responses are higher, and the differences between the two groups are smaller. More than 83 percent of the surveyed Christians strongly agree that they should teach moral values to their children, compared to 77 percent of those who are not self-identified Christians. Of course, our bias asks how one can know moral values without some type of absolutes based on a faith system.

What does the Bible say about misalignment in relationships? Second Corinthians 6:14 is discussed and debated among Christian scholars: "Do not be mismatched with unbelievers. For what partnership is there between righteousness and lawlessness? Or what fellowship does light have with darkness?" Some other translations use the phrase "unequally yoked" instead of "mismatched."

The debate and discussion often centers on the nature and extent of being mismatched or unequally yoked. Does the text mean a Christian should not marry a non-Christian? Does it mean that a Christian should not go into business or work directly with a non-Christian? Or does the text have a broader application? For example, does it mean that Christians should not associate with non-Christians to the extent that the relationship would hinder their own Christian walk?

The discussion continues to this day, but our research clearly indicates that those who identify themselves as Christians often have a different perspective on relationships from those who do not. The danger for misalignment is great.

Let's take one example: We asked the respondents if they believed they would stay married to their current spouse until one of them dies. More than 76 percent of the married Christians strongly agreed that they would, but only 64 percent of the non-Christians felt that way. Just looking at a response like that makes us wish we had the luxury of asking follow-up questions to the predetermined questions. We did, however, have the opportunity to listen to some married persons from each perspective. Ron from Kansas City is representative of the non-Christians' responses.

"I can't say for sure I will be married to the same person for life," he began. "I mean, who can? Things happen, you know. People change. I've got no plans to leave my wife, but I'm not going to lie and say that I know we'll both be married to each other for life."

We must be clear that not all the non-Christians expressed that same uncertainty of commitment. More than one-third of that group did respond that they had a lifelong commitment to marriage. And almost one-fourth of the Christians did *not* have such a commitment. In fact, lest we overstate our case, we should remind you that the differential between the two groups was only 12 percentage points.

But our point is still the same. Those with different faith perspectives may have different perspectives on relationships. And those different viewpoints can result in misaligned relationships.

Imagine this scenario. It's probably not too hard to imagine since you've seen it played out before. The wife/mom (we'll call her Janna) believes it is important to take the two girls to worship service on Sunday mornings on a regular basis. The husband/dad (Jay) disagrees. He thinks it's a waste of time. The children would do better, he believes, to get needed sleep and then do something with the family.

Janna and Jay are able to keep their disagreements from the girls. They even had some heated arguments about this issue, but the girls remained oblivious.

Until they asked the question.

"Mom, why doesn't Dad go to church with us?"

Then the private argument becomes a fight in front of the kids. Husband is angry with wife. Wife is mad at husband. Two young daughters are confused and hurt at the scene they witnessed.

Sound familiar?

Our survey indicated that such scenarios are likely, if not common, in many homes. Among self-described Christians, 38 percent believed strongly that they should have their children in a weekly worship service. Among the non-Christians, not surprisingly, the number was much lower at 9 percent. That's a 29-point differential. Even with this subsample, the difference is huge.

We guess that our bias is reflected in our surprise that less than four of ten Christians strongly believe that it is important to have their children in a weekly worship service. We could speculate on some of the reasons for this low response. We have noted in other research the anti-institutional sentiment among a number of Christians who don't believe that the local church is that important ("I love Jesus but not the church").

We could guess that some Christians don't feel they should impose their beliefs on anyone, including their own kids. In fact, we have enough comments from this study to suggest that this reason may be more than conjecture.

A third reason is that some of the self-described Christians are not Christians at all. They may call themselves

Christians because their parents were Christians. Or they may see Christianity as the default religion of Americans, even though they have no personal commitment to Christ themselves.

These comments from Ron in Tulsa bolster this likelihood. "I checked 'Christian' on the survey because my parents were both Protestants. At least I think they were. They really never attended church, and I've only been in a church three or four times in my life. But I guess 'Christian' would be the closest description of me, whatever it means."

Not only are matters of faith and worship attendance potential points of conflict with those who are not aligned religiously, but other issues surfaced in our survey as well. For example, among the self-described Christians, 61 percent strongly agreed that they had a strong marriage. Among the non-Christians, the number was 49 percent.

Parenting issues also reflected this disparity. The self-described Christians were more likely to assess their parenting skills as good (59% strongly agreed) than the non-Christians (47% strongly agreed). Of course, we have already noted where issues of faith could present conflicts between parents and children.

It appears from our study that relational misalignment dealing with faith issues is more likely to take place within the family. While relational challenges related to faith may occur between friends, coworkers, or other relationships, the challenge is most acute within an immediate family. It only makes sense. Our faith determines so much of who we are and what we do. When we do not agree on this critical issue, the chances for problems to arise are much more likely.

Commitment Inconsistencies

Thom remembers well the first time he encountered this issue. It would be the first of many similar counseling situations. He was a pastor in Florida, and the wife of the couple requested the time with him. It was immediately apparent to him that the wife was there out of desperation and that the husband was there with great reluctance.

The wife was a professing Christian. The husband was not.

The wife was tearful, even sobbing. The husband had no tears; his demeanor was stern.

The marriage was falling apart, and the wife was willing to do almost anything to save it. The husband was resigned to the marriage's failure and wondered what he was doing in a Baptist pastor's office.

One had taken a vow for life. The other had repeated those same words at the wedding, but he gave no indication on this day that he would live up to his promises.

The counseling session was of little value. Thom saw quickly that he couldn't help the situation when the husband had no intention of keeping his commitment.

The marriage failed. Divorce came shortly thereafter. And four children, all under the age of eight, saw their father sporadically from that point forward. It was tragic, but unfortunately it was a tragedy that is repeated hundreds of times each week.

We could have addressed this issue in the previous discussion of gender differences. Or we could have included it in the section on differences of faith. But we believe that the issue is broader than any one demographic difference. The problem is one of commitment.

Misalignment occurs in a relationship when one or both of the parties are not truly committed to the relationship. And yes, we did see some correlation with demographic profiles and the level of commitment to a marriage. For example, when we asked the respondents if they would marry their same spouse if they had to do it over again, the differences were significant.

Slightly less than 60 percent of husbands strongly agreed that they would marry the same wife if they had to do it all over again. Among the wives, the number was higher at 69 percent. When a self-described Christian responded to this statement, 66 percent strongly agreed. But, among the non-Christians the number dropped to 54 percent.

It is not surprising to discover, therefore, that female Christians were the most committed to their marriages (69%). Conversely, male non-Christians were the least committed (50%). What is surprising, if not disconcerting, is that one out of three married persons expressed doubt that they would marry the same person if they had the chance to do it over again.

The simple life in relationships requires alignment. Unfortunately many marriages aren't aligned because the commitment is just not there. And this commitment issue is not limited just to marriages. The same issue is present in other relationships as well.

Thom and Art were standing in a reception line shortly after Thom had been installed as the president of LifeWay Christian Resources. The gentlemen spoke to both of us, as well as Sam and Jess, Art's brothers. This man was a prominent leader in Christian circles, and he had retired about a year earlier.

He spoke first to the three sons. "Guys," he said, "your dad will be in an important position, and he will have a lot of new friends. You keep him grounded because many of those so-called friends will be friendly to him only as long as he is president. They will disappear the moment he steps down from this position. I know," he said carefully and wistfully. "I've been there."

The simple life.

Clarity. Movement. Alignment. Focus.

And alignment can't take place in relationships unless there is true commitment.

The Time Issue

Misalignment in relationships also takes place if there is not sufficient time for the relationship to grow. Since we have presented an entire section of time and the simple life, we will not stay at this point long. Here is the bottom line. We don't have to write a book to tell you that you need to be spending more time for things that really matter.

And relationships really matter. That's what the simple life is all about.

Before we yield this section to an entire section on the simple life and money, we can make our point with a couple more statistics. And you thought we were done with all the numbers!

Of all the married persons in our survey, 43 percent agreed strongly and 41 percent agreed somewhat that they need to spend more time with their husbands or wives. Simple math tells us that 84 percent is a pretty strong indicator.

Relationships are misaligned if there is not sufficient time for the relationships to grow. Simple enough.

The Money Issue

Gender differences can cause misalignment in relationships. So can faith issues. And uneven commitment in relationships. You have to include insufficient time. But if we didn't mention this one, you would think we were negligent.

We're talking about money differences and money problems. That is the issue that can really cause problems in relationships, particularly within immediate families.

Volumes have been written about it. Seminars abound. Tens of thousands of people make their living advising about it.

But money problems still exist. In fact, money problems are pervasive. It's such an important issue for the simple life that, like the time issue, we devote four chapters to it in this book.

Relationships get out of whack when there are disagreements or problems with finances. So stay tuned. We'll be discussing this issue in detail shortly.

The Aligned Simple Life

There you have it: the five most common areas of misalignment: gender differences, faith differences, commitment problems, time problems, and money disagreements. Do you recognize any of them as misalignments in your relationships? One of them? Perhaps more than one?

Take a time-out then. We want to challenge you. Make a few basic commitments to recognize where relationship misalignment might occur. It may not be simple, but we believe it will help move you toward the simple life.

The next step? Read below and begin.

APPLICATION

SIMPLE LIFE: ALIGNMENT

DIFFERENCES IN RELATIONSHIPS

We challenge you to recognize where misalignments in your relationships may exist. Of course, you will need to decide which relationship will get your attention for this exercise. Spouse? Friend? Child? Parent? Fiancé? Coworker? Boyfriend or girlfriend? Other?

You will not totally solve the problem of misalignment, but you will be able to recognize where and how it takes place. In our study we found that recognition goes a long way toward better relationships in the simple life.

Okay, decide whom you want to focus on now. Think about how the person is different from you. Now put those differences into the categories below. You might not have any differences to put in one or two of the categories. Or you might have several that fit into one category. Fill in only where it's applicable.

Gender Differences

_____

_____

_____

_____

_____

_____

_____

Faith Differences

_____

_____

_____

_____

_____

_____

Commitment Differences

_____

_____

_____

_____

_____

_____

Time Differences

_____

_____

_____

_____

_____

_____

_____

Money Differences

_____

_____

_____

_____

_____

_____

_____

CHAPTER 8

Focus, Relationships, and Sacrifice

Clarity → Movement → Alignment → FOCUS

The simple life requires focus in relationships.

Sounds simple, doesn't it? Hardly.

Focus requires that we abandon everything that interferes with our having the best possible relationships. That abandonment is not just letting go of the bad stuff in our lives. It includes eliminating the not-so-bad stuff and even some good stuff. We can become so overcommitted to many good things that we do few of them well. Including relationships. And that's where the problems begin.

We both like to watch television. We both particularly enjoy football games on television. But if we watched all the games we wanted to watch, our wives wouldn't see us much in the fall season.

Not seeing our wives is not good. Okay, that's a double negative, but you understand what we're saying.

Thom has another example of watching televised sports. He's an Atlanta Braves baseball fan. The Braves were one of the first teams that had all their games televised. So Thom started watching Atlanta baseball early in his marriage. The regular season of baseball has more than one hundred games, and each game lasts between two and three hours. If Thom had continued his early pattern, he would have watched about three hundred hours of baseball in one season. That's the equivalent of watching more then twelve days of baseball for twenty-four hours straight. That's not good. Thom soon quit watching so much baseball.

For both Art and Thom, watching sports on television is not bad. It's just that we can be involved in so many good things that relationships suffer. That's the challenge with this thing called focus. You have to let go of some good stuff.

Sacrifice is not easy, or it wouldn't be called sacrifice. But if we're really serious about the simple life and if we are really serious about healthy relationships as a part of the simple life, sacrifice is an absolute necessity.

What areas of your life might require sacrifice? Let's look at a few possibilities.

Sacrificing the Material for the Relational

As we mentioned earlier, the movie *Fireproof* and its companion book, *The Love Dare*, were blockbusters beyond almost anyone's expectations. The movie, released in late 2008, commanded box office receipts for movies of ten times its budget. And then the release of the book, *The Love Dare*, shocked many as it quickly moved to number one in its category of the *New York Times* best sellers.

Though pundits to this day are still trying to figure out the success formula of the movie and the book, it's really simple to understand. The message of both was counterintuitive to cultural norms: In order to have truly meaningful relationships, you must be willing to sacrifice your needs and desires for the good of others.

In the *Fireproof* movie, Caleb is the neglectful and self-centered husband who verbally abuses his wife, Catherine. One of his primary goals in life is to buy the boat of his dreams. But (with apologies to those who may not have seen the movie) he finally discovers that the boat can't be his source of happiness. He gives his hard-earned savings to Catherine's parents who have medical and financial needs.

Get the picture? There was nothing wrong with Caleb's desire for a boat. And he was willing to save methodically for his dream rather than put it on credit. Yet Caleb sacrificed his desire for the good of others. And in that he found true joy.

Financial and material sacrifices are often closely connected to relational health in the simple life. That basic principle was true for the lowest to the highest incomes in our study. More than 13 percent of the families in our survey had an income below $20,000. And 24 percent had incomes below $30,000. Yet 15 percent of those we surveyed had incomes above $100,000.

The results were the same regardless of income. It is a cliché, but it is true: money can't buy happiness. Or, since Thom is such a fan of the Beatles, money "can't buy me love." For those who are clueless about sixties music, please disregard the previous sentence and read on.

Hartley is forty-one years old and has a good upper-middle management position in a Fortune 1000 company in the Northeast. He and Diane have been married twelve years and have an eight-year-old son and a six-year-old daughter. Because he is on a fast track for a promotion, he works around sixty hours each week. He sees his wife and two kids much less than he should. Hartley is miserable.

"There's been a lot of tension in our family the past few months," he admitted. "The kids are whining that they want me to do things with them, and Diane and I have been fighting a lot."

We asked the self-evident question. "Why don't you just cut back on your work hours?"

Hartley's response was defensive.

"You sound just like my wife," he said with a few more decibels. "She just doesn't realize that I am doing these extra hours for the family. If I get this promotion, I will get a big raise, and we will have a lot more as a family."

Well, we asked slowly, if Diane were making the choice, would she like more money for the family or more time from you?

Silence. Hartley wouldn't answer the question.

All three Rainer sons spoke at Thom's installation as president of LifeWay Christian Resources. Jess was first.

Jess recalled fond memories he had of his dad when he was growing up. But this youngest son said something that caused curious looks in the crowd. He said his best time with his dad was the "Squeaky" trip.

The Squeaky trip?

Jess spoke of traveling with his father to one of Thom's speaking engagements. The two traveled eighteen hours round-trip in the car together, just the two of them. Along the first leg of the trip, Thom and Jess stopped in a convenience store. Jess, only four years old at the time, asked his dad if he could get a small stuffed animal that looked like a colorful bird. Thom agreed but became annoyed when Jess discovered that if you shook the toy lightly, it made a birdlike squeaking sound. Thus the bird was named Squeaky.

So Thom's purchase of a toy was one of Jess's highlights of moments with his dad? Wrong.

Jess spoke with emotion as he told the crowd that the fond memory was not the purchase of another toy. Squeaky was simply a point of reference. The joy of that trip, he said, was the fact that he had his dad's undivided attention for eighteen hours. Even two decades later, Jess recounted what really mattered. And Thom sat in the audience as tears streamed down his face.

Perhaps too many things are keeping you from a closer relationship with those you love and friends who mean much to you. Perhaps you are pursuing those things through long hours and tiring work. As a consequence, you have little time for the relationships that really matter.

The material items and the toys you possess are not inherently evil. And the long work hours are not bad examples of your character unless they interfere with what really matters—like relationships. Then it's time to focus, time to eliminate, time to sacrifice.

We found in our survey that many were chasing the material at the expense of the relational, and they weren't happy. For example, only 28 percent of the respondents could strongly agree that they were living within their financial means. Nearly four out of five had some level of concern about the debt they carried. And a mere 5 percent felt that they were saving enough money.

We cover the financial issue in the next section. Our point here is that we were hearing clearly that the material world was not bringing joy to families. To the contrary, the pursuit of the material often was at the expense of the relational. We heard from hundreds who understood they needed to cut back somewhere in their lifestyles. They just didn't know where to begin.

And what's really tough is that we will be eliminating some things that are really good. But good is not really good if it becomes a distraction from the best—like healthy relationships with those who really matter in our lives.

Sacrificing Self-focus for Other-focus

Our friend Brad Waggoner often says that one of the characteristics he seeks in a leader is self-awareness. If we can at least get a glimpse of who we really are and how others see us, we can make significant progress.

The problem is that no one is completely self-aware, and few are even mostly self-aware. We tend to see ourselves in a way that is often significantly different from how others view us.

Frank, for example, is in the midst of marital difficulties. His wife, Ellen, is ready to proceed with divorce. She's had enough of the marriage.

Frank can't understand. "I'm a good guy," he exclaims. "I do a lot of good things for her. Why can't she see that?"

Your turn, Ellen. "He is totally self-absorbed. Even his so-called friends see it, but they are afraid to tell him. He always talks about himself. He's always promoting himself, and he never does anything for me. I'm tired of it, and I'm tired of him."

There is a chasm of perceptions here.

The simple life means that we sacrifice self for others. It means that we're highly intentional about doing for others. Frankly, it brings us back to the description of love in 1 Corinthians 13. Do you remember how love is described? "Love is patient; love is kind. Loves does not envy; is not boastful; is not conceited; does not act improperly; is not selfish; is not provoked; does not keep a record of wrongs" (1 Cor. 13:4–5).

Notice the common thread in all of these characteristics of love. They all point to how we should put others and their needs before our own. They are characteristics of sacrifice and selflessness.

No, it's not wrong to want something for yourself. And it's not wrong to do something for yourself. But the simple life means there will be times when you sacrifice your own desires for the good of others. That's the nature of focus. You have to eliminate some things, even some good things. And sometimes those good things may be what you desire for yourself.

About two thousand years ago, the mother of the disciples James and John approached Jesus and asked Him to allow her two sons to sit on either side of Jesus, one on the right and one on the left. Such positions indicated the lines of authority and power. Those closest to the authority figure were of the highest rank.

Jesus looked at James and John and said to them, "You don't know what you're asking. Are you able to drink the cup that

I am about to drink?" (Matt. 20:22). The two brothers
responded positively even though Jesus knew better. He was
referring to the suffering He would soon endure on the cross.
James and John were looking for position and perks, not
suffering.

Then word about the brothers' question got to the other
ten disciples, and they were ticked! "When the 10 disciples
heard this, they became indignant with the two brothers"
(Matt. 20:24).

Do you see what's taking place here? James and John
wanted position and power for themselves. The other ten
disciples were mad because they wanted the same for themselves. So how did Jesus handle this self-centered group of
men? He told them that they had the simple life all messed
up. (Okay, He didn't use the phrase "simple life," but it fits
well here.)

Listen to Jesus' words: "You know that the rulers of the
Gentiles dominate them, and the men of high position exercise power over them. It must not be like that among you. On
the contrary, whoever wants to be great among you must be
your servant, and whoever wants to become first among you
must be your slave; just as the Son of Man did not come to be
served, but to serve, and to give His life—a ransom for many"
(Matt. 20:25–28).

Jesus turned the tables upside down for the disciples.
As they were seeking fulfillment in life through power and
prestige, He told them that a meaningful life is possible only
when we put others before ourselves. And He spoke of the
cross that was to come, the ransom for many, as the supreme
example of self-giving.

Are you struggling relationally? With a spouse? Another family member? A friend? A coworker? A fellow student? A neighbor?

Only about a third of the respondents strongly agreed that their spouses offer them words of encouragement. And nearly 100 percent wish they did. The problem is ubiquitous in all relationships, not just the marriage relationship. It seems that many relationships are suffering because one or both of the parties are focused on self.

Perhaps the relationship needs more focus. And focus means we are willing to eliminate some things, even if those things aren't bad in themselves. So we look at areas of self-focus, and ask ourselves if we could sacrifice those for the sake of others. Consider some of these questions:

- Could I eliminate some activities that are focused on my needs and desires so that I can give attention to others?
- Do I often focus on what the other person should do for me instead of what I could do for him or her?
- Is my pursuit of material gain and higher position coming at the sacrifice of relationships?
- Am I angry with someone because of what they haven't done for me?
- Do I each day intentionally do something sacrificially for someone?
- Do others honestly see me as selfish or selfless?

Sacrificing Busyness for Relationships

We have dedicated nearly one fourth of the book to issues of time, but we must also look at this issue as it relates to relationships.

We discovered several interesting things about people and their relationships in our study. Below is a summary of these findings.

- The higher the income, the more likely the person would be to complain about being too busy. The chase of the material gain actually seems to bring more problems.
- One half of the respondents want to slow down but don't know how.
- Concerns over children being too busy were far higher among parents of teenagers than among parents of younger children.
- Only 13 percent of those responding agreed strongly that their families have enough relaxing times together.
- Four out of ten said they were on emotional edge because of their schedules.
- Nearly half of the respondents said they will probably have health problems if they continue at their current pace.
- Only one fourth of the respondents agreed strongly that they spend relaxed time with their children.
- Seven out of ten surveyed said they would change their daily routine if they could.

Do you see where the problems noted in the list could present relational problems? Parents don't spend relaxed time with their children. A significant number of people can't enjoy healthy relationships because they're on emotional edge with their schedules. Hardly any families have relaxed time together.

The simple life demands that you focus. You must eliminate much of your busyness. We can imagine your quick response to that statement: "There's no way I can eliminate all the things I'm doing."

Jayne Ellen, for example, is from a Chicago suburb. She agrees wholeheartedly that she and her family are too busy. "Okay," she begins. "Let's see what's keeping our family so busy. My husband and I both work. We really don't put in any more than forty or so hours a week, but with the commute our work is nearly fifty hours a week. We can't quit our jobs. If either one of us quit, we couldn't pay the mortgage.

"Our son and daughter aren't old enough to drive yet. The bus takes them to school, but we have to drive them to soccer games and practice, piano lessons, and different doctors' appointments. Then they have homework most weeknights, and they need our help a lot."

Jayne Ellen paused. "I'm just beginning, but it's more of the same. You tell me what we can eliminate. I don't see anything that can change."

We asked her if she felt she was giving the kids and her husband the quantity and quality of time she would like. "No, no way," she responded. We then asked her if relationships were strained because of the busyness of their lives. Again, she didn't hesitate, "Absolutely."

We didn't have an easy answer for Jayne Ellen. But her own responses told her something had to give. She had to focus. Relationships were frayed because schedules were just too packed.

The simple life demands focus. Relationships are in the balance. There is no easy solution, but something must be eliminated. Our relationship with someone we care about is simply too important to keep on doing all that we have been doing.

Five Questions for Focus

We realize that, in each of the four sections, focus will often be the most difficult to execute. Focus means that we eliminate some things, and often it means we eliminate some good things. That's tough. In fact, some of the respondents told us it was impossible.

While we don't offer a magic bullet, we are proposing some questions for you to consider. Some may apply to your life; others may not. Some of them call for radical action; others do not.

What we do know is that we are hearing all across our land that life has gotten too complex and relationships are suffering as a consequence. Something has to change.

If the other party in your relationship could change some things about your life, what would they be? "I was surprised," Allen admitted. "I asked my wife what she would like to see changed in my life, and she told me she would like me to get back into teaching. I was shocked. She knew that the money was less than I'm making now, but she was ready to downsize and make the necessary adjustments. When I asked her why she wanted me to do this, she just said that she knew I would be most fulfilled teaching. And she knew that my happiness affected all of our family. She's a wise lady."

Thom had a similar experience many years ago. He left the world of business to attend seminary. At the time Thom and Nellie Jo had two young sons. So he attended seminary for three years to get his master's degree. He started preparing to move toward full-time church work and, thus, to leave the seminary.

Thom was really surprised when Nellie Jo said they needed to stay at seminary for three more years so Thom could earn a doctorate. Thom had assumed that Nellie Jo was ready for a more stable life financially since they had barely been getting by for three years. But she simply said that Thom had a gift to teach and that he should pursue the educational route that would best open those doors.

Both Thom and Art know that Thom married an amazing woman.

The simple life may seem to be an unrealistic goal because we think there are some things in our lives that just can't be eliminated. Focus seems difficult if not impossible. Have you considered asking someone close to you? You may be surprised at their suggestions about how your life and relationships can improve.

Could I eliminate some material possession that may be hindering a relationship? We both know a guy who loves boating. He loves the water and all the activities related to boating. He spends a lot of time taking care of the boat and enjoying all the water activities. Guess what he did recently. He sold his boat.

There was nothing inherently wrong with his boating activities. But he discovered that he was so busy with those activities that he was neglecting his wife and two children. Yes, the family shared some of the activities with him, but the overall time involved in working with his boat was just too much. So he sold his boat.

There was some financial benefit to selling the boat, but that was not his motivation. He was neglecting his family. And by selling that one possession, he made a major step toward the simple life. By the way, he does hope that he and his wife can get another boat after the kids are out of the house.

Could I eliminate a job? Now that really sounds radical. But plenty of people have done it. Your current job may be interfering with your relationships. It could be taking too much of your time. It could be so stressful that you are on edge when you are with others you care about. Or you might just be bored.

We all know that lack of happiness and fulfillment in our vocations affects our relationships. But, sadly, most people live with the pain and drudgery of an unfulfilling job. Changing jobs may seem to be a radical step. But it could be the step you need to take to simplify your life and improve your relationships.

Are casual activities interfering with my relationships? Thom confesses guilt on this point. His time is too consumed on the Internet and his iPhone. He checks his e-mail incessantly. Thom was recently on a retreat with LifeWay Christian Resources executives. He asked them to share with him his weaknesses and challenges.

There was a moment of awkward silence. After all, everyone in the room reported to Thom. Finally one brave soul spoke: "You have trouble giving us your full attention. Look what you are doing right now. Even though I'm speaking to you, you are looking at your iPhone and checking e-mail."

Ouch.

Some of us are addicted to the e-world. Others spend hours watching television. Some are totally consumed with sports. And even others may often have their noses in books, newspapers, and magazines.

At best these are distractions from healthy relationships. At worst, these casual activities may be causing deep fissures in relationships. Are there casual activities you need to eliminate or reduce?

Would my children like to eliminate some of their activities? If you still have children at home, have you looked at their activities lately? Are they busy? Are they *too* busy?

Try something different. Ask them if they could change their activities, would they change them, and what types of changes would they make. Granted, we can't do everything our kids ask us. Many of them might eliminate school as an activity. Not a good option.

Still, you might be surprised at some of the choices they would make. You may have them involved in activities "for their own good," only to find that they're really not happy with what they're doing. You may discover that they would like to slow down and simplify as well. And when they are better focused, the parents can be better focused as well. When they slow down, so will you.

What Really Matters

Jesus said: "Love the Lord your God with all your heart, with all your soul, and with all your mind. This is the greatest and most important commandment. The second is like it: Love your neighbor as yourself" (Matt. 22:37–39).

It's really simple, Jesus said. The most important thing that matters is our relationship with God. And the second most important thing that matters is our relationship with others.

In this section we have shared with you the hopes and struggles, the dreams and disillusionment of making relationships work. Jesus knew it best. When our lives are done, what really matters is not the things we have accumulated or the positions we have attained.

What really matters is our relationship with God. What really matters is our relationship with others. We need to focus to give attention to these things.

That's the simple life, and that's what really matters.

APPLICATION
SIMPLE LIFE: FOCUS
ELIMINATING FOR HEALTHY RELATIONSHIPS

Remember, the purpose of focus in the simple life is to eliminate some of the good things that interfere with our relationships. This is often difficult since you are eliminating things in your life that aren't inherently bad.

1. Ask a person with whom you desire to have the best possible relationship the following question: "What would you want me to change about my life so we can have an even better relationship?"

2. Can I eliminate some material possession that might hinder my relationship with someone? We often get too busy with our toys!

3. Can I eliminate a job? Admittedly, that's a radical question. But it might be absolutely necessary for a healthy relationship.

4. Are there casual activities that interfere with my relationships? Remember the story of the iPhone addiction.

5. Would my children (if you have kids at home) eliminate some of their activities if they had a choice?

PART 3

Simple Life: How to Simplify and Build Healthy Finances

CHAPTER 9

I Want to Provide Financially for My Family

CLARITY → Movement → Alignment → Focus

Josh found a seat in the corner. The coffee bar was a little more crowded than usual. The university had just finished up their last week for the semester. So for a brief moment before diving into the summer, many students were without school and without work. Soon most students would either make their trek home or start their three-month job before the fall semester brought on another year of school.

Josh took a sip of his coffee and looked at his view. Others seemed to be enjoying themselves, talking and laughing. It seemed as if they didn't have a care in the world, and maybe they didn't. Josh reminisced about his college years. Life seemed so simple then. The future was wide open; his dreams were limitless. Money was not an issue. Sure, he had debts, but he was certain that they would somehow work themselves out. After graduation he would get a job and pay everything off. It would be fine.

He couldn't help but think how much life had changed. Now he hides his occasional visit to the coffee bar from his wife. The justification of paying three or four dollars for a quick energy boost was difficult for Elaine to understand, especially while he and Elaine were wrestling with the decision of whether they would be able to pay for one of their kids' final field trips for the school year.

As Josh thought of this, his 10-percent recycled cup became filled with hot, liquid guilt. His eyes glazed; he slowly twirled the cup on the small table. He took another sip. He had already paid for it anyway.

As he shifted his eyes back to the room of students, he smiled. The college years were well behind him now. He wondered if he had known then what he knew now, would he have ever left school. If he had only known the stress and the complexity that would follow down the road, he might have forgone the opportunity to walk across the stage, shake the president's hand, and take hold of the rolled piece of paper that was supposed to symbolize freedom. He might have passed at throwing his cap in the air. At the moment, becoming a career student sounded pretty enticing.

Life took some unexpected turns. Now all he could think about was how he was going to make it out of the hole in which he and Elaine found themselves. Josh didn't want to become one of those people who was unable to pay their bills, but it was getting close. With the increase in interest rates, his mortgage payment had just adjusted to a couple of hundred dollars more per month. The credit card balances that they swore would be paid off before the zero percent offer ended were still there, now with a looming double-digit rate. The minimum payment was all that they could afford last month and probably this month as well. He didn't even want to think how many more years of lease payments they had on their cars. Driving a luxury car just seems stupid now.

Josh took another sip; this time it was accompanied with a deep sigh.

What was he going to do about the cheerleading trip? He couldn't tell his daughter no. She didn't do anything to put them in this situation. Besides, he never missed any type of camp or trip growing up. His parents always took care of everything. He was supposed to build upon the life that his parents had given him, not take steps backwards. He was not going to be the type of parent that limited his child's dreams.

The coffee was getter cooler so he drank a little bit more.

Maybe he would get a decent bonus at work this year. If he could just tread water until Christmas, then he could take the extra money and pay off some of their debt. Of course, he and Elaine normally used that money to pay off the gifts they had bought for the holidays. Well, maybe they would try to be more frugal on gifts this year and then use the rest to pay off some of their debt. At least, they could put a little dent in their balances. Even at this thought he knew it wouldn't work. They wiped out the bonus on gifts every year, even before he had received it. They had to spend at least as much on others as others spent on them. It was only right.

"Man, I need some more money," Josh mumbled to himself.

He finished off the last bit of coffee, got up, and threw away the cup. Before leaving, he went to the counter where he was met by a hyper-caffeinated, college-aged employee.

"Are you guys hiring?" asked Josh.

"Always, bro," replied the employee as he reached for an application.

Josh took the application from the guy's hand.

"Thanks," said Josh with a solemn head nod.

He walked out of the coffee bar, application in hand, with a lingering sense of embarrassment. Did he really just ask for this?

Why We Hate Finances

Finance can seem like such a dirty word. Along with religion and politics, it is one of the three topics we are supposed to avoid in a conversation. Finance is a word that simply carries baggage. For many it's like a bitter taste in the mouth; it evokes memories from a previous financial problem. We tell ourselves that money is not important, that there are more important things in life.

And at least in the latter, we are correct.

But we still find it difficult to ignore the abundance of teachings in Scripture about finance. Money was one of the most frequent topics of discussion for Jesus.

So we sit, hating finances while trying to convince ourselves of their importance in our life's journey. Here are some quotes from our respondents:

"I would like to have complete financial freedom, to be without worry about any money matters."

- "We need to pay down a lot of debt."

- "I would love to know that my kids and I would have no worries when it comes to money in the future."
- "I wish I could afford to quit my second job and spend more time with the family."
- "I want a sound future for myself and all of my family members."

In our survey more than 45 percent of the respondents admitted that they did not have enough income for their lifestyles. For many of us, money is a ball and chain attached around the ankle, limiting our life's movement.

We feel that if we could just get a few extra zeros added to our bank account, then just maybe the weight would start to lighten, the clasp around the ankle would start to loosen. So many of those surveyed told us that money was a limiting factor to doing what they wanted to do. One forty-something man commented, "If I were just independently wealthy, then I could pursue what I really want out of life." And every now and then, we jokingly find ourselves wishing for the old bartering system, where a handful of goats would get you some land to grow your crops, and maybe even a couple of spouses depending on your negotiation skills.

Those were simpler times (except for the couple of spouses).

Those who have had some type of financial trouble in their lives can attest to the amount of stress it places on them and their families. Half of those who took our survey told us that finances caused strain in their marriage. When money gets thin, life can get scary. What do we do? Where do we go? Which bill do we pay? How are we going to pay for her education? What is going to happen to us? Difficult questions must be answered.

Time does not wait for the decisions. It keeps advancing toward the deadlines, dancing toward the due dates. It would be great if we could just put everything on pause for a little while, allowing us to get our bearings, decide our next steps; but life continues, with or without the money.

We are in disarray. The financial stress suddenly engulfs our lives. The smile we once had is no more. The bounce in our step is more of a slow drag. Life's shine has dulled, and every day becomes just another battle.

The complexity of finances does not help. Credit scores, amortization schedules, interest rates, total cost of funds, budgeting, stocks, mutual funds, IRAs, and investment strategies. Even those in the financial field understand this. That is why for a mortgage you typically go to someone who specializes in mortgages; for retirement planning you typically go to someone who specializes in retirement planning. The tremendous array and complexity of finances limits even those who are in the financial field from fully understanding every little detail.

If it is too overwhelming for them, what about everyone else? How is the elementary teacher supposed to figure these things out when her life is about her students? When is the factory worker supposed to figure these things out when all he wants to do is justifiably rest after a long shift? Many of us find ourselves just "not worrying about it" and skip over this part of life.

But we know this does not help.

Money can make life a mess. And it doesn't matter how many zeroes you have on your paycheck, financial trouble can find any of us. With each of these beginning chapters, we have tried to demonstrate the need for clarity with time and clarity with relationships.

Finances are no different.

In our crazy world, it is so easy to get encompassed by a fog of confusion and misdirection that ultimately results in our financial mess. Everyone seems to know what our money is supposed to accomplish except us. Our mailboxes are filled with offers and ideas on what we should do with our money. Retailers tell us that our money should be spent at their stores. Banks tell us that we should save, invest, and take out loans. Auto dealerships tell us that our money is meant for that perfect new car. Credit card companies don't care what you do with your money as long as you use their cards to make those purchases. Some ideas are good; some are bad. All seem to be presented as the right thing to do.

There is too much noise. We are disoriented. What are we trying to accomplish with our money?

Making Finance Simple

In Matthew 25:14–30 Jesus told a story about a master and his three servants. The master was going out of town for a while, and he left the servants to take care of the property. Before he left, the master met with the three servants. He knew each of them well and their ability to handle his finances. To the first servant he gave five talents, a form of money. To the second servant, he gave two talents. To the third servant, he handed just one talent. No specific instructions were given. It was just expected that these servants would take care of the money as their master would if he were still there, trying to find the most productive place for his funds.

Now try to imagine yourself as that third servant. You just watched as one of your peers was entrusted to double what you received and the other was given five times what you were given. At this point would you not want to disprove your master's expectations? Would it not fuel a fire within you? Would this not challenge you?

But the master knew his servants well. The first servant turned his five talents into ten. The second also doubled what he had received and turned the two talents into four. The third servant would have been better off not even receiving his one talent. He took the one talent, dug a hole, and hid it in the ground. He completely eliminated any potential to do good with what the master gave him.

The master eventually came back. When he saw that the first two servants gave him a 100-percent return, he was excited. He praised them for what they had accomplished and promised to give them even more to watch over. And why not? They proved themselves more than capable.

The third servant approached the master. The servant told the master that he was scared of what might happen if he lost the money so he hid it in a hole. After watching the other two servants hand back double what they had been given, he presented his one, now probably somewhat dirty, talent.

The master was furious. He took the talent from the third servant and tossed it to the first servant, a far more produc-tive servant. The master chastised the third servant and threw him out of the house and into the darkness.

So it is here that we try to find clarity in our fiscal haze. And though Jesus' story is not limited to financial steward-ship, we do know that we're supposed to do something with the financial resources He has entrusted to us.

But what do we do? We need clarity.

Finding financial clarity requires a big idea. There must be an all-encompassing direction from which we make monetary decisions.

Should I buy this? Should I invest in that? Should I pay this off first? Can I splurge on this? There are a lot of questions out there, each with its own nuances.

Just one idea captures them all. Stewardship. It is the only concept that provides clarity to our finances.

Stewardship is a word we often hear from behind the pulpit but rarely hear outside the walls of the church. Much like the servants in Jesus' story, a steward is traditionally one who takes care of another's household. A steward watches over the domestic affairs so that the master may focus on whatever he deems most important. Much trust is placed in the steward by the master. He is expected to act in the best interest of his master, with or without his oversight. So stewardship consists of managing those obligations given to the steward.

By the nature of the word, stewardship requires some type of higher authority. It is a position of submittal to a greater good. It is the denying of oneself and the exalting of another. It is commitment to the well-being of another, knowing that his happiness will result in your happiness.

The story Jesus gave about the servants was about this idea called stewardship on a much larger scale. It was about God calling all of us to take care of His things while we are on this brief journey in life. And though this chapter is about money, the concept of stewardship reaches far beyond the boundaries of our bank accounts. Everything we have, everything we are belongs to the One who created us. Our entire being demands stewardship.

Why does God want us to be guardians of His money? So His will is done on Earth as it is in heaven.

For God to give the title of *steward* to us, His own creation, is remarkable. In an incredible twist, God, perfect and righteous, has chosen us, fallible and sometimes just idiotic humans, to watch over much until He returns. Knowing of our imperfections, He still put together a human portfolio in which He would invest to accomplish His goals.

Money is not the root of all evil. When properly used, it is a means that can produce all kinds of good in our world. But to the contrary, so many of our financial decisions reduce the potential impact we could have on this earth. They can diminish our fulfillment as God's agents of change.

Odds are that the monthly interest you are paying on your credit cards could give a kid in Uganda a chance of surviving her childhood. Maybe one in the Ukraine as well. But our potential impact on that life is negated because in our abundance we choose not to be God's stewards.

Stewardship is not some mathematical formula or a list of dos and don'ts. Stewardship is about the heart.

It is about waking up every morning ready to listen to what God wants us to do for the day. It is about wanting to take care of what God has given us while we are on this little blue planet. It is about acknowledging that His plan is much greater than anything we could imagine. It is about developing a heart that is willing to make financial decisions based on His wants and not ours. A steward who is stubbornly trying to capture God's desire for His resources is simply beautiful.

Components of Stewardship

A steward has two critical components: detachment and wisdom.

Though he is intimately involved in the affairs of his master, a caretaker must never begin to think that the possessions he watches are his own. He cannot allow himself to consider that he is somehow deserving of all that he oversees and dub himself the rightful title-owner. Only when the steward is completely detached from his master's belongings is he able to determine how his master's property may be most productive.

In Mark 10:17–22, we find this story:

> As He was setting out on a journey, a man ran up, knelt down before Him, and asked Him, "Good Teacher, what must I do to inherit eternal life?"
>
> "Why do you call Me good?" Jesus asked him. "No one is good but One—God. You know the commandments: Do not murder; do not commit adultery; do not steal; do not bear false witness; do not defraud; honor your father and mother."
>
> He said to Him, "Teacher, I have kept all these from my youth."
>
> Then looking at him, Jesus loved him and said to him, "You lack one thing: Go, sell all you have and give to the poor, and you will have treasure in heaven. Then come, follow Me."
>
> But he was stunned at this demand, and he went away grieving, because he had many possessions.

Depressing.

Jesus was looking at the man; the man was looking at Jesus. A decision had to be made. With emotions pulsating through his body, the young man turned his eyes from Jesus, turned around, and walked away. He had just looked Christ in the eyes, and though no words were spoken, he made his answer clear. His attachment to money and possessions twisted his decision making so much that he was able to look directly at the face of salvation, a face that loved him, and turn and walk away.

One of the primary rules of stewardship had been broken.

After Jesus told him to get rid of his wealth, the man went away grieving. Jesus' words broke his heart. He could not envision a life without all of the luxuries to which he had become accustomed. On one side of the scale were earthly riches; on the other side stood Jesus.

He made his choice. The attraction and comfort of wealth were too strong for the young man.

Detachment.

Wisdom.

Stewardship.

Your Financial Statement

So it is with stewardship that we approach our money. Our study indicated that many are in dire need just to get the basics in order. Exactly 50 percent of those we surveyed indicated that they often have more bills to pay in a month than they have money.

Instead of taking a more traditional path of setting up a budget and making long-term financial plans, we will begin with the simple path of deciding our financial purpose. By now you understand the importance of creating a definitive statement behind which you can rally. With this statement you have already defined clarity with time and relationships.

Your financial life has many variables that we do not know, and we are fine with that. You may or may not have a need to get out of debt. You may or may not be concerned with retirement. Whatever situation you find yourself in, whether it may seem like a blessing or a curse, your statement must be piloted by stewardship. Stewardship will guide you through the movement, alignment, and focus phases until you have simplified your financial picture. Let's start working on that statement.

Three categories of finance need to be addressed:

1. *The Now (0 to 10 years):* Those financial concerns that will impact our immediate to a ten-year time horizon. Some of those concerns may be paying bills, credit cards, short-term loans, or emergency funds.

2. *The Future (10+ years):* Recognizes the decisions that will affect our lives outside of the decade mark. For many this includes retirement, college funds, and mortgages.

3. *The Far Future (Your Legacy):* In Proverbs 13:22, the writer indicates that the finale of one's relationship with money comes at death, that when we pass away, we can leave an inheritance for the next generation. It is a consideration that rarely makes it into financial planning, but it is imperative for the Christian. Even in our death we love others.

Of course, as we move through our dash, our life's time line, our financial concerns evolve. The decisions for the future (retirement, advanced fund planning) may become part of the now as they develop into an immediate concern.

As circumstances change, so will our finances. Your future may be someone's now. Your now may be someone's future.

To develop your statement, we recommend that you write down the three categories: the now, the future, and the far future. Under the appropriate time horizon, write down and rank your financial goals. This is the time to paint your ideal financial picture. Have fun with it but be real. Your fifty-five-foot yachts in Florida and Maine can wait until you tackle some more important issues.

Recall Josh at the beginning of the chapter. The contemplating coffee-drinker knew that his finances were out of control. He felt the despair and stress of an increasingly overwhelming burden from the result of past financial decisions. Here is what he wrote:

The Now
1. Give back to God.
2. Pay off credit cards.
3. Have more available money each month.
4. Create an emergency fund.

The Future
5. Retire at sixty-five.
6. Pay for kids' college.
7. Be mortgage-free.

The Far Future
8. Have enough life insurance to care for family.
9. Give each child $200,000 upon death.
10. Have a will.

Of course, if you are married, discuss and develop your goals together. You might be surprised to find that your spouse's big financial priority is not your own. Josh discovered that his wife was most concerned about the financial security of the family if something were to happen to him. Hence, the importance of life insurance entered into his planning, something he hadn't even considered was a major cause of concern for his wife. There should only be one list of priorities. A house divided and chasing after separate goals quickly finds itself in disarray. Finances will continue to be strained if there are not priorities where both have agreed.

After categorizing and ranking our priorities, we want to set about creating a mission statement that allows us to pursue goals in each of those three categories.

We know what many of you are thinking: *My only concern for the moment is what is happening in the now. I can't focus on the future, much less the far future. I will get to that stuff later. Just let me deal with the now.*

Because of the evolutionary nature of each financial category, it is important to strive for goals under each heading. We must create a balance in how we pursue our financial goals. Retirement may be twenty-five years down the road but, God willing, that twenty-five years will suddenly arrive, and the entryway into retirement will no longer be in the future but the now. Without preparation you will be faced with another seemingly insurmountable mountain to climb. Your future and far future priorities should be just as much of a concern in the present as they are in the years ahead. We prepare today for the needs of tomorrow.

Josh thought about his statement. It had to be an attainable goal. He knew that achieving any of his goals would take some effort, but he did not want to create further frustrations for himself and his wife by creating an impossible goal. He also wanted the statement to be dated. He needed to have an ending time by which these goals were to be accomplished. This would help him and his wife stay on course and not become lax in their pursuit.

Here was Josh's statement:

Over the next year, I will give to God my first 10 percent of every paycheck, reduce my credit card debt by 50 percent, max out the company match on my 401(k), and find a way to budget a life insurance policy.

Josh was eager to see this thing fleshed out.

Keep in mind that your financial mission statement needs to be flexible. Something amazing starts happening when we have clarity with our financial mission: we start reaching our goals. Many of us find that the reason we became so plagued with money problems is because we never opened our eyes and hearts to what was happening. We turned a blind eye. So if you find yourself achieving your goals before the allotted time, keep going. Input the next priority on your list. Use the momentum to reach for something higher, something better.

Of course, unexpected financial problems do happen. This is another reason to keep your statement flexible. If an unexpected financial crisis arises, do not give up. Adjust your statement to the situation, but keep going. You picked up this book because you wanted something different, something simple. Do not allow yourself to fall back into the life that you so desperately wanted to escape.

Remember, it all comes back to stewardship. It doesn't matter if we only have a few cents in our pockets or a couple million in our bank account. None of us are deserving of what we have. Everything we have been given is a gift, and we are the stewards. If you are reading this, you have life, and that in itself is amazingly beautiful. This money thing is just something extra that has been given, a responsibility that He thinks you can handle. As we take the next step toward financial simplicity, use this mission statement to demonstrate yourself obedient as God's steward.

At this point you should have some sense of clarity for your finances, not that everything has been figured out but that you understand what your money is meant to accomplish. Your statement of stewardship will aid in engaging some of life's difficult financial decisions. Your compass will keep you on the right track.

Simplifying finances is not an easy task. For many who have found themselves in trouble, it can be a long and weary road to travel. When you want to quit, when you want to give in, remember that you have an incredible God who wants you to succeed and wants to see you get out of the mess you may be in. After all, it is His money, and He wants a good return.

APPLICATION
SIMPLE LIFE: CLARITY
MISSION STATEMENTS FOR STEWARDSHIP

We challenge you to do mission statements for your finances in three categories.

Remember, a mission statement is a basic declaration of intent with actionable items. For example, Josh's mission statement for the now was:

Over the next year, I will give to God my first 10 percent of every paycheck, reduce my credit card debt by 50 percent, max out the company match on my 401(k), and find a way to budget a life insurance policy.

Now, prepare your mission statements for the following three eras of your life:

The Now (0 to 10 years):

_____

_____

_____

_____

_____

_____

The Future (10+ years)

_____

_____

_____

_____

_____

_____

_____

_____

The Far Future (Your Legacy)

_____

_____

_____

_____

_____

_____

_____

CHAPTER 10

Making Sense of Money Matters

Clarity → MOVEMENT → Alignment → Focus

For many of us, our financial situation is less than ideal. Okay, for some of us, it stinks.

Bills have stacked up. The income we were expecting at this stage in our life has not materialized. We may be donating blood just so we can buy a movie ticket and a small bag of popcorn. We find ourselves trying to fund a lifestyle that doesn't fit with our paycheck.

Many of those in our study were perplexed about how they got in this financial mess. They were just living their lives, and then suddenly, without warning, everything turned south. They looked up to find themselves in the midst of a financial nightmare. They couldn't escape. They were stuck.

And then the tears come. I (Art) hate the tears. I sit in my office with clients and rummage through their financial mess, and as we rummage, reality hits. They're in trouble.

I don't hate the tears because of my lack of sensitivity. It is the opposite. I truly hurt for these people because I know that the road ahead is going to be tough. There are no easy ways out. I want to reach out to them, tell them that it will be okay. And it will—but not for a while. For a while it will be tough. And once they step out of my office and into the world, life will be different. Their situation demands that it be different.

But before they leave, the statement almost inevitably comes out: "I just don't know how we got here." And in saying this, they unknowingly reveal the heart of the problem.

We don't know how we got here. We don't know how things should really be and the potential outcomes that come along with having a sound financial plan.

So it is with our lack of awareness that we begin this chapter. Our failure to see how we got into the mess is our barrier. It prevents movement from occurring in our financial lives. And we need movement; we need to start moving toward fiscal simplicity.

Past decisions litter the pathway. They block us from moving forward, from making our mission statement become more than just goals. The removal of these barriers will get us back to our responsibility of being wise caretakers.

As we noted earlier, 50 percent of respondents to our survey said that they have more bills than money each month. Another 46 percent agreed that their credit card debt was too high. And a whopping 72 percent did not have the equivalent of six months' living expenses saved in case of an emergency.

Those are scary numbers.

Obstacles need to be removed. You picked up this book to get away from this stuff. Let's take the next step to achieving our financial goals.

Understanding Your Barrier

In Acts 5:1–11, there is an intense story about a husband, a wife, and their offering. It had not been that long since Jesus left Earth, and the church was in its infancy. First, let's back up to Acts 2:44: "Now all the believers were together and had everything in common." The body of Christ, the church, was beginning to take shape, and it was becoming something beautiful.

Ananias and his wife, Sapphira, were part of the church's beginnings. They felt compelled to sell a piece of their property and present it as an offering to God. Though nothing was asked of them, they decided to keep part of the pledged sale for themselves but present it as if they were giving the earnings in its entirety.

Plain and simple, they lied.

Ananias approached Peter and placed the funds at his and the other apostles' feet. The Bible does not indicate how Peter knew that the offering was not the total of the sale. It may have been revealed to him by God; it may have been told to him by someone who caught word of the intentional deception. Either way, Peter confronted Ananias about his dishonesty.

There was no time for apologies. At the end of Peter's words, Ananias fell dead and was taken outside to be buried.

About three hours later, there was a repeat performance. Sapphira, clueless to what had recently transpired, stood in the same room where her husband had just died. As he had done with Ananias, Peter confronted Sapphira: "'Tell me,' Peter asked her, 'did you sell the field for this price?' 'Yes,' she said, 'for that price'" (5:8).

After a few words from Peter, Sapphira fell dead as well and was taken outside to be buried next to her husband.

That's scary.

The Bible is explicit about the cause of the disaster: "Wasn't it yours while you possessed it? And after it was sold, wasn't it at your disposal? Why is it that you planned this thing in your heart? You have not lied to men but to God!" (5:4).

The gift itself was good, but the deception ruined it in God's eyes. Maybe Ananias and Sapphira desired to be seen as supersacrificial. Maybe they wanted a couple of acknowledging head nods and a few holy grunts given on their behalf. Of course, maybe they just didn't feel like giving it all up. They wanted their fair share of the sale and not what they had committed to God.

The outcome was death. The cause was desire.

A couple's attempt at misleading God in their giving results in death.

Could you imagine if this were to happen on a regular basis? A wave of sighs would be released as the plate passed down the rows, knowing that they will live to see another Sunday. And, of course, there would always be a little bit of excitement when Johnny Liar collapses next to you. It would make you want to think twice about dropping that envelope in the offering plate.

In a similar but not nearly as dramatic way, many of our financial struggles are the result of some outside factor, something more personal than many of us would like to admit. It would be easy to say that a credit card balance is the barrier that needs to be eliminated to achieve a simple financial structure, but rarely is that the cause. The debt is the outcome of a barrier, not the barrier itself.

Let us hear from Erin to illustrate: "Look, I know that my budget is strained. Trust me, I realize this every time I open the mailbox and see a bill. I get a little nervous, hoping that I will have enough to pay it. So far, I have been fine. Every bill has been paid, and I never have had any late fees. So I guess that I am fine for now."

It does not take a financial expert to realize that Erin is not fine. Actually, she's in a serious situation. One misstep and she is in trouble.

"I guess I could try to trade in my car for one with a lower monthly payment, but once you have a car like mine, it's hard to take a step down. Everyone loves it; I get so many compliments. I don't know, I guess it just makes me feel good. I feel like I'm somebody when I drive around in it. I don't know if I want to let that go."

Do you see Erin's barrier? Do you hear the real cause of her financial strain?

It's not the bills. It's not the car. It's deeper than that. Her problem isn't her financial state; that's only where it has manifested itself. Her struggle is with herself. Her struggle is with her identity.

These types of barriers cause us to make decisions that are fiscally irresponsible. We want to point the finger at someone or something else, but many times our financial situations arise out of our own self-identity. These personal obstacles are preventing us from moving forward with our mission statement. They are hindering our potential to becoming solid stewards of our gifts.

Certainly there are times when we experience circumstances that are out of our control. But such times are the minority. We find it easy to blame the credit card companies for our situations due to exorbitant interest rates. And though some of their practices are questionable, it was not the credit card company that put the original balance on that card. They did not swipe the Visa or MasterCard in the terminal. They did not purchase more than we could afford to pay off.

And much like our ability to blame financial institutions, we must be careful when we use our lack of financial resources, also known as our paycheck, as an excuse for our burdens. We know that money limits us in our decision-making, but acquiring additional funds does not necessarily mean that our financial burdens will be resolved. Often our monetary problems have nothing to do with money. And even if we were to get a raise or win the lottery, the issues would still exist inside of us, giving us the same problems on a much grander scale.

No matter how much money we make, we must first uncover our motivations for our financial decisions.

Moving Your Motivation

What motivates your financial decisions?

We come into this world naked and knowing nothing except that which is innate. We have no clue how to communicate except through a simple scream that is used for anything from hunger, to sickness, to sleepiness, to loneliness. We don't know why the sky is blue, why the grass is green, or why our little planet has two settings, night and day. Our mind is a blank canvas.

At some point we learn to communicate our curiosity about this mysterious place. We discover how to ask simple questions about a complex world. And when we are young, we ask with only one word because only one word is needed. "Why?"

Or we flavor it up with a "But why?" And thus, the "Why?" game begins.

It is a simple game. The child asks a question, and if the answer is not sufficient in the mind of the child, then he asks another question. "Why?"

This process is repeated until either the kid becomes happy with the answer or the adult gets annoyed and tells the child to go play with her toys.

One of the beauties of this game is that it gets down to the heart of the matter. It requires us to dig deep, uncover something that lies beyond the surface. A quick, nonchalant answer does not suffice. And as you may know, when it comes to money, there are often motivations that are buried deep beneath the topsoil of our hearts.

Sometimes they are beautiful. Sometimes they are ugly.

Some we will acknowledge. Some we won't.

One of the reasons the Bible discusses money is because it is such a telling indicator of what's going on inside of us. Our monetary decisions are an outflow of our heart. Jesus said it clearly in Matthew 6:21, "For where your treasure is, there your heart will be also."

The cliché says that if you want to look at someone's priorities, just take a look at their checkbook. There is truth behind this. Recorded in the register are the places or persons we deem important enough to ration a portion of our financial resources.

When we truthfully answer the *why* question, we come face-to-face with our heart. We see our motivations for what they really are, not as we pretend them to be.

Is debt a problem? Absolutely.

Is debt the cause of our financial problems? No.

When we dig deep to the root cause of debt, we often find a common obstacle. Debt is primarily caused by overconsumption. Overconsumption is caused by a desire to have something that is beyond our financial reach. We want something beyond our financial means because we think that somehow it will make us more complete.

So we buy that something, even when we don't have the money. We just pull out our little plastic savior and swear that we will pay it off by the end of the month, before the interest kicks in. And the balance builds.

We are immersed in a culture that teaches consumption as a way of life. We think that our purchasing habits, our ways of entangling ourselves with debt, are normal. Satan is great at molding our minds to fit his purposes. If he can just get us to justify the one purchase we can't afford, then he knows that the next will come easier. The result is often frustration and stress that complicate our life and ultimately our relationship with God.

We know that it is not just debt that hinders financial simplicity. There is typically much more. If our answer to the final *why* falls short of being acceptable to God, then we must fervently seek to remove that obstacle.

But do not leave it up to your own wisdom. Reach for help from the Maker of all things. The *why* is not hidden from Him.

He already knows your struggle; He has seen your heart's true motivation. And most important, He understands.

> For we do not have a high priest who is unable to sympathize with our weaknesses, but One who has been tested in every way as we are, yet without sin. Therefore let us approach the throne of grace with boldness, so that we may receive mercy and find grace to help us at the proper time. (Heb. 4:15–16)

Dig deep for answers. And then present them to the God who came to this tiny rock of a planet to better understand what you are experiencing. With Him, move your motivation.

The Far Future, the Future, and the Now

As we discussed in the previous chapter, each one of these eras is separate but highly dependent on the others. These three areas of finance are always with us, whether you have just started on your own or have been retired for many years.

We will continue to use these categories as an aid in our quest for financial simplicity. Each category holds its own obstacles that, unless removed, limit the movement of reaching our desired destination.

Proverbs 13:22 says, "A good man leaves an inheritance to his grandchildren, but the sinner's wealth is stored up for the righteous."

We should make financial decisions not because it will improve our situation but because it will benefit someone else. This idea swims completely upstream against the suggestion that because we worked hard for it all, we deserve to enjoy it all.

Is there anything wrong with enjoying the fruits of your labor? Absolutely not. But the Bible does give an indication that there is something wrong when we hoard the fruits of our labor. Why? Because it is not ours to hoard. There is more beyond our life, and our death provides one final opportunity to show love.

Only occasionally do we hear concern about the well-being of the generations that are to come after us, generations that we may never physically meet. We have conversations about environmental awareness and government spending. But rarely do we concern ourselves with producing an inheritance that will aid our children's children.

And it is not just our grandchildren with whom we need to be concerned. Those who are presently living with us need us to show concern for their future financial security. Four out of ten (41%) male respondents and 51 percent of female respondents indicated that they did not have enough insurance. Unfortunately they are probably right.

What barriers prevent us from caring for those who will potentially outlive us? Is it a preoccupation with ourselves? Do we think tragedies will never occur? Do we think we have plenty of time? Sadly many will be left without because we never placed any importance on our financial legacy. We never figured out ways in which our fortune, whether thousands or millions, could benefit those beyond our graves.

We need not paint ourselves into a corner of ignorance. We can remove the barriers that hinder our movement to a lasting financial legacy.

Movement: The Future

We have to be careful with our words here. Good people with good intentions get hurt when they are unprepared for retirement. God watches over each and every one of us and cares for us more deeply than any of us will ever understand while on this earth. But He allows for His followers to make mistakes and suffer the consequences of those mistakes. For those who choose not to plan properly for retirement, results will probably align with the lack of preparation.

We see an elderly man and his wife purchasing food with stamps and wonder what put them in that situation. Were they always without, or were they once living as they wanted, not thinking that they would ever see this moment?

For example, 73 percent of men and women in our survey had concerns about whether or not they will retire comfortably. From this number come cries of distress, fear, and discomfort about what the future will bring. We are a culture that spends first and saves if we have anything left over. We splurge in the present at the risk of the future. Without sufficient income, we are no longer able to support the lifestyle we once had. We rely on Social Security just to get us from one month to the next. The government becomes our lifeline.

And the future is not always about retirement. It's about saving for your daughter's education. It can be about preparing for that house you have wanted. It is about whatever may be coming up in your financial path beyond the next ten years.

Like the barriers we face in the far future, obstacles in the future often arise out of a lack of concern. We push it off as something that is too far down the road. We live as if the future will never come. Tomorrow will not be here until today is done, and today has not reached its completion.

So we set plans aside. We don't prepare. And when the future becomes the now, we are left in despair, wondering where the time went and what we could have done differently.

How do we overcome mental barriers? Do we talk to the father who has had to tell his daughter that, even though he promised to take care of college tuition, the money is just not there? He thought he could catch up but never could. Do we sit across from an elderly couple who, in their youth, were the life of the party, splurging on anything and everything, and now share a meek meal of canned tuna and wait for their Social Security check to arrive so they can survive another month?

Movement: The Now

Many of us find ourselves wanting to set aside something for retirement, desiring to leave some type of legacy to the next generation, but the concerns of today are like a thick, grey fog around us. We can't see beyond the present. We just want to make it through today. If we could just figure out how to make the present work, then we might be able to look toward the future.

Some who read this book are starting afresh, with little financial baggage. Others might have two or three U-Hauls filled with heavy, old, dusty luggage. Some have not even had the opportunity to make a poor financial decision; others have a stack of them sitting on the kitchen table, each with its own envelope, waiting to be paid. Wherever you find yourself, good, holy things can come from your finances when you dedicate this part of your life to God.

The barriers that are present in the now phase are powerfully destructive. Satan knows that if he can get us to construct solid, constrictive blockages to our financial well-being in the present, then we will be potentially affected for the rest of our lives. They are blockages that we sometimes carry with us for many years.

Remember Erin? She found her identity in a car. The metal and glass that encased her as she moved down the road made her feel good. She liked who she was; no, she liked how she was perceived by others as she sat behind the wheel. And for that feeling, she was willing to risk her finances.

Maybe you dismissed the far future and the future as a lack of understanding, more of a mental barrier than anything else. The obstacles we face in the now are a little bit more difficult to write off.

As we played the *why* game with our finances, most of our final answers probably ended up here in the now. Most of our struggles are in the present and are impacting our day-to-day living. Prayerfully focus on the now. Try to find those personal struggles that are preventing you from moving toward the simplicity you want. For many this will mean literally a radical change of lifestyle. Your house may no longer look like the storefront of Pottery Barn. Your clothes might not be found in *Vogue* or GQ anymore. Your child may not be wearing threads from the Ralph Lauren kids' department. And that's fine because, if we are honest, these issues are probably not just causing financial disruption but interfering with our relationship with God. And no designer is worth that cost.

Catching Up with Josh

Josh, our friend from the previous chapter, took another look at his mission statement:

Over the next year, I will give to God my first 10 percent of every paycheck, reduce my credit card debt by 50 percent, max out the company match on my 401(k), and find a way to budget a life insurance policy.

Then he looked back at his list of priorities in each of the three (The Now, The Future, and The Far Future) categories. He knew that a lot of barriers were preventing him from moving toward his goals.

Josh decided to pick one from each category and prayerfully submit it to God for help. They were:

> *The Now*: Materialism
> *The Future*: Complacency
> *The Far Future*: An overt focus on self

He looked at what he had just written and shook his head. Money was not the issue. *He* was the issue.

As we follow Josh's lead, many of us will find ourselves facing some difficult realities about the state of our hearts. In the space at the end of this chapter, we want you to confront the obstacles you are experiencing in each of the three main categories and seek God on each one of them. Remember, these barriers are not just obstacles that are hindering our financial simplicity but are also hurting our development as Christians. Removing these obstructions will help us reach our financial goals and allow us to take another step closer to becoming more like Jesus.

Sadly, financial difficulties have almost become an accepted way of life, the norm. For those who choose to pursue the simple life, it is time to break through the barriers that have been keeping you from experiencing the simple life in finances.

APPLICATION
SIMPLE LIFE: MOVEMENT
THE OBSTACLES TO FINANCIAL SIMPLICITY

Honest self-assessment is required here.

Identify barriers that hinder your movement toward financial simplicity. And realize that often these obstacles are the result of our focus on self.

The Now (0 to 10 years)

What barriers should you remove for financial health and simplicity for now and the next several years?

_____

_____

_____

_____

_____

_____

_____

The Future (10+ years)

What barriers should you remove for financial health and simplicity for the period beyond the next ten years and into retirement if you're not already there?

_____

_____

_____

_____

_____

_____

_____

The Far Future (Your Legacy)

What barriers should you remove to provide a financial legacy after your death?

_____

_____

_____

_____

_____

_____

_____

CHAPTER 11

Aligning Your Money and Mission

Clarity → Movement → ALIGNMENT → Focus

What goes through your head when someone mentions the Jeep automotive brand in a passing conversation? Do you imagine a rugged vehicle, splashing through mud on some backwoods trail with the windshield wipers creating the only clear spot in the mud that has covered the body? Do you picture an SUV driving through some arid, Moab-like terrain with ease, spraying up sand with every sharp turn? Or maybe you think of a Wrangler with the top down, sun drenching its passengers as they cruise along a seemingly undiscovered, wide-open stretch of beach.

There is just something about Jeep and adventure.

What about Lexus? What images come to mind? Do you picture a car whisking through a city's downtown, the buildings' lights reflecting off a perfectly buffed exterior? Can you smell the leather that is but a part of the wood-grained, perfectly sculpted interior? Do you imagine its passengers stepping out at the valet, adorned with modern suits, trendy dresses, and shiny jewelry that catches your eye?

There is just something about a Lexus and luxury.

Then we have Toyota, a relative of Lexus that gives off a completely different vibe. You may envision a car that embodies reliability. For some the picture of an odometer, pushing the 200k mark may come to mind. Others may see a family emerging from the car after another successful and desirably uneventful trip. Still others will conjure an image of a vehicle that passes by numerous gas stations because of the fuel-efficient engine.

There is just something about Toyota and quality.

It's amazing how the characteristics of certain brands are so deeply ingrained into our minds. Once we have developed a perception of a brand, it often takes some dramatic event to move us away from that image.

What is it that makes us have the perceived images, both good and bad, of certain brands? In the simplest sense, it is a process those in the marketing industry dub "branding."

It happens everywhere.

Think about it. Is Starbucks just about good coffee, or is there something more? Do you think that the design, layout, colors, and overall theme of each store were accidents? What about the music that seems to fit so well with the store's environment? Is it just random coincidence?

You know the answer. It was all done with purpose. Everything is intentionally devised to support that over-arching intangible "it" that Starbucks has, the "it" that you experience when you sit down in one of their stores with a mentally stimulating read and a fresh, hot latte. "It" is what goes beyond the caffeinated liquid in the cup.

Jeep, Lexus, and Toyota marketers made sure that the brand of the automobile lined up to reinforce the perceived image of the vehicle. Jeep commercials are typically shot at some off-road location. Lexus commercials seem to consistently take place in a downtown hot spot or at some house that typifies wealth. Toyota likes to keep the family involved.

This concept of branding provides us with an important understanding of how alignment works in regards to our finances. We first must recognize the core. For us, this is our mission statement. And around this core we try to line up everything, every action taken, to support the overarching goal. But unlike branding, we are not trying to make the tangible intangible; we are attempting to make the tangible, well, tangible.

Many times we may find ourselves, having made our purpose clear and having removed many obstacles, still feeling a little out of sync. We have our core, but all that surrounds the core is not necessarily supportive. We need to make sure our financial activities are aligned with our mission statement.

Our "it" needs to be developed with our finances.

How is alignment created and maintained in our finances? We have put together five sections in this chapter that will aid you as you continue on this journey:

1. An honest assessment
2. Accountability
3. Matching activities with priorities and personalities

4. A willingness to realign
5. Acceptance of imperfection

We will start at the top.

Honest Assessment

Let us introduce you to two characters: Down Dan and Up Udolf. (Yes, we struggled to find a name that started with *U*.)

Down Dan was always bummed about his attempt to simplify his finances. He claimed to have tried to align everything to his mission statement, but every area of his money seemed to be a struggle. Whenever the topic of finances came up, he would typically say that he was "just getting by" in his typical Eeyore-like voice.

Nothing was ever good enough. One of the primary objectives of his mission statement was to save money. Though he had made progress and started saving, it was not good enough. Curiously he seemed to be on pace to reach his goal, but his verbiage was quite to the contrary.

Up Udolf was quite the opposite. He was always on a high note about his money. Everything was always perfect. According to him, "Everything is great!"

Of course, he was quick to tell you about his supposed financial success. He declared to have already accomplished his first goal and was in the process of updating his mission statement to give him additional challenges. One time during his progress, Up Udolf lost his job, but this did not faze him; everything was under control and going according to his plan. He would never give any specifics, and no one could tell any changes in the way he lived.

It was almost as if Up Udolf was hiding something.

Down Dan and Up Udolf both had an issue when it came to the assessment of their financial predicament. Both were giving extreme and inaccurate views of their progress. Even if they were to tell us specific activities, it would be difficult to gauge their advancement because of their skewed perceptions.

Maybe Down Dan was afraid of admitting success because of a fear of creating unrealistic expectations. Maybe Up Udolf was scared of revealing his struggles because he did not want to be perceived as a failure.

When assessing our ability to align activities with our goals, we must become honest with ourselves. A skewed assessment will only inhibit our ability to accomplish our mission. If we were to ask Down Dan and Up Udolf about their alignment, we would know no more about their situation than if they had just remained silent.

And this can easily happen with us. Whether it is to make us appear lesser or greater, we have preferences on how we want others to perceive us.

Of course, it is not just about an honest exterior, the one the world sees. Even more important is the interior.

Have you ever convinced yourself of something that you knew was not true? It sounds ridiculous, but we think you understand what we mean. It happens when you want something so badly that you are willing to compromise your own intelligence and your own reality to avoid some truth that you do not want to recognize.

Sure, it is pathetic, but we've all done it. As we assess our financial realities, we must be brutally honest.

When we are trying to determine the state of our financial alignment, it is best to focus on our three stages of finance:

the now, the future, and the far future. Within each category, ask yourself the following questions:

- What was my goal?
- What changes did I make to meet my goal?
- Am I seeing progress?
- If no, what adjustment needs to take place?

We refresh our memory as to what our goal is, evaluate the outcome of those decisions, and, if necessary, determine the types of changes needed for us to see our heart's desire become reality.

We have spoken of our role as God's stewards. This honest assessment is an integral part of our stewardship. It is how we can personally hold ourselves accountable to the actions, or lack of actions, that we take.

In our study, 55 percent of our respondents felt that they had too much debt. How is your debt doing?

And 72 percent admitted that they did not have six months' worth of expenses set aside. How is your savings?

Only 25 percent of males and 36 percent of females said that they had enough homeowners insurance. What have you done to cover yourself and your family in case of disaster?

Be honest with yourself. Do not sell yourself short; do not consider your alignment better than it is. Honesty holds no bias.

Remember, detach yourself and be wise. This is about more than just you. Be stewards of honor.

Accountability

In Luke 12:13–21 we find Jesus surrounded by a crowd. And from the crowd comes a voice, "Teacher, tell my brother to divide the inheritance with me" (v. 13).

The Bible does not indicate who this man was; all that we know is his appeal. His request was so disappointing. This random man gets a shot to grab Jesus' ear, and "tell my brother to divide the inheritance with me" was the best that he could do? What about an explanation of eternity? What was it like before creation? At the very least, he could've asked Jesus to part another sea.

There was an unquestionable blindness about this man. Though he came to see Jesus, his eyes could only focus on himself. He did not understand the opportunity before him. He let us all down with his question.

Of course, Jesus responded, "'Friend, . . . who appointed Me a judge or arbitrator over you?' He then told them, 'Watch out and be on guard against all greed because one's life is not in the abundance of his possessions'" (vv. 14–15).

In summary, Jesus had better things to do than worry about some greedy man's brother's inheritance. He was there to save the world, not some selfish man's wallet.

But Jesus did not leave it at this. He told a parable:

A rich man's land was very productive. He thought to himself, "What should I do, since I don't have anywhere to store my crops? I will do this," he said. "I'll tear down my barns and build bigger ones and store all my grain and my goods there. Then I'll say to myself, 'You have many goods stored up for

many years. Take it easy; eat drink, and enjoy yourself.'" (vv. 16–19)

At this point, the man in the crowd had to be wondering
where Jesus was going with this. Jesus continued, "But God
said to him, 'You fool! This very night your life is demanded
of you. And the things you have prepared—whose will they
be?' That's how it is with the one who stores up treasure for
himself and is not rich toward God" (vv. 20–21).

We imagine that this guy didn't stick around.

The parable itself is extremely appropriate for a discussion
on finances. However, the action of this man in the crowd
brings us to the topic of accountability.

Like the man in the crowd, we are often blinded to what
is most important. With our money it is easy to get distracted
by activities that do not align with the mission statement and
do not aid in the realization of our goals. We ask the wrong
questions. We ignore the opportunity at hand.

We wonder how we can afford a new bedroom suite
when we should be figuring out how to save six months'
living expenses for an emergency. We get distracted by that
showroom shine of a new car when we should be focused on
getting rid of credit card debt. We get enamored by the things
that are fun and bored by the things that are considered con-
ventional. Few find it more entertaining to save than to figure
out a way to spend that extra dollar in the pocket.

So many of our financial decisions don't align with our
mission statement. We quickly find out that we cannot do
this on our own. There is a need for some type of accountability. Christ called out our random guy; Jesus cut right to
the heart of the matter. Most of us need that same type of
reality-crushing news in regard to our finances.

Proper accountability with another will help you stay on track, get you to take off the blinders, and provide incentive to see your goals flesh into reality. We recommend that you don't take the opportunity lightly to have someone hold you responsible for achieving your mission statement.

Here are some basic recommendations when seeking out someone to hold you accountable for your finances:

- They must have similar values.
- They must understand or have similar goals.
- They must understand money, at least on a basic level.
- They must be trusted.
- They must be willing to provide honest feedback.
- They cannot be a family member.

A good accountability partner will give you a nudge when you start veering off track. She will encourage you when you do right. He will walk with you, step-by-step, as you develop a life that exemplifies financial simplicity.

Priorities and Personalities

The methods of managing money are like snowflakes. Stephanie likes everything electronic. Mr. Graham gets freaked out if paper is not involved. Larry does everything over the phone. Ms. Tishner would be lost without her debit card.

If ten people were to walk into a bank, there would be ten different ways of handling money. Sure, there is no statistic (that we know of) to back this up, but we know that the ways in which individuals take care of their finances vary widely. We all have our own little methods.

Now we have purposefully tried not to get into specifics in regards to finances and will continue not to do so. We only desire to provide an outline into which you can enter your own specific situation.

The handling of finances is all about preferences. Many are uncomfortable doing their finances with gadgetry and technology. On the opposite end of the spectrum, there are those who could not function without some sort of electronic device. If they were not able to see their finances through the computer or phone, they would be lost.

"You mean people actually go into those bank buildings? Why?"

Often our means of handling our money is dictated by previous experience.

Mr. Tucker, an elderly man, has never used a computer and never will.

Tina, who is in her twenties, had her account hacked twice over the Internet, so she, like Mr. Tucker, has vowed never to use the computer again.

Same preferences, different reasons.

Sometimes it is a generational thing. Those who are younger are more likely to place trust in new technology. Some like to have a document for everything; others think this is just a waste of a tree. Some trust their banker; others think bankers are just crooks in suits, figuring out some way to scam them out of their money.

Needless to say, whether you are a tech-superstar or a loyal pencil-only register fanatic, we understand. And we are not trying to change your ways in that area.

While we are trying to simplify our finances, we will inevitably run across and implement some ideas or methods that go against our nature. Most of us have heard the old saying, "There's more than one way to skin a cat." We're not really sure who said this first, but we're pretty sure that we don't want to meet him.

The point of the odd maxim is relevant to our alignment. We can fulfill our mission statement in numerous ways. And since God has gifted us differently and given us different personalities, why would we not try to find a means by which we can reach our goals with greater ease?

"I have to admit that I had been struggling to reach my goal. I wanted to reduce my monthly spending, but all of the number crunching just got annoying."

Herman didn't like the details. But instead of giving up, he tried to find an approach that would not only meet his goal but also better match his personality.

"After doing some investigation, I found out that my bank had plenty of options that would allow me to keep track of my spending without having to concentrate too much on those tedious little calculations."

Herman made an important realization: the means by which he was attempting to rein in his spending was not aligned with his personality. This made the process of simplification a burden on his life. And even though the activity itself was aligned, there were better options for Herman. Fortunately he was able to discover better ways, ways that lined up with who God created him to be.

Our uniqueness goes beyond the obvious physical features. The layers of individual distinction make us like a rare jewel that is precious in God's sight. We were all designed with specifics on how we should operate. And our personalities will either react positively or negatively to how we do our finances.

If you find yourself feeling like your actions are not *you*, you're probably right. You can handle your money in numerous ways. Seek out those that align with who you were meant to be.

Willingness to Adjust

So if we recognize the need to change, then there must be a willingness to implement that change. While this may sound obvious, change often does not come easy. We typically hesitate when change is demanded of us.

We like our ways. They are what we know. We like what we know especially when it comes to our money.

As life continues to take you on its journey, your financial situation will inevitably see makeovers. There will be highs and lows, valleys and peaks. External factors such as income increases and decreases, financial emergencies, and the birth of a child will impact your situation.

Simplicity requires flexibility.

The lack of flexibility can have dramatic consequences. Take a quick walk with us down the street. We want to show you somebody.

Look over there. Do you see the guy whose attire looks like he just stepped out of the eighties? No, he's not retro; he's too old for that.

See those jeans; they're authentic.

Disturbing isn't it?

What about that hyper-color T-shirt?

The permanently splotched shirt nicely draws attention away from his beautifully manicured Kentucky waterfall (aka the mullet).

Somewhere along the line this guy gave up. He became comfortable, settled in his ways, and let the world change around him while he didn't budge. Now he cruises in that Firebird he's waxing down, blasting some Motley Crew, wondering why everyone he passes just seems to point and laugh.

Sure, we find humor in this, but we can also learn some lessons. Maybe it's that sometimes a refusal to accept change and adapt will leave us looking foolish.

Activities to which we have become accustomed may no longer be the best route. Change could happen in a week, a month, or a year. We must be ready to adjust as the roller coaster of life gives us its quick turns, sharp drops, and sometimes gut-wrenching loops.

Be prepared. Be flexible.

The Acceptance of Imperfection

We find our friend, Josh, back at the coffee shop.

"Look, man, as always, I appreciate your meeting with me. Trying to get a good grasp on my money is such a difficult thing to do. I need all of the support that I can get."

Josh set up a time when he and Lucas could get together on a biweekly basis to talk about the progress with his finances. It had been a crucial step for him as it kept him accountable to someone other than his wife.

"Are you sure that you don't want any coffee, Josh?" Lucas asked.

"No, man. I am trying to cut back on caffeine," replied Josh.

He was also trying to cut back on expenses.

As the conversation went on, Lucas asked Josh some tough questions about his pursuit to simplify his finances. Josh appreciated Lucas's seriousness about the matter. He could tell that Lucas knew how critical this issue was for him. It took a couple of meetings before Josh was completely comfortable divulging all of his money issues with another person, but it was worth it. These little meetings had kept him on track so far. Well, except for one area.

"So tell me about God's 10 percent," asked Lucas.

This had been an issue for Josh. It was the first goal of his mission statement.

> *Over the next year, I will give to God my first 10 percent of every paycheck, reduce my credit card debt by 50 percent, max out the company match on my 401(k), and find a way to budget a life insurance policy.*

He had taken steps to reduce his credit card debt, increase his 401(k) contribution, and get a life insurance policy, but it seemed that there was never any money left over after those things were done.

Josh had become frustrated with this. He hated facing Lucas and telling him the same thing each time they talked. It was embarrassing.

He had contemplated removing the goal from his mission statement altogether, but he knew that this was not just something he wanted to do, it was something that was required of him. He knew that he needed to make it happen.

For the next twenty minutes, Josh and Lucas discussed how Josh could create an activity that would align with this goal. After bouncing around a few ideas, they determined that it would be best if Josh gave his company permission to directly deposit a portion of his paycheck into a savings account, opened for the specific purpose of setting it aside for God.

It was "God's savings account."

His desire to give back to God a portion of his earnings would be accomplished by directing those funds to come out of his pay first. This would help eliminate the temptation to use it for other purposes.

Josh was satisfied. "You know, I think I will grab a cup of coffee," he said with a smug look on face.

"Really?" inquired Lucas. "I though you were trying to cut back on caffeine."

Josh thought about it again for a second. It would be difficult to hide his coffee breath from his wife. She would know. He couldn't take the risk of having to explain his little splurge.

"You're right. I'll hold off. That's why I need you, Lucas. You're there to look out for me," Josh said as he slapped Lucas on the back.

They stepped outside the coffee shop and shook hands.

"I'll see you in two weeks," Lucas said with a smile.

"I'll be there," replied Josh with a matching smile.

They then got in their cars and drove home to their families.

As we review the story of Josh, we see that even though he had the desire to meet his goal, he still had an alignment issue. He gave priority to all parts of his statement except the first. By reevaluating his alignment, he figured out a way to adjust his actions to meet not only the first but all of the other desires as well.

Josh could have wallowed in defeat because his plan had not succeeded as he had hoped. He could have given up on this one aspect of his mission statement, declared it impossible. But he didn't.

Fortunately Josh did not dwell too long on his miscalculation. He quickly moved from being frustrated to being determined to reconstruct his alignment to ensure success in all areas of his mission statement.

Like Josh, you will find areas in your life that do not match up with your desired outcome. If you get it right the first time, great. If you find yourself needing to adjust, that is okay. Remember, this is a process, and it must be treated as such.

Approach errors as an opportunity to learn, grow, and further define who you yearn to be. Do not strive for perfection. Strive for the goal.

Aligned with Hope

As you can see, your alignment will play a critical role in simplifying your finances. When all is aligned between your mission statement and your activities, everything seems to make sense and hope remains. However, when things just don't seem to mesh, frustration ensues and hope diminishes.

You cannot lose hope. Hope fuels action. Hope gets you to the next step. The next step is focus.

Prayerfully consider your alignment. Ask God to reveal ways in which you can set up your activities to parallel with your priorities, to make sense with who you are and who you desire to be. Find hope in your alignment.

APPLICATION
SIMPLE LIFE: ALIGNMENT
FINANCES AND THE UNIQUENESS OF YOU

Countless books, seminars, and other resources are available on managing your finances. We didn't replicate much of that information in this book. So you don't have much guidance here on the specifics of budgets, mortgages, savings, investments, retirement, and the like.

Instead, in this chapter, you should ask if the way you are handling your finances best matches who you are. Look at the following five sets of questions. Answer them to get an idea if you need to make any adjustments toward the accomplishment of your mission statement.

1. Have you honestly assessed your current financial situation? If not, can you do it, or do you need outside help?

2. Do you need someone to help you stay accountable in your finances? Who would you trust? How would you establish that accountability?

3. Does your financial plan match who you are? If you are not a detail person, a detailed budget may drive you crazy. If you have trouble disciplining yourself to tithe or save, you may need a plan that does it automatically for you.

4. Are you willing to make the changes you know you need to make or those that someone you trust recommends you make?

5. Are you willing to accept your imperfections and start afresh when you don't stick with the financial plan according to your mission statement?

CHAPTER 12

Keeping Focus on Your Finances

Clarity → Movement → Alignment → FOCUS

We find Josh back at his regular stomping ground, the coffee shop. But this time he did not sit inside. The weather was right, and a nice, gentle breeze was carrying across the area so he chose to sit outside. The coffee shop had some wrought-iron chairs and tables in front of the entrance for those patrons who wanted to enjoy their beverage in the fresh air. Though Josh had since given up his three-dollar cup of joe, he reasoned that his previous purchases more than afforded him the right to take his place in their chairs.

So he sat.

Though he had taken many steps to improve and simplify his finances, he still felt some weight on his shoulders. This is why he came to this spot alone. He needed to think.

Josh reached in his left rear pants pocket and pulled out his wallet. He opened the wallet up and sifted through a couple of dollar bills. For a brief second he was tempted to trade those bills in for a cup of the black stuff, but then his fingers came upon his purpose for opening the wallet.

Josh pulled out a small piece of paper. It was a little worn, a little dirty, and folded in half. He opened it and read the words:

Over the next year, I will give to God my first 10 percent of every paycheck, reduce my credit card debt by 50 percent, max out the company match on my 401(k), and find a way to budget a life insurance policy.

It was his mission statement. Whenever he felt like he needed clarification, he would view it as a reminder of his goals. It provided him with a little kick of inspiration to keep on pursuing simplicity.

He had been successful in giving God the first 10 percent of his paycheck. Though not by 50 percent yet, he and his wife had reduced their credit card debt by spending a little less and putting more toward that debt. He had maxed out his match with his company's 401(k) and had gotten a life insurance policy. Though he would like the policy to be more, it was a good start.

As he sat there looking at his worn piece of paper, a car pulled up. Two parents and their young daughter emerged from the car and then went into the shop. He felt the weight again.

He had made a lot of right choices on this path to simplicity, but one question still lingered: What about his daughter's cheerleading trip?

The coach needed the payment in two days. Josh and his wife, Elaine, had deliberated over this for some time. The trip was expensive, especially for their financial position. The funds needed for the trip could make a good dent in their credit card debt. But wasn't this considered an investment into their child's future? Getting a good return on that is priceless.

Well, almost priceless. There was definitely a cost involved. A cost they couldn't afford.

Though his eyes were not closed, Josh prayed, "God, help me. You know the burden of our finances. You know the stress it has caused. You know that we need out of this mess as quickly as possible. Give me the strength and wisdom to do what is right for the family. Help me with this decision. Help me."

Josh caught a whiff of coffee as a customer swung open the shop's door. It was almost hypnotic. Without a cup in hand, this would have to do.

Saving the Ship

Jimmy Scroggins, a pastor in West Palm Beach, Florida, gave a compelling illustration that relates to some of the financial decisions we must face as we pursue the simple life.

He told of an aircraft carrier, warring on open seas. The number of sailors and airmen, the most crucial resources on the ship, was limited. As the war raged, planes were quickly taking off from the carrier until none were left. Soon most of the men were in the air, and only a few remained on the ship.

While the planes flew, the ship came under attack. The men who remained on the carrier did the best they could to fend off the attack, but it was a futile effort. The ship soon had holes in it, and the carrier was taking on water.

The men on the ship tried to fix them, but with most fighting in the air and some fighting on the ship, there was not even manpower to mend the holes.

The captain soon realized what was happening and ordered the planes to come back. They needed to save the ship. Without the ship the planes could not land or take off again. The men in the air would be stranded, and the situation would ultimately lead to their deaths. It was great that they had many planes in the air, but without the ship the fight was lost.

One by one they landed on the ship. With each aircraft that arrived, more and more men became available to fend off the attack and fix the holes. The carrier was saved.

The captain had made the right decision. And because the ship was saved, they were able to live to fight another day.

The final chapter in this section is dedicated to helping you answer some of the most difficult decisions that you will have in regard to your finances. Like Josh, you probably have made a lot of great decisions and followed through with action. But at the same time you realize that there is more. Some weights still burden your progress.

Choosing to get out of debt was easy. Finding yourself in a place where it is either your child's cheerleading trip or a notable decrease in that debt can be gut-wrenching.

We all have our planes in the air. They are doing what they are supposed to be doing, fighting the battle. But as the planes fly above us, our ship is under attack. We are taking on water and do not have the resources to fix the holes.

Our study revealed the battle on many different fronts. Notably, 60 percent of the respondents indicated that finances were causing significant stress in their families. And remember the statistic stated earlier that 50 percent of those surveyed typically have more bills than money in a given month. Nearly half (46%) of the respondents said that their credit card bills are too high.

A decision must be made. Do we keep the planes flying, or do we call back the planes and save the ship? Choose one and both the planes and the ship could find themselves on the ocean floor. Choose another and the entire crew may live to fight another day.

What is your decision?

Welcome to focus.

A Briefing on Focus

At this point you should understand the concept of focus, a willingness to eliminate even that which is good but does not contribute to the overall pursuit of your goals, at least for the time being.

The aircraft carrier illustration demonstrates the importance of keeping the core intact. Our core is our goals. If we're not able to pull our resources together and tend to the core for a while, our attempt to simplify our money will remain under the same attack that brought us to this point. And as that struggle continues, our core becomes even more embattled, and the complexity of our finances persists.

You may have some great ideas about where your money should go, how it should be spent. And you may have great intentions and a clear mind, but if you do not narrow your focus, at least for a season, you run the risk of losing all the work you have done until this point.

In a war at sea, keeping your planes in combat is important, but keeping your ship afloat is vital. As we continue to chase after stewardship, we must focus on that which allows us to be the best managers of God's resources.

Josh was burdened by an upcoming decision. He had a daughter who wanted to go on a cheerleading trip. Even if he scraped the funds together, those funds could have an impact on his debt. Part of Josh wants to provide for his daughter. Part of him wants to pay off his debt. Both are good options.

To help Josh and you out, here are some characteristics of focus for the simple life:

1. *Focus sees the whole picture.* All financial decisions are connected; each impacts the others. For every dollar you spend on gas, you have one less dollar to spend, save, or invest somewhere else. No financial decisions stand alone or are unconnected. Focus requires us to see this big picture, that everything, and sometimes everyone, is intertwined, for better or worse.

Josh needs to consider the fact that his debt has and will continue to have a direct impact on his entire family. Consider the stress. Consider the shifty ground on which his family's finances sit.

Is it more important to create a solid surface upon which Josh and his family can continue to build for many years, or is it more important to send his daughter on this trip? Will it benefit his daughter more to have a family that is solid in their finances, or will it benefit her more to learn how to develop some new cheerleading skills?

This is more than a trip. It is a piece of the picture. And whatever the decision may be, the picture will be affected.

2. Focus is blind to the externals. Those of you who have been around horse racing understand the concept of blinders. Blinders are placed on the sides of a horse's eyes so that his vision is limited to see only what is in front of him.

In a race, several horses are on the track; most are running within inches of another competitor. Distraction comes easily as a horse has the tendency to check out who is running next to him. This distraction can cause the horse to slow down and remove himself as a contender for the victory.

In our financial life a lot of things are going on around us. Distraction comes easily. Strapping on a pair of financial blinders can aid us in reaching the final goal. As we proceed with this journey, we must be willing to look ahead and allow the externals to fade away.

No competitor enters a race without the intent to reach the finish line. As a horse dashes around the track with a single goal, so you must continue this race and be purposeful about reaching the intended outcome, the point where you find yourself crossing the finish line.

3. Focus distinguishes between the good and the good. You will find yourself in a situation where you must distinguish between a necessary good and an unnecessary good in relation to your mission statement. Our finances can provide us with the opportunity to do many great things. We can feed the hungry, give to the poor, and take care of our family.

But sometimes that which is good will limit us in this particular pursuit of simplicity. God does desire us to take care of others, but rarely does God ask us to put ourselves in financial ruin and become another's burden. We can give until it hurts, but then we find ourselves hurt.

So you might have to ask yourself, "To what extent?" To what extent do you continue to do those things which are of pure intent but are of ill consequences to your goals? You have already determined what is important in your finances. Anything above and beyond needs to be prayerfully questioned until you are on solid financial ground.

Make sure one good is not preventing another good from occurring.

Focus on the Now, the Future, and the Far Future (Your Legacy)

Focus on the Now (0 to 10 years)

Our survey showed that the respondents desired a better lifestyle for their children than they had experienced as a child. More than 77 percent of the men and 68 percent of the women said that they wanted to give their children more materially than they had growing up. And 50 percent wanted to currently give their children more than they had already given them.

Desiring to care for our children is by no means a poor motive. It's a natural yearning to want to provide the best for our kids. But at what cost? We now see parents who are living month to month with their three-year-old wearing a Ralph Lauren polo, a shirt that will be useless by the time he turns four.

Companies push our emotional buttons to convince us to provide the best for our children. But they make the branded goods the standard by which some gauge and compare their love for their kids. We want them to wear the best, drive the best, and experience the best. For those who can't afford to do so, this desire to provide materially for their children beyond the child's needs is a barrier. And that barrier hinders the family from ever seeing simplicity in their finances.

What can be a good desire can turn into a money pit. And even though there is nothing inherently wrong with the desire to provide our children nice things such as name-brand goods, we can't make the mistake of finding our parental worth in such an endeavor.

Focus on the Future (10+ years)

It's simple. We need to set aside money for the future. But 50 percent of our respondents did not have a financial plan for the future. Another 73 percent have concerns about whether they can retire comfortably. And these surveys preceded the stock market crash in late 2008 that demolished most retirement accounts. The need is there.

Money is finite. This reality requires us to make decisions on the pursuits that we take for our future. It would be nice if we could simultaneously set aside the full amount preferred for our distant plans and have the funds for everything we desire right now, but life typically dictates something different.

Maybe you determined that your retirement was your greatest need, but you also need to start saving for your son's college expenses. Your mission statement reflects the next step in your retirement planning and, like most, your funds are limited. If you split the funds, there remains little impact on either. You need to focus.

This is why you created a mission statement. You need to reflect back on your statement and let it guide your focus. Maybe you can help out with college at a later date. Maybe your son can start saving some for himself.

It is admirable to want to help your son in his college expenses. But trust us, he will be much more appreciative when you're not knocking on his door, asking to live with him and his future family because you ran out of funds during retirement.

Focus on the Far Future (Your Legacy)

Trent thought about his legacy more than most. He had a wife and two beautiful children. Trent was the primary wage earner in the household, and so while they were dependent on him, he wanted to make sure that, even in his death, they had enough. Trent also wanted to have some type of insurance money go to his church.

Trent looked at his financial situation. There was no way he could do both. The premium on both of those insurance policies would push his available funds. Trent knew that he and his wife had created a mission statement that addressed the insurance need for his family.

Focus required that Trent make priorities. His family was his priority.

Our survey showed that 41 percent of males and 51 percent of females in our survey believed that they did not have enough insurance. Like Trent, the lack of insurance is a reality that many face. There are many reasons to have insurance, including legacy building. As you pursue your legacy, do not stretch yourself out too far. Focus on the mission statement and allow it to govern the direction of your legacy. As time progresses, you will be able to build your legacy and be a blessing to future generations.

What Focus Cannot Eliminate

The act of offering up our money to God has two purposes:

1. To participate in God's work
2. To reveal our hearts

God does not need our money. God does not function on dollars and cents. His purposes in this world are not dictated by a well-managed budget. He has no need for proper accounting methods. He is not even worried when a nation falls on tough economic times. His plan is already set in motion, and the final chapter will reach its last page. That piece of paper in your wallet, the one that our world values so much, has no authority in regard to His plan. He is much greater than that.

God did not fill the Bible with lessons on giving because He has a need. God created the concept of giving so that we may be a part of His plan for our obedience to Him. He wants us to live beyond what is humanly capable, to tap into the spiritual. Giving was fashioned out of His love for us.

In 2 Corinthians 8:3–4, the apostle Paul tells of a Macedonian church that seemed to get it: "I testify that, on their own, according to their ability and beyond their ability, they begged us insistently for the privilege of sharing in the ministry to the saints."

They wanted to be a part of something beyond themselves. They begged to participate in the work of God through their gifts. Like you and us, they were beings created for all the good that God originally designed, including the spiritually fulfilling act of giving.

They were meant to give. We are meant to give.

And in the same letter to the Corinthians, Paul writes about the connection between the heart and one's offering: "Each person should do as he has decided in his heart—not out of regret or out of necessity, for God loves a cheerful giver" (2 Cor. 9:7).

Many Christians argue that we need to give 10 percent of our earnings to the church, basing their position on texts from Malachi 3 and 1 Corinthians 16. But then we also run across the verse above. What are we to make of this?

A good way to answer this question is to take a look at the Ten Commandments. When God presented these commands to the Israelites, He set the bar pretty low. Do not kill. Do not have sex with someone other than your spouse. They were the basics.

But then came additional teachings from Jesus. He did not make these commandments optional but taught that there is so much more. Everything, including these basics, is about the heart. And when the heart is involved, a change occurs.

Now anger at your brother is on the same level as murder. Now adultery is merely lusting after someone other than your spouse. God wants more than a mind full of dos and do nots. He wants the heart.

The same goes for Scripture on giving. Offering one tenth of your earnings is the basics. Supporting the ministry of your local church is the low bar. When God starts to look at the heart, the bar bumps up. We are no longer just offering what is determined by Scripture as appropriate but by what the Holy Spirit instructs us. It is a gift only known by you and God.

One day Jesus was in the temple, watching people drop off their offerings. Men and women of great wealth dropped off their bags of money, but Jesus was not impressed.

Then a poverty-stricken widow passed by and dropped two copper coins, practically nothing, in the tabernacle's treasury. Jesus called His disciples over to Him and said, "I assure you: This poor widow has put in more than all those giving to the temple treasury. For they all gave out of their surplus, but she out of her poverty has put in everything she possessed—all she had to live on" (Mark 12:43–44).

The rich offerings could not match the heart of this widow. Her gift, the gift of her heart, was worth more than any bag of money.

Withdrawing your offering is dismissing an invitation to participate in God's work. This is one area that should not be eliminated by your focus. To miss out on giving is to miss out on one of the beautiful acts of obedience that God provided for us.

Giving is a gift created for you. Immerse yourself in the experience. Pray for God to direct your heart in your offerings, and be a part of something beyond your human capability.

Welcome to the Beginning

You have clarified, moved, aligned, and focused. For most, this is not the end but merely a beginning. It is a time to create a new standard for the handling of money. It is a time to shift one's view on the role finances can play during a lifetime.

Finances can be the source of many ups and downs, highs and lows. And we would be careless to say that simplifying the management of your money will eliminate all concerns. Unexpected twists come; unanticipated turns suddenly appear.

Purposefully we tried not to become too entangled in specific products, specific tools that could aid in your management. There are already many writings about those aspects of finances, and they should be used when necessary.

In the same breath it is also important to find someone who is both financially competent and trustworthy. There are some areas, such as retirement planning, which are best suited to be discussed with a professional.

Money has its place in each of our lives. Matthew 6:20–21 says, "But collect for yourselves treasures in heaven, where neither moth nor rust destroys, and where thieves don't break in and steal. For where your treasure is, there your heart will be also."

Money is a matter of the heart.

Throughout this section we stressed the need for us to excel at stewardship. God gives us this awesome responsibility and opportunity. He gives us responsibility so that we may be used in this life. Like giving, stewardship is a gift. When God requests stewardship, He hands us a gift that allows us to develop spiritually and to make a positive difference on His planet.

Take the gift. Tear the wrapping. Open the box. Explore the contents. Experience how stewardship can make a difference not only in your life but throughout all eternity.

Application
Simple Life: Focus
Spending Less on the Good Things

In the broadest of terms, you are in one of two categories: good financial condition or bad financial condition. But most of us are willing to admit that we could do better.

For the person in bad financial condition, the motivation to make changes is obvious. You really would like the simple life financially, but you know you have a long way to go.

If you are fortunate enough to be in good financial condition, the pressure to change is not so great. But is it possible that you could give more to your church and other worthy causes? Is it possible that you could save more and set aside more for retirement? Is it possible that you could provide more for those you love? Would you like to leave a financial legacy to them?

We challenge you to make a list of those good expenditures that are not absolutely necessary. Estimate the amount you spend in a year for each item on the list.

Think hard. Think about the money you spend on the expensive cups of coffee, on snacks, on clothes, on a nice car. Think really hard. You may be surprised how you can focus and really eliminate some good expenses for better causes. Then you might truly be able to have clarity for your mission statement.

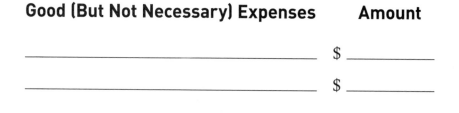

Good (But Not Necessary) Expenses   Amount

_____ $ _____

_____ $ _____

_____ $ _____

_____ $ _____

_____ $ _____

_____ $ _____

_____ $ _____

_____ $ _____

_____ $ _____

_____ $ _____

PART 4

Simple Life: How to Get Closer to God

CHAPTER 13

Looking for God in All the Wrong Places

CLARITY → Movement → Alignment → Focus

"T he fool says in his heart, 'God does not exist'" (Ps. 14:1). Those are not our words. They come straight from the Bible.

Apparently most of those we surveyed agreed. Eight out of ten respondents said they were Christians. Another 7 percent held to some other religious belief. And another 11 percent believed in God but had no preferred religious system. Only 2 percent were either agnostics (persons who claim neither faith nor disbelief in God) or atheists (persons who deny that God exists).

So how do Americans feel about their relationship with God? Not so good. At least that's what they told us.

Nearly seven out of ten (69%, for you statistical sticklers) said that they needed to spend more time on spiritual matters. The vast majority believes in God. Most of those are Christians. And most of the Christians say that they need to simplify their lives so that they have more time for God.

"Isn't it ridiculous?" Stephanie questioned. "I say that I believe in God. I say that God should be the most important priority in my life. I claim that God sent His Son to die for me. But I somehow can't make time for Him. No, I take that back. I *don't* make time for Him. What is wrong with me?"

Stephanie is not alone in her sentiments. We heard stories like Stephanie's throughout our survey. Jack is a good representative of those who are looking for God in all the wrong places.

God, Jack, and the Simple Life

Jack is forty-three years old. He is vice president of a midsize software company in East Tennessee. He married at age nineteen, but that marriage only survived a little more than two years. He met Laura when he was twenty-five. They married a year later and have been happily married for seventeen years. They have three sons.

Work consumes Jack's life. "I know that I should not work as much as I do. But our company has grown in good and bad economic times, and we never seem to have enough qualified employees. Those of us who have been here a while really put in a lot of hours because we know the company best."

We asked Jack where he would spend more time if he could. "I guess there are at least two or three immediate answers to that question," he responded. "My wife needs more of my time. The boys are involved in a ton of sports. I miss too many of their games. But, if I had to pick just one area where I would spend more time, it would be with God."

Jack was raised in a Christian home. His parents took him to church "every time the lights were on in the church." The influence of the church and his Christian parents on his life is "one of the most important factors that shaped who I am today."

He was a member of the Nazarene church in his childhood and youth, and he and Laura are members of a nondenominational church today.

"Yeah, we are members. But I bet the other members wouldn't recognize me if I showed up next Sunday. I haven't been to church in more than six months, and I have only taken the family three times in the past two years. Laura sometimes takes the boys without me, but she gets tired of being a single church parent. So she really doesn't go at all that much any more. I really can't blame her."

Jack's faith and his church were formative in his life. He even admits that they were the most important influences in his life. Yet, despite his background and beliefs, he has, for all practical purposes, left the church.

Jack continued, "Sometimes I get so frustrated with my schedule and so filled with guilt about my neglect of spiritual matters that I cry out to God and ask Him where He is. I really feel guilty watching my three sons grow up without church being a part of their lives. I keep asking God for help, but I guess I just need to slow down and listen to God. I know I'm looking for God in all the wrong places."

The Big Discrepancy

Nearly nine out of ten of those we surveyed felt that it was important for them and their families to have a spiritual foundation. More than eight out of ten said that they agreed it was important for them to live by the values of the Bible. And another eight out of ten indicated that they try to provide good spiritual leadership in their families. But most of these same people said that they weren't making enough room in their lives for God.

That's the big discrepancy between the desire and reality. Between what they know is right and actions that fail to follow what is right. Between saying that God is their priority and making Him their priority.

The first cry of the respondents for the simple life was a life more focused on God. A life where God is in the center rather than on the periphery. A life where spiritual desires meet spiritual realities.

Clarity: A Plan to Move God to the Center

Allow us the pleasure of redundancy for just a moment. In the introduction we said that the simple life would focus on four major components: clarity, movement, alignment, and focus. In the first chapter of each section, we have focused on clarity. Where should you be going? Where are you going? What is your blueprint?

We do not have to convince many of you that God is important in your life. In fact, most of you would agree that nothing is more important than God. He is our Creator. He is our Savior. He is our reason for being. So why do we push Him to the periphery?

Most said that their priorities were mixed up and messed up. Most realize that they needed a simpler life that puts God in His rightful place. Some of you may be reading this book primarily to move to the simple life where God is at the center.

So it's time for a change.

In the first step, which we call clarity, you need to state your intention to change. That's a simple first step. We'll talk about actually making the change later.

We heard from Jack earlier in this chapter. He knew that he wanted to put God back at the center of his life. He knew that he needed to provide spiritual leadership for his wife and three sons. So he told us that he would make a change. But we wondered if his desire for change would have any specificity to it. Or would it be some ambiguous statement like, "I want to get closer to God"?

So we were pleasantly surprised to hear Jack state his intentions with some degree of specificity. "This survey has been a wake-up call for me," he began.

> I will move closer to God by beginning to read the Bible at least fifteen minutes a day, by taking my family to church each week, and by talking about spiritual matters with my family at least once a week.

Wait a minute. Let's get a rerun of Jack's statement.

He will get closer to God with three clear action items: fifteen minutes of Bible study every day, taking the family to church on Sunday, and talking about spiritual matters with his family at least once a week.

Now we know that growing closer to God is not some magical formula. And we know that it is possible to read the

Bible, go to church, and talk about spiritual matters, and still not have God at the center of your life.

When Jesus walked this earth as a man, He recognized that someone could have all the outward manifestations of spirituality and still be distant from God. In fact, He encountered a group of such people often. They were the Pharisees.

The name *Pharisee* means "separated ones." These guys took seriously refraining from any defilement at all. They had a pretty good theology too. They believed in the resurrection of the body after death, and they believed in rewards and punishments in a life after death.

There were probably a few thousand of them at the time of Jesus. They rigorously kept the laws of the Old Testament. And then they added some other rules to assure obedience to these laws. They had dietary rituals. They had rituals of purity at meals. They had rules for keeping the Sabbath holy. They even had a set of rules on what work could be done on the Sabbath.

The strict traditions of the Pharisees caused some of them to be legalistic. Instead of having an internal change, they externalized God's law. They relied on different types of external obedience in their attempts to get closer to God.

These guys didn't make Jesus happy. To the contrary, He was disgusted with them. Just listen to an excerpt of His denunciation of the Pharisees: "Woe to you, scribes and Pharisees, hypocrites! You are like whitewashed tombs, which appear beautiful on the outside, but inside are full of dead men's bones and every impurity. In the same way, on the outside you seem righteous to people, but inside you are full of hypocrisy and lawlessness" (Matt. 23:27–28).

Wow! Not exactly the picture of people getting closer to God.

A checklist of items marked off does not make someone get closer to God. Still, if those actions are the result of a true desire to put God at the center of one's life, it is not bad. Certainly it is not like the Pharisees.

In fact, if we have a desire to get closer to God and we have no actions that move us in that direction, we are probably not getting closer to God. The Bible says clearly, "In the same way faith, if it doesn't have works, is dead by itself" (James 2:17).

You see, 69 percent of those we surveyed indicated that they really wanted to move closer to God. They had no need to lie or to impress. They seemed sincere in their desire.

Our research indicates that desire without specificity typically leads nowhere. So we aren't proposing that you just have outward manifestations of religion like the Pharisees. Instead, we are proposing that you plan concrete actions that will demonstrate your inner desire.

A mission statement will aid the process of clarity.

Jack's statement a few pages ago could make a perfect mission statement:

> *I will move closer to God by beginning to read the Bible at least fifteen minutes a day, by taking my family to church each week, and by talking about spiritual matters with my family at least once a week.*

Do you see how clear his statement is? It is not just some nebulous thought about getting closer to God; it is a mission statement that is an action plan.

Now hear us well. We know that there is not a checklist of items that move someone closer to God. We are suggesting an action-oriented mission statement that reflects a heartfelt desire.

Can this process of clarity to getting closer to God really work? We think so, but we would like to offer a few caveats.

First, the mission statement must be preceded by intentionality. If your heart does not desire to change, the actions you plan will put you in the camp of the Pharisees. And, as we learned from Jesus, that's not a good place to be.

Second, the mission statement must be a process. It can't just be some lofty ideas with no concrete plans. It must be faith demonstrated by action.

Third, we suggest you share your mission statement with someone. Ask them if you can be accountable to them for six months or a year to stay on track. That person may be a friend, spouse, or coworker. But it needs to be someone with whom you don't mind sharing your struggles and your victories.

Finally, your mission statement is likely different from that of others. Even as I (Thom) wrote parts of this chapter, I began to desire my own simple life, my own plan for getting closer to God. May I share with you my personal mission statement for getting closer to God?

In the next year I plan to read the entire Bible, to pray with my wife at least twice a week, to share my faith at least once a week, and to spend a minimum of thirty minutes in prayer every day.

Now I hope I can do better than the mission statement. But I certainly should not do worse. In our survey we heard from hundreds of people about how they wanted a simple life closer to God. And they had specific ideas about what that meant. Let us share the three biggest steps they wanted to take.

Simple Life and the Local Church

I (Thom) have a story that is not unlike many of those who participated in this study. I was raised in a home where my parents attended church regularly. In fact, until I became a teenager, church was very much at the center of my life.

But then the church was torn apart in a contentious and prolonged battle between two sides, both of which knew they had the will of God on their side.

It was ugly. Really ugly.

My parents were not involved in the fighting, but they had to choose one of the two churches that emerged from the split. They did so, and I followed them, at least for a while. But the bitterness that continued on both sides of the fight left a bad taste in my mouth. As I progressed through my teenage years, I attended church less and less. By the time I was fifteen, I probably attended less than once a month. And when I got my driver's license at age sixteen, I was out of there.

At age sixteen I was "unchurched Thom." I didn't return to church for several years. That is another important part of the story.

At about the time I got my driver's license, I saw this gorgeous girl in my high school. I was smitten. (That word really shows how old I am!) Her name was Nellie Jo King. We dated throughout high school and college, and we got married a month after Nellie Jo graduated from college. We dated six years, and we have been married nearly thirty-two years. Almost four decades with the same "girl," and I still love her more each day.

Excuse me, I need to get back to the purpose of my story.

Nellie Jo was a churchgoing girl, and she wished that I would return to church. In fact, she has told me on more than one occasion that she wished she had been more insistent to me about the matter.

But we married, and I still stayed out of church. Then, after two years of marriage, something happened that turned my priorities upside down.

Nellie Jo told me that I was going to be a father.

Even in my early childhood, I can remember dreaming about becoming a dad. I always wanted to have children. I really wanted to have sons, though I know I would have felt blessed had God given us daughters. Soon into her pregnancy, I learned that my first child would indeed be a boy.

What a wake-up call!

My life had become mixed up and confused. I needed a simpler life with priorities in order. And the first action plan I made was to get back in church. And so I did. I needed to get back in church, but I also needed a church home for my growing family.

The local church gets a bad rap. And we Christians often deserve the reviews we get. The church is full of hypocrites. The church does have its problems. The church often does present a bad story to the watching world.

But it's the same church Jesus gave us two thousand years ago. The church in Jerusalem had people complaining that their ministry needs were being ignored. The church at Corinth had terrible infighting, immorality, and abuse of spiritual gifts. The churches in Galatia were struggling with doctrinal issues. And even the joyous fellowship at Philippi had a curious battle taking place between two women in the church.

These are but a few of the not-so-pleasant stories we learn about the churches of the New Testament. But we still hunger for the fellowship we find in the church.

The writer of Hebrews reminded us why we hunger for the church: "And let us be concerned about one another in order to promote love and good works, not staying away from our meetings, as some habitually do, but encouraging each other, and all the more as you see the day drawing near" (Heb. 10:24–25).

No claims that the church is perfect. No denials of hypocrisy. Just a simple reminder that the church is the place where Christians come together to encourage one another, to worship God together, to love one another, and to do good works together.

Those who responded to our survey seem to understand that void. They seemed to know that, in order to get closer to God, they needed to be around others who worshipped God. They understood that Lone Ranger Christianity is not the Christianity of the Bible.

Just 29 percent of our respondents attend church weekly. Only 51 percent of born-again Christians did so. And among evangelicals, those Christians with conservative and specific doctrinal beliefs, nearly one-fourth were absent from church on a weekly basis.

And many of those with whom we spoke know something is missing in their lives. They realize that the simple life is one of priorities. And if those priorities don't include the church, then their lives are too busy.

Let us say a word to those of you who are active in churches. We have spent thousands of hours in past studies listening to those who are not in church. Most of them are not antichurch. Most of them don't harbor resentment toward Christians in the church.

But when these unchurched people decide to visit a church, they often have to summon great courage to walk into a place where they know few, if any, people. And they often tell us that they feel excluded and on the outside ("not a part of the club," one person said matter-of-factly).

It looks like a lot of people may be looking to return to church. I hope we Christians don't run them away.

The Simple Life and the Bible

For Jennifer, a partner in a prestigious law practice in Philadelphia, the completion of our survey struck a nerve. "Our family has two high-powered attorneys," she began. "I work in a firm that focuses on criminal law, and my husband has done well specializing in real estate law. We have a good family income, and I know a lot of people who would like to trade places with us."

The "but" qualifier could have been anticipated.

"But we are not really a happy family. Our family reminds me of that country song that says the successful life has us fending like the Hatfields and McCoys. We really need a simpler life."

Jennifer wasted no time defining her understanding of the simple life.

"Our family is so busy. My husband and I work fifty to sixty hours a week. Our two daughters are involved in the best activities money can buy. But we are not happy."

Jennifer continued, "I want everyone in my family on the same page. I wish we could just live the values of the Bible. Of course, that means that we need to know what the Bible says, and I doubt any of us could tell you much about that book."

The results of this study were fascinating in many ways, but the responses on issues of spirituality were among the most surprising. Nearly nine out of ten (89%) respondents indicated that having a spiritual foundation is important. More than eight of out ten (81%) told us that they needed to provide stronger spiritual leadership for their children.

And here is where it really gets interesting.

More than eight out of ten of those surveyed told us that they needed to live by the values of the Bible. A whopping 82 percent said that the Bible should be their moral compass, their family's guide, and their blueprint for the simple life.

But here's the catch. The vast majority of Americans, including churchgoing Christians, are really ignorant about the Bible. We could cite some of our previous research, or we could share with you countless other research projects, but the conclusion is the same.

Most of us don't know the Bible. And most of us don't know the Bible because (prepare yourself for a profound statement!) we don't read the Bible.

If those who participated in this study were anything, they were frank and open with their feedback. They admitted that the Bible should be foundational for their lives, but relatively few people know the Bible well enough to live by it.

So they told us. They wanted to be closer to God. And they said they needed to be in church. Then they said they needed to know the Bible, so they could live by the Bible.

While these two realities were not a big surprise, the third confession caught us a bit off guard. The simple life that they desired meant that they needed to be more open about their faith.

The Simple Life and Open Discussion about Faith

We've noticed something lately. Up until this point we have not been able to quantify it. It seems that matters of spirituality have become more and more part of the common discourse in our society.

During the 2008 presidential elections, we read countless articles and heard countless interviews about the faith of McCain and Obama. Major newspapers now have entire religious sections, and some of the front-page articles are on matters of faith. Secular radio and television highlight spiritual issues daily. And we have lost count of the number of blogs on the Internet that deal specifically with faith issues.

Faith is back in the public square.

We shared with you earlier that we are born-again, evangelical Christians. We didn't want you to have doubts about our perspectives and potential biases. And we readily admit that the openness to and discussion about spiritual matters is much broader than Christianity. Our society is truly pluralistic (the presence of multiple religions or beliefs) and even syncretistic (the attempt to combine different religions or beliefs) in its collective beliefs.

But faith is back in the public square. And since eight out of ten respondents indicated, at least in broad terms, that they were Christian, most of the respondents said that they needed to be open about their Christian faith.

More than eight out of ten (81%) of those surveyed indicated that it was important for them to demonstrate spiritual leadership in their families, their places of work, and in other relationships. A smaller but still significant majority (69%) told us that they needed to focus more of their time on spiritual matters. And six out of ten bluntly said that they should be discussing openly spiritual matters with others.

So much for keeping your religion to yourself.

Mitchell, a twenty-eight-year-old married man from Iowa, expressed the sentiments well: "If something really means something to you, you end up talking about it openly. I am originally from Indianapolis, and I am a diehard Colts fan. You can't get me to shut up about my Colts. So I don't think you can really grow in your faith unless you are open about it. That's what I need to be doing more, especially with my family."

Faced with further persecution and possible death, Peter and John were told by the religious authorities to stop speaking about their faith in Christ. Their response was bold and straightforward: "We are unable to stop speaking about what we have seen and heard" (Acts 4:20).

The simple life for many means getting closer to God. And for them that closeness with God comes when they speak about their beliefs unashamedly.

Bill is from northern California. His story speaks well to this issue. "My nine-year-old son came home from school excited a few weeks ago," he began. "I asked him why he was so excited. He told me that someone taught him a lot of things about Jesus today. Curious, I asked him how that happened. My son said, 'Oh, I just decided to ask someone since you don't ever talk about Him.'"

His tearful eyes spoke volumes. "I think," he said carefully, "it's time for me to speak up about what really matters."

Clarity, God, and the Simple Life

Many of you realize something is missing in your life. Perhaps you realize Someone is missing in your life. And you also realize that you will never get your life in order until you give priority to the One who created you.

We shared with you earlier our beliefs. We are Christians. We believe that God revealed Himself through His Son, Jesus Christ.

We believe what the Bible says about us humans. All of us sin; all of us cannot enter into the perfection that is God because we have sin in our life. That which is imperfect can't be in the presence of that which is perfect. The Bible says clearly: "For all have sinned and fall short of the glory of God" (Rom. 3:23).

Did you catch the word *all?* That's everybody. That's Art and Thom. That's people who seem to have it all together. That's you.

None of us are good enough or can do enough good things to get to God. Sin keeps us from Him. That's the bad news.

The good news is that God provided a way for our sins to be forgiven. He sent His Son Jesus to die for us, to take the punishment for our sins. The Bible says it clearly: "He made the

One who did not know sin to be sin for us, so that we might become the righteousness of God in Him" (2 Cor. 5:21).

Why did God willingly give His Son to die for us? "For God loved the world in this way: He gave His One and Only Son, so that everyone who believes in Him will not perish but have eternal life" (John 3:16).

The beginning point of getting closer to God is knowing God through His Son, Jesus Christ. You must first admit that you are a sinner and that you want God to forgive your sins. That is the turning away from sins called repentance in the Bible.

You must, by faith, accept what Jesus did for you by dying on the cross. He took the punishment for us. And you must believe that Jesus not only died but rose from the dead. He conquered death. And when we trust Christ to be our Savior, He forgives our sins and gives us the promise and hope of eternal life in heaven.

Such is the greatest gift ever offered and given.

Some of you may already be Christians. Yet you know that you are not following Him as closely as you should be. Now is the time to turn back to Him. Some may need to connect with a church. Others may need to spend more time in the Bible or in prayer. Still others need to get involved in some type of ministry or service that you have been reticent to do. And some may need to speak freely to others about God and spiritual matters.

Now is the time for clarity. Now is the time for making a simple statement, a mission statement, to get closer to God. We will talk later about how all this takes place. For now, make a simple statement to get closer to God. Get clarity about it.

That's an important step toward the simple life as you seek to follow God more closely.

So . . . what is your plan?

APPLICATION
SIMPLE LIFE: CLARITY
A MISSION STATEMENT FOR GOD

Write a simple and succinct mission statement about the changes you need to make spiritually. And if you have doubts that you are a Christian, go back and read the last portion of this chapter. You can't begin to grow until you are first born again.

As you think about what will be in your mission statement, remember some of these salient points:

- You must have a desire to have a mission statement to get closer to God. If you see this exercise as a legalistic checklist, you have missed the point completely. Only write what you know in your heart you need and want to do.

- You must be *intentional* about following this mission statement. It can't just be an idea or concept. It must be a plan where you do plan to make progress. You should seek God in prayer that He will give you the strength to carry it out.

- The statement should be a process. It should state your specific plans. "I plan to love God more" is not a mission statement. "I plan to love God more by spending thirty minutes a day in prayer with Him" is a mission statement. The first sentence has no plan. The second one does.

- The statement should be a starting point. You should not try to conquer the world in thirty days.
- Here is the sample mission statement from Jack in this chapter: *I will move closer to God by beginning to read the Bible at least fifteen minutes a day, by taking my family to church each week, and by talking about spiritual matters with my family at least once a week.*

Get the picture? Now write your mission statement below:

_____

_____

_____

_____

_____

_____

_____

_____

_____

_____

_____

_____

_____

_____

_____

_____

CHAPTER 14

Moving Closer to God

Clarity → MOVEMENT → Alignment → Focus

No one likes congestion.

We have never heard anyone say that one of his or her favorite moments is to be tied up in traffic for two hours.

And if you live in the Southeast like we do (Thom in Tennessee and Art in Florida), you are likely to experience a flight delay in the Atlanta-Hartsfield-Jackson International Airport. Wow, even the name of the airport is congested! In fact, we often plan flights so that we don't have to fly through Atlanta. The chances are great that we will be delayed getting in or getting out.

The reason? Congestion.

Oh, they will tell you that it is due to weather or some other reason, but the reality is that there is no margin for error or bad weather or anything else. The slightest glitch means that some of the planes will have to wait before they can leave to go to Atlanta (that wonderful airline-speak phrase called "ground delay"), or they will have to wait in a long line to depart.

Congestion is bad.

Both of us have allergies, but Art really has it bad at times. In fact, he has asthma. His airways constrict, becoming inflamed and lined with excessive amounts of mucus.

Excessive amounts of mucus? Ugh.

Okay, we have made our point.

But the reality is the same. Congestion is bad.

The problem with congestion is that it hinders the best or most natural process or progress. We need to move in one direction but congestion stops us or detours us. We aren't our best or we can't do our best when congestion gets in the way.

Now let us ask you a simple question. Do you have congestion in your relationship with God? Perhaps you answer that question with a resounding no. That's great! But it's not the norm. In fact, our research shows that a significant majority of people readily admit that they need and desire a healthier relationship with God.

Let's look at some of the evidence. Nine out of ten of those surveyed believe in the importance of a spiritual foundation for them and their families. That's a lot. When you consider that 16 percent of the respondents indicated that they had no faith preference at all, the significance of the response is amplified.

Okay, now we know that most people want a strong spiritual foundation. They want to get closer to God and to spend more time with Him. But how do they think they are doing? Not so great.

Nearly seven out of ten (69%) in our study desire more time for church and other spiritual matters. God is not in the picture in many lives. Congestion is in the way.

Jeannie is an artist who lives in Thom's hometown of Franklin, Tennessee, a suburb of Nashville. We asked her what she thought she needed to have a more complete life. Her response was straightforward.

"That's easy," she said quickly. "I would like to get closer to God."

So, we asked, where do you attend church?

"I don't."

How often do you read the Bible?

"Not much."

Do you pray regularly?

"Nope, sporadically."

"Look," Jeannie told us. "You can ask me questions all day about my spirituality, and I'm not going to fare well. That's what I'm getting at. I'm not close to God, but I want to be. And I really don't have a good excuse. I just have never made a habit of those things I know I should be doing. I'm too busy for my own good. I guess I'm too busy for God."

We earlier cited the apostle Paul's sole determination to get closer to God. But we need to be clear. Even Paul knew he had a ways to go. "Not that I have already reached the goal, or am already fully mature, but I make every effort to take hold of it because I also have been taken hold of by Christ Jesus" (Phil. 3:12).

Paul had not reached his goal. Paul was not fully mature spiritually. Paul had not arrived. But he didn't quit. In fact, he was able to move forward (there's that "movement" word) because Christ has already done the work. Paul could make every effort because his strength was Christ.

He could then say with confidence, "Brothers, I do not consider myself to have taken hold of it. But one thing I do: forgetting what is behind and reaching forward to what is ahead, I pursue as my goal the prize promised by God's heavenly call in Christ Jesus" (Phil. 3:13–14).

Paul had movement to get closer to God. He reached toward what was ahead. He pursued the goal. He removed the congestion and had clear movement toward God.

Notice what he said. He forgot what was behind. No, Paul did not have a sudden attack of amnesia. But he did say that he would no longer dwell on his failures. He knew that Christ had forgiven him, so he was ready to move on.

Ready to move closer to God in the simple life?

That's what we heard from the overwhelming majority. And now that you have clarity, a clear goal in mind, let's see what is next toward a closer relationship with God. Movement toward God can be summed in five words: *prayerful, forgetful, incremental, immediate,* and *resilient.* Let's look at each of these words.

Movement toward God: Prayerful

I (Thom) can't even pray without first being prayerful.

Yeah, I know, that sentence is totally confusing.

I struggle with consistency in my prayer life. I read about great prayer warriors who spent hours in prayer, and I am ashamed. I have trouble focusing for thirty minutes. I begin my conversation with God, and I often start thinking about my to-do list for the day. When I lose focus in my conversations with my wife, she lets me know quickly.

So I asked God to help me with my prayer life.

I prayed for a better prayer life.

In that same book of Philippians, Paul said, "Don't worry about anything, but in everything, through prayer and petition with thanksgiving, let your requests be made known to God" (Phil. 4:6).

You can't miss it. He said in *everything* let your requests be made known to God. Everything. Every big thing. Every little thing. Everything.

So now, my first step in a better prayer life is to pray for a better prayer life.

Simple? Yes. But profound.

God wants to take all our needs, our burdens, our worries, our cares. We are to take everything to Him in prayer.

In the previous chapter you established clarity. You set some goals that you would like to reach to get closer to God. We heard from Jack in the previous chapter. Jack's statement in that chapter made a perfect mission statement:

I will move closer to God by beginning to read the Bible at least fifteen minutes a day, by taking my family to church each week, and by talking about spiritual matters with my family at least once a week.

It's a great mission statement. It encapsulates everything we said about clarity.

But the next step is action. Clarity must shift to movement. The goals must also be an action plan.

That's where we fail often, isn't it?

We plan to spend more time with the kids, but we don't do it.

We plan to lose weight, but we don't do it.

We plan to read the Bible, but we don't do it.

And we plan to get closer to God, but we don't do it.

Clarity says have a good plan. *Movement* says act on the plan. And that's often where the breakdown occurs.

That is why we begin with prayer. That is why we begin with God and not ourselves.

We are asking for His strength and not our own.

You have a great plan, but you are afraid of failure. Stop everything. Stop everything right now. Pause for a moment. Pray. Ask God for His success as you seek to get closer to Him. Stop depending on your limited ability and start depending on the One who has no limits.

Pray. Nothing moves congestion like prayer.

Movement toward God: Forgetful

I (Thom) absolutely love my wife, Nellie Jo. She is beautiful. She is godly. She is smart. She is fun. She is also blunt.

Nellie Jo does not mince words. Now hear me well. She certainly follows the biblical pattern of submission. She has followed me all over the nation. She has taken care of three boys while I pursued my goals and dreams. She always put the boys and me before herself. But that does not mean she lets me get away with anything.

For example, one of my greatest joys is spending time and talking with my three sons. They are now grown and married, but we still stay in touch almost every day. And when Nellie Jo hears me tell one of the boys that I will do something for him, she typically tells me that I will forget.

THOM: Okay, Sam, I will send you that book.

NELLIE JO: No you won't; you'll forget.

THOM: Art, I will call him for you.

NELLIE JO: No you won't; you will forget.

THOM: Jess, I will send you a check for the tickets.

NELLIE JO: No you won't; you'll forget.

Sigh. I do forget a lot.

Then Nellie Jo tells me to leave Stacy (my assistant) an e-mail or voice mail so that she will remind me. Hmmm, does that mean Nellie Jo thinks Stacy is more diligent than I am?

Still, I can't argue the point. I do tend to forget too many things. I do get distracted.

You get the point, I'm sure. Forgetting is always bad. Right? Wrong.

Do you remember the words of the apostle Paul noted earlier? "But one thing I do, forgetting what is behind . . ." (Phil. 3:13). It's really amazing. The apostle talks about his singular focus in life, and the first thing he mentions is that he forgets.

You see, forgetting is not always bad. In fact, it can be positively life changing.

We often set goals. We often plan to get closer to God. We often think that this time it will work. But it doesn't.

We are paralyzed from moving forward because of past failures. Listen to Stephanie's story.

"I am a divorcee," she began with her eyes looking downward. "My husband left me three years ago. And he had every right to leave. I had an affair with his best friend. Well, I guess you would say his former best friend. I can't explain myself to this day. I didn't love his friend. I loved my husband. I still love him."

Stephanie responded in our survey that she wanted to move closer to God. She had begun attending church, reading her Bible regularly, and praying every day. But then she stopped.

Why?

"I just feel like such a failure," she admitted. "I don't know if I can ever love or be loved again by anyone, including God."

Jesus encountered a woman who probably felt a lot like Stephanie. The story is in John 8:1–12. The woman in the story was actually caught in the act of committing adultery. The accusers brought her to Jesus. Their primary intention was to trap Jesus even more than shaming and accusing the woman.

The scribes and the Pharisees wanted to see if Jesus would really follow the law of Moses, which called for the stoning to death of one caught in adultery. So they asked Him what they should do with the adulterous woman.

Jesus was writing something on the ground, but for a moment He stood up and answered them, "The one without sin among you should be the first to throw a stone at her" (John 8:7). One by one, all the accusers quietly walked away. Only Jesus and the woman remained.

Jesus stood up again from His writing, and He spoke directly to the woman, "Woman, where are they? Has no one condemned you?" (v. 10).

Don't you wish you could have been there? Don't you wish you could have seen the expressions of those who left and the woman who remained?

She answered simply, "No one, Lord" (v. 11).

And Jesus, the One who is God, responded, "Neither do I condemn you. Go, and from now on do not sin any more" (v. 11).

Forget. Leave that behind. Go and sin no more.

Some of the respondents in our study just had trouble forgetting. They had trouble believing they could move forward.

Congestion precludes movement. Is it possible that some of the congestion you are experiencing is because you can't forget?

"He has rescued us from the domain of darkness and transferred us into the kingdom of the Son He loves, in whom we have redemption, the forgiveness of sins" (Col. 1:13–14).

He has forgiven. Now you must forget and move forward.

Movement toward God: Incremental

We keep returning to the mission statement of Jack for several reasons. For one, it is simple. For another, it is realistic. Jack does not state that he will read the Bible in its entirety every month, spend fifteen hours a week in prayer, and share his faith with at least twenty people each week.

Those goals are admirable. And in God's power, all things are possible. But most of us will become discouraged and frustrated if we set such lofty goals.

Jack's plans were to spend only fifteen minutes a day reading the Bible, take his family to church just once a week, and talk with his family about spiritual matters only once a week.

We can anticipate some of you superspiritual types dismissing Jack's plans as superficial or inadequate. But remember, this plan is a beginning, not an end. We will talk later about incremental movement, or eating the elephant one bite at a time.

For now you have clarity through your mission statement. You are beginning to act upon the mission statement. You began the movement with prayer. You then learned that you needed to forget the past and move toward the future. And now you are learning to move at a pace that is sustainable.

The simple life means that you enter into this process simply. If you have concluded that one of your main deficiencies in life is a closer relationship with God, start moving in that direction.

Have you ever seen a Christian meteor? She begins to get serious, real serious about getting closer to God. She spends fifteen hours a week at the church. She prays two hours a day. She reads the Bible two hours a day. She goes on three international mission trips in one year. And then she flames out. Totally burned out.

We are not discouraging you from a life totally committed to God. We are simply asking you to consider a slower, more incremental pace.

I (Thom) shared a few details of my weight loss earlier. I have been on many diets: low carbohydrates, extremely low calories, one-food diets, etc. They all failed for one simple reason: I tried to lose my weight as quickly as possible by dramatically changing my eating habits.

But this last time the weight came off and stayed off. How? I modestly reduced calories and modestly increased physical activity.

Today I'm walking as much as ten miles a day, but I didn't start that way. One mile a day was the beginning.

Now we don't mean to compare a diet with a relationship with God. But relationships often take time to develop, at least from our human perspective. Begin with a mission statement that is both simple and incremental. You will remove a lot of congestion that way. And one year from now, you may be surprised at the progress you've made.

Movement toward God: Immediate

Let's return to the story of the adulterous woman. Jesus clearly communicated to her that she was forgiven. But what then did He tell her? "Go, and from now on do not sin any more" (John 8:11).

Notice what Jesus did not say. He did not say, "Give this serious thought and after a few weeks change your lifestyle." No, He told her to sin no more. Right then. At that moment. Without delay.

We have lots of statistics in this research. Reams of data. Page after page of numerical responses. So much that if we put just 10 percent of all the results here, you would have a book of statistics and graphs. And most of you would be bored silly.

So we spent hundreds of hours going through the data so you wouldn't have to do so. One of our main quests was to discern patterns. And we did discover several patterns, one of which probably won't surprise you. One of the main sources of congestion was "soon."

"I will start back going to church soon."

"I plan to begin reading my Bible every day soon."

"I will start talking about spiritual matters with my family soon."

Of course, "soon" never happens. It's put on the shelf of good intentions. But "soon" becomes "never."

One good example is that last quote: "I will start talking about spiritual matters with my family soon." For whatever reasons, people have a strong desire to talk about those issues that really matter but a desire that often does not translate into reality.

What is curious is that discussing spiritual issues is a big priority for most, yet only 23 percent of those who responded to our survey agreed strongly that they discuss such issues regularly in their families. It's the "want to" and "am doing" disconnect.

Meet Shelly from Wyoming. She considers herself a Christian. She and her family attend church "usually three times a month." Her plight is common.

"My family and I love to talk," she said. "We talk about school, work, football, the girls' boyfriends . . . almost everything but God."

The obvious question came next. Why?

"I really don't have a good answer. I don't believe there is anything more important to talk about. But we just never do. It seems awkward for some reason. Still, I keep telling myself that we will make spiritual matters a part of our regular talks, but I just never get around to it. I have good intentions, but I don't follow through."

The story is common. And it seems in two of the four big issues, God and money, it is more common. Movement is hindered by congestion, and one of the most common forms of congestion is procrastination.

The writer of Hebrews addressed this issue in an unusual way: "Watch out, brothers, so that there won't be in any of you an evil, unbelieving heart that departs from the living God. But encourage each other daily, while it is still called today, so that none of you is hardened by sin's deception" (Heb. 3:12–13).

Notice how the writer dealt with the idea of encouraging each other daily. He said do it "while it is still called today." Daily doesn't mean soon. Daily doesn't mean tomorrow. Daily doesn't mean when you get around to it. Daily means today, now, at this very moment.

You have established a mission statement. You thus have clarity. But a mission statement by its very nature requires action or movement. You have thus prayed for God to give you His strength to accomplish it. You have moved beyond past failures and sins. You have determined that you will take baby steps and not try to accomplish so much that failure is a near certainty.

Now you must simply do it. No excuses. No waiting. Just do it.

Movement toward God: Resilient

The apostle Paul provides an example for so many aspects of the simple life. In 2 Corinthians 11:24–28, he gives us a glimpse of the trials he endured:

> Five times I received from the Jews 40 lashes minus one. Three times I was beaten with rods. Once I was stoned. Three times I was shipwrecked. I have spent a night and a day in the depths of the sea. On frequent journeys, I faced dangers from rivers, dangers from robbers, dangers from my own people, dangers from the Gentiles, dangers in the city, dangers in the open country, dangers on the sea, and dangers among false brothers; labor and hardship,

many sleepless nights, hunger and thirst, often without food, cold, and lacking clothing. Not to mention other things, there is the daily pressure on me: my care for all the churches.

Not such a pretty life, is it? But you know what Paul did. He always bounced back. He never gave up.

Why? He answers the question well. "So because of Christ, I am pleased in weaknesses, in insults, in catastrophes, in persecutions, and in pressures. For when I am weak, then I am strong" (2 Cor. 12:10).

Paul was truly resilient.

The simple life means that we start taking some serious steps toward getting closer to God. But, for some of you, the fear of failure is just too great. You've tried in the past. And you've failed. You tried. You failed. What's the use of trying yet again?

Margaret is from upstate New York. She speaks for many of our respondents. "I know some of the things I should be doing," she began. "But I also know that any efforts I make will end in failure. I said I would read the Bible every day. I failed. I said I was going to have a daily prayer time. I failed. I said I would attend church at least once a week. I failed. Why should I expect that I'll get it right this time?"

Movement means that we try again. And if we fail, we try again. It means that we are resilient and do not give up.

Not too long ago, one of the most viewed YouTube videos was "The Last Lecture" by Randy Pausch, a professor at Carnegie Mellon University. Though we would like to have seen a greater emphasis on eternal life, the story of Randy Pausch is one of the most compelling visions of the simple life and never giving up.

Pausch, at age forty-six, was diagnosed with pancreatic cancer. Instead of going into a shell and giving up, he continued to live his life to the fullest. He could have had a pity party that he would be leaving a loving wife and three young children. He could have said that life isn't fair. He could have been angry. He could have given up.

"The Last Lecture" is just that. It is Randy Pausch's final lecture at the university where he served as professor. And what is amazing about the lecture is the indomitable spirit and the incredible attitude of this man. One of our favorite quotes from Pausch in this final lecture is: "I have fun every day of my life, and I am going to continue to have fun every day that I am alive."

Randy Pausch died on July 25, 2008, at age forty-seven. But he never gave up.

Movement and Getting Closer to God

Now let's review the pattern we have so far of the simple life. The first step is *clarity*. We even suggested that you write a mission statement about your intentions. And we gave you an example of one man's mission statement for getting closer to God.

The second action is the subject of this chapter, *movement*. Movement is the removal of obstacles or congestion.

The big stumbling block in the early phases of the simple life is movement. Why?

Movement means we have to change our habits. And by our nature, we are creatures of habit. How many of you drive the same path to work? Do you eat the same type of unhealthy foods each week? Do you spend more time watching television than you do reading the Bible? Do you work so many hours that the kids get shortchanged?

Work habits. Eating habits. Leisure habits.

Movement means that you have to break many of those habitual patterns. Why aren't we moving closer to God? We have not broken enough habits to have time for Him or His Word. Perhaps we have declared Sunday a sleep-in day rather than getting to bed earlier on Saturday night so that we can attend church. Perhaps we give more lip service to that which really matters. But talking does not get the job done. We have to break out of the patterns that hinder us.

Also movement means immediate. If you are reading this book and you begin to think, *That sounds like a good idea; I might try it in a week or so,* you have missed the point and failed to move to the simple life. We heard many of those surveyed say that they plan to "get around to it" soon. But those "roundtoits" are the cries of failure. Movement means right now, not tomorrow but now.

Is there really anything more important than getting closer to God? If you have read this far in this book, you probably have formulated in your mind or, for some of you, in writing, a mission statement for moving closer to God. So you really are a person of serious intentions.

Now is the time to begin. Break the habits that hold you back. And make the decision in God's strength to do it now.

APPLICATION
SIMPLE LIFE: MOVEMENT
THE PRIORITY OF PRAYER

Look at Philippians 4:6: "Don't worry about anything, but in everything, through prayer and petition with thanksgiving, let your requests be made known to God."

Before you go any further, take time to pray. Pray that God will draw you closer to Him. Pray that you will practice those spiritual disciplines that will draw you closer to God. Pray that God will use this book on the simple life as a resource for a life closer to Him. Pray that God will give you His strength to move closer to Him *right now*.

Take a few minutes to pray.

Now answer the following questions from Philippians 4:6.

1. How is worry related to prayer?

_____

2. What does it mean to present "everything" to God in prayer?

_____

3. How does thanksgiving relate to prayer?

_____

_____

_____

_____

_____

_____

_____

_____

_____

_____

CHAPTER 15

God in the Background

Clarity → Movement → ALIGNMENT → Focus

The success of the movie *Facing the Giants* took most of us by surprise. The low-budget production, $100,000 by some estimates, opened in the fall of 2006 in a paltry 441 theaters nationwide. The actors and actresses were all volunteers, most of them from local churches in Albany, Georgia. And the staff from a local church, Sherwood Baptist Church, produced the movie.

How could such an effort ever succeed? We were surprised.

By 2007 the movie had grossed $10 million, and its impact is still felt today. It truly became a wonder film in the eyes of many.

How do you assess the factors of success? Certainly the movie had favorable buzz as many in the national media began to take notice. And a spirited debate over the PG rating didn't hurt either. Undoubtedly the response of evangelical Christians and churches played a major role in its success. And ultimately one just has to acknowledge the sovereignty of God and His favor upon the production.

Still one cannot deny the simple but effective story line. It's a modern-day David and Goliath parable. The struggling and losing Shiloh Christian Eagles football team has a football plot reminiscent of the *Hoosiers* basketball movie of earlier years. But this time the hand of God is portrayed vividly and powerfully.

One of the most dramatic moments takes place when Coach Grant Taylor sees his life falling apart and a parental conspiracy afoot to have him fired. He reexamines his life, and realizes that his motive for coaching was wrong. It's not first about winning; it's about bringing honor to God in all that we do.

It takes Coach Taylor a while to persuade the players to buy into this new purpose. But when a spiritual awakening takes place on the small Christian campus, not only do the football players get it, but most of the school gets it too. The purpose is no longer to win games; that would only be an ancillary benefit. The real purpose is to glorify God.

Facing the Giants has a predictable plot, but it is nevertheless engaging and inspiring. The little Christian school faces a behemoth opponent, the perennial state champion aptly named the Giants. And, of course, the little school wins the state championship with a record-setting field goal by a new player on the team, the smallest guy on the team. His name is David.

Isn't it amazing how we are inspired when we see teams, people, and churches come together for a common purpose for the good? Maybe we are inspired because such scenarios are relatively rare. We don't often see efforts and energies and resources aligned for a common purpose. Alignment is good. Yet alignment is rare.

We have discussed the concept of *clarity*, understanding what your true purpose and goals are. We dealt with *movement*, getting beyond congestion and blockages. Now we are looking at the issue of *alignment*, making certain that all we do moves us toward accomplishing our purpose.

Take a moment to reflect. Have you written your mission statement for your simple life in relationship to God? How do you plan to get closer to God?

You probably found some blockages and congestion that were hindering this process, so you began to work on those issues. Now you have the rest of your life's activities. How many of those activities will align with your mission statement? How can you bring unity to your own life? How is your alignment?

The obvious question is: Where do I begin to align my life's activities to get closer to God? In this chapter on alignment in our relationship with God, we will address five major areas toward alignment. And the first requires that you look in the mirror.

Looking in the Mirror: Honest Self-Assessment

We mentioned earlier *The Last Lecture* by the late Randy Pausch. One of the bits of wisdom that Pausch consistently gave his students was his insistence that they ruthlessly evaluate themselves. He told them to "look in the mirror" and to be honest about the reflection they saw.

In his classes the students were divided into workgroups, and the peers in each group evaluated one another. How much did the student contribute? How well did he or she work with others? What type of attitude did he or she have? What was his or her work ethic?

Then on a regular basis Pausch would provide computer-generated results based on the periodic evaluations. The students would discover the quartile in which they were ranked and why they fit within that ranking.

One particularly obnoxious student offended everyone and was not a stellar worker. When the first evaluations were distributed, he was in the fourth, the last, quartile. Simply stated, he was among the worst students.

Instead of honestly looking at himself in the mirror, the student was unfazed. Instead of seeking to heed the input and find ways to improve himself, he rationalized his rankings. He presumed that he was at the top of this worst group, a fact that he could not know since individual rankings were not provided. He also rationalized that, if he were at the top of the worst group, he was really closer to the third quartile group, which made him closer to average.

Talk about rationalizations!

Pausch took the student aside for a frank one-on-one discussion. He told him that, despite his twisting of the feedback, the student was dead last in the last group. He told the student that he was obnoxious, lazy, and, worst of all, had no self-awareness. Pausch did not pull any punches. Under no uncertain terms, he told the brash young man that he was headed for failure despite an abundance of skills and academic abilities.

The bold confrontation worked. The student would later become a star in his field.

The simple life means that we have to face the reality of who we really are. It means facing some tough issues.

In our research we asked if the respondent was a good spiritual leader in his or her family. On the surface the results were encouraging. Slightly more than two-thirds of those surveyed either agreed strongly or agreed somewhat that they were good spiritual leaders. Now, if 68 percent of American adults are good spiritual leaders, our national and spiritual problems should be quickly eradicated.

But we all know differently. Where is the disconnection?

Only 22 percent *agree strongly* with the contention that they are good spiritual leaders. Nearly half, 46 percent, only *agree somewhat*. The remaining 32 percent admit that they are not good spiritual leaders. It's the "agree somewhat" group that got our attention.

Why would nearly half of those surveyed respond with uncertainty about such an important issue? Many in this group are just not being completely honest with themselves. They are hopeful but not realistic.

Karl, for example, is a software developer in a suburb of Kansas City. He was among those who responded "agree somewhat" to the spiritual leadership statement. Why, we asked, could he not answer the question with greater certainty?

"Well," he began hesitatingly, "I think I do a pretty good job of being a spiritual leader in my family. And I am known at work as the guy who doesn't cuss or drink. I do pray sometimes, so I guess I can't be all that bad as a spiritual leader."

If you caught some comments without much conviction, we did as well. "I think . . . ," Karl said. He rates his leadership as "a pretty good job." He prays "sometimes." And as a spiritual leader he can't be all that bad, he "guesses."

Our sense of most of the "agree somewhat" group is that they really were not evaluating their spiritual lives with much honesty. For example, we asked Karl if his wife and children would describe him as a spiritual leader. "I'm not sure what they would say," he responded curtly. Are you a regular Bible reader? "Who is?" he questioned in response. "Do you attend church regularly?" His curious response to that question was, "I don't know."

We did not need to spend much time with Karl to see that he really doesn't have an honest self-assessment of his relationship with God, at least as it is manifested in certain activities. To remedy this problem, Karl could take some type of discipleship inventory. Our favorite is included in Brad Waggoner's book *The Shape of Faith to Come*. We encourage you to take that inventory for a more objective view of your relationship with God.

But, realizing that many people who are seeking the simple life won't take time to do an inventory, perhaps a few self-evaluative questions would help.

- Am I closer to God today than I was a year ago?
- Is prayer a regular part of my day?
- Do I read the Bible at least two or three times a week?
- Am I truly connected to a local congregation?
- Do I talk freely with family and others about my faith?

These questions are, of course, nowhere close to being exhaustive. They do provide, however, a quick glimpse into our spiritual lives. And the first step of alignment is an honest, if not ruthless, self-evaluation.

When we presented these same questions to Karl in an informal discussion, he was at first defensive and curt. But after a few more moments of conversation, his tone changed. "Look," he began, "I guess I have not really been honest with myself. I'm not really walking with God. I have a long way to go. But I guess I need to start somewhere."

Karl is taking the first step toward alignment.

Talk to Someone: Accountability

Brad Waggoner, whom we mentioned earlier, wanted to shed a few pounds. Like many of us (Thom more than Art), he has struggled with getting those last pounds off. We have known Brad to try two approaches that seemed to work.

The first time he made a deal with his two sons. He would pay them some predetermined amount if he did not meet his goals. Brad is a generous guy and doesn't mind giving to anyone, especially his sons. But he is also competitive. He didn't want to admit defeat to his sons. The pounds came off.

More recently he jumped into an online accountability group with some peers who work out at the local YMCA. They are required to weigh in every month. If they don't meet their goals, they have to pay a small fine. But the real humiliation comes when the successful weight losers are unmerciful in their comments to the unsuccessful guys. It's all done in fun, but it is very competitive.

Many of us need alignment in our spiritual walk, and many of us need accountability to keep us on the right track. In married households only 39 percent of both parents attend church worship services at least once a month. In nearly half of the households, neither parent attends.

Now let us suppose that you decide in your mission statement that you desire to attend church regularly. What form of accountability works best for you? Ella from Oregon responded without hesitation.

"I just told my three kids that we needed to start going to church," she said with a grin. "I'm a single mom with absolutely no time, so I have pushed God out of my life. But when I told the girls that we were going to church, they started reminding me every Saturday night and waking me up on Sunday mornings. That was all the push I needed."

Indeed, many of the respondents in our study indicated a lot of accountability approaches, some formal and others informal. "I got involved in a Bible study group at a church a few miles from me," Sandra told us. "The people in the group are great, but if I miss a study, they text message me before the day is over." Sandra doesn't miss many Bible studies.

While some of the accountability approaches are highly structured, more are informal and natural. Billy from Arkansas needs the discipline of calling Dino every week. "If I don't make that call, I just slip back into my old patterns," Billy told us.

But Susie from Sacramento does not need that much structure. "I talk to Barbara almost every day, by phone and in person," she began. "We talk so much that spiritual matters will come up at some point. Though we never think of our conversations as accountability sessions, they do have that element."

Susie then related to us how important it is for them to talk regularly. "There used to be three of us who were so tight with one another that we all talked together on a regular basis. Then Laverne gradually withdrew. In fact, it was so gradual that we didn't really pay much attention. I wish we had. Maybe we could have helped her not to have that affair and destroy her family."

A few of the respondents were accountable to themselves. If such a statement sounds contradictory, that was our first reaction as well. But George from Texas disagreed. "I keep my relationship with God strong by writing in a journal," he said. "I write with total honesty. And I can tell if I am getting off track by what I write in my journal. And I know I'm really getting off track if I fail to write something in my journal every day."

Recognizing Who We Are: The Personality Match

You'll find countless self-assessment tools on the market today. Some of them help us to understand our strengths and weaknesses. Others tell us something about our leadership style. Still others inform us of our personality traits and idiosyncrasies. Yet others can help us to discover our spiritual gifts.

All of these tools help us understand our uniqueness. They give us a perspective that we may not often see of ourselves. We like the inventories and tests. We have found that they are truly helpful in our attempt to learn more about the way God made us.

But you don't have to take an inventory or test to know some things about yourself. You know what you like and what you don't like. And you know what works in your life and what doesn't. In fact, we found that many people are out of alignment in their relationship with God because they are trying to do something that goes against the grain of their personalities and the way God made them.

I (Thom) am president of a company, LifeWay Christian Resources. Though I don't particularly like meetings, it's a way of life in my position. The people who report to me have learned some things about me in how they relate to me in those meetings.

First, please don't come into a meeting and talk about peripheral issues unless it's college football. Be prepared to get right to the point. Second, please don't let the conversation drag on. I can get bored and distracted easily.

I have learned that those same personality traits affect my relationship with God. I have trouble focusing during prayer time. My mind often wanders. And I feel guilty about it. My prayer life has been a struggle all of my Christian life. When someone would ask me about my quiet time, I would become uncomfortable. I don't like quiet and still.

For years I felt guilty because I just didn't do well being quiet and still. Then I tried something different. I began praying while I walked. While some people may be totally distracted praying while walking in the neighborhood, I learned that I could focus much better than in solitude in a room by myself. My personality was better suited for activity, even in times of praying.

Many are struggling in their relationship with God because they are trying to be someone else. God accepts us as we are.

Listen to the comments of some of those who get this idea:

- "I read my Bible in fifteen-minute increments. It helps me to grasp the meaning better than if I do one long reading."

- "My prayer time is the first thing in the morning before the kids get up. It is the only time I have alone, and it is my best time of day."
- "I started becoming more faithful in my church attendance when I began going to the early morning service. That's just a better time of day for me."
- "I used to force evangelistic conversations on people, which was really not my style. I changed that and started praying that God would give me opportunities for more natural conversations. It has been amazing! I am now sharing my faith more than ever."

The simple life requires alignment. And alignment means understanding who you are and playing to your strengths, personality, and gifts.

The Willingness to Realign: Flexibility

"Sometimes," Michael told us, "I just wonder if I will ever get this right. Since I became a Christian more than ten years ago, I have tried to have a closer walk with God. When I was single, I had no problem with time for prayer and studying God's Word. But now I am married with two preschool sons. I'm having a tough time doing things the way I used to."

Guess what, Michael? You probably can't do things the way you used to.

Michael has family responsibilities he didn't have a few years ago. He has time constraints that are different. He has to realign. Sometimes we just can't do things the way we've always done them.

The apostle Paul was the master of realignment. Shortly after he became a Christian, he began speaking boldly about his newly found faith. But remember, this was the same guy who, just a while earlier, was threatening and persecuting Christians. Some of Paul's old anti-Christian buddies had trouble accepting the new Paul, who was still called Saul at this point.

In fact, they were so irritated with him and his changes that they decided to kill him. Now that's a good reason to realign.

We learn in Acts 9:28–30: "Saul was coming and going with them in Jerusalem, speaking boldly in the name of the Lord. He conversed and debated with the Hellenistic Jews, but they attempted to kill him. When the brothers found out, they took him down to Caesarea and sent him off to Tarsus."

Okay, maybe Paul had some encouragement realigning. The "brothers" (we love that name) "took him down" and "sent him off."

Maybe that's forced realignment.

But on several other occasions, Paul made other moves that demonstrated his flexibility and his willingness to realign. Look at this story in Acts 16:6–8: "They went through the region of Phrygia and Galatia and were prevented by the Holy Spirit from speaking the message in the province of Asia. When they came to Mysia, they tried to go into Bithynia, but the Spirit of Jesus did not allow them. So bypassing Mysia, they came to Troas."

Paul adjusted. He and his companions wanted to share the message of Christ in Asia, but the Holy Spirit prevented them from doing so. We don't know why or how the Holy Spirit did this, but Paul adjusted.

Plan B was next.

They then came to Mysia and tried to go into Bithynia, but this time the Spirit of Jesus did not let them move forward. Again, we don't how or why the Spirit said no. We just know that He did.

Plan C was next.

They bypassed Mysia and made it to Troas. Now Paul and gang get settled. Right? Wrong. The story continues in Acts 16:9–10: "During the night a vision appeared to Paul: a Macedonian man was standing and pleading with him, 'Cross over to Macedonia and help us!' After he had seen the vision, we immediately made efforts to set out for Macedonia, concluding that God had called us to evangelize them."

Plan D was the solution.

Most of us are willing to throw in the towel after one failed attempt. And we certainly won't make it after two unsuccessful ventures. But not so Paul. He saw every closed door as an opportunity to find an open door. And on the fourth try he finally found his place.

Oh, by the way, Paul did have a successful ministry in Macedonia. Some heard the gospel message and believed. But Paul ended up in prison there, beaten with rods, and feet placed in stocks. So he had to leave again, this time for Thessalonica.

Plan E. Realignment. Total flexibility.

Alignment will probably lead to realignment. And realignment means that you won't always get it right, but then you try again. And realignment means that you may get it right for a while, but you have to adjust or change as God changes the circumstances of your life.

Accepting Your Humanity: A Willingness to Be Imperfect

Imperfection comes in two different types of packages. The first type of imperfection is when we disobey God. We sin and thus fail to meet His perfect and holy standards. The Bible is clear that all of us carry that guilt: "For all have sinned and fall short of the glory of God" (Rom. 3:23).

The Bible also teaches that those who repent or turn from sin and place their faith in Christ will be forgiven of those sins. We addressed this issue earlier, but allow us to focus on another of the many great passages of forgiveness, Romans 3:24–25: "They are justified freely by His grace through the redemption that is in Christ Jesus. God presented Him as a propitiation through faith in His blood, to demonstrate His righteousness, because in His restraint God passed over the sins previously committed."

That seldom-used word *propitiation* refers to the appeasement of God's wrath against all sinners, meaning all of us. In other words, we deserved the full vengeance of God's fury against us as sinners, but God showed restraint because of what His Son, Jesus, did on the cross. Jesus took the punishment for us.

Pretty heavy stuff.

But it's just another reminder of the great gift of salvation by grace. Yet becoming a Christian doesn't mean we stay sin free. Even our favorite apostle, Paul, talked about this struggle: "For I do not do the good that I want to do, but I practice the evil that I do not want to do. . . . What a wretched man I am! Who will rescue me from this body of death? I thank God through Jesus Christ our Lord!" (Rom. 7:19, 24–25).

We are all sinners. And our sinning doesn't stop after we become Christians. And while our sin nature doesn't give us an excuse to sin, we do have the promise of forgiveness, even as Christians.

But we already addressed the forgiveness earlier. Just a few paragraphs ago, we spoke of the imperfection issue coming in two packages. The first was our sinful nature, but for this chapter we want to focus on the second package of imperfection. Simply stated, no matter how hard we try, we will never get everything done perfectly.

And some of you have not entered the simple life because you are a perfectionist. If you don't do things exactly right, you consider yourself a failure. Are we talking to you?

Meet Rebecca from Des Moines, Iowa. Rebecca is a perfectionist, and it is about to kill her.

"I was told by my pastor that I needed to have a one-hour quiet time every day," she said nervously. "I did fine the first three days, and then, boom, a dozen urgent matters got me off focus. The same thing has happened to me in my Bible reading time. In fact, it seems like every time I try to do something right, I fail. I really wonder if it's worth the effort at all."

You've heard the story hundreds of times with different variations. The child comes home with a great first report card: seven As and one B. And the perfectionist parent asks why she didn't make all As. That child will likely grow up thinking she can never please anyone, including God.

While we should strive to draw closer to God, we also need to understand that amazing thing called grace. Because of what His Son did for us, God loves us unconditionally. We don't seek to please Him so that He will love us. We seek to please Him because we desire to respond to His grace and love.

Both Art and Thom are married to amazing women. It may be cliché, but we know we married above ourselves. We both like to do things for Sarah and Nellie Jo. But we don't seek to please them because we need to earn their love. We seek to please them because of the abundance of love we have for them.

Some of you perfectionists need to relax in the simple life. Your alignment may need to be removing the heavy burden of perfectionism.

Jesus said it best; He always does: "Come to Me, all of you who are weary and burdened, and I will give you rest. All of you, take up My yoke and learn from me, because I am gentle and humble in heart, and you will find rest for yourselves. For My yoke is easy and My burden is light" (Matt. 11:28–30).

Shed the perfectionism and rest in Jesus.

Back to Clarity

Let's return to the simple chart for the simple life:

Clarity → Movement → Alignment → Focus

We began with a mission statement that was simultaneously a statement of process for simple life. And we heard from Jack from Tennessee in the previous two chapters. Jack's statement in those chapters made a perfect mission statement:

I will move closer to God by beginning to read the Bible at least fifteen minutes a day, by taking my family to church each week, and by talking about spiritual matters with my family at least once a week.

Jack had clarity. It was his mission statement.

Jack had movement. He dealt with those negative things that stop him from accomplishing his mission statement. We called that congestion. And now he seeks alignment, the arrangement of all of his activities and priorities so that the process of the simple life can be accomplished.

Finally, Jack needs to focus, which means getting rid of the good stuff. Getting rid of the good stuff? Yeah, the good stuff. We'll talk about that in the next chapter.

APPLICATION
SIMPLE LIFE: ALIGNMENT
LOOKING IN THE MIRROR

You have written your mission statement; you gave clarity to what you need to do to get closer to God. Now take time to think about aligning your life and personality.

Use the blanks below to write down several words that describe your personality, your gifts, your background, and your abilities. Some of the words may be positive, while others may not be so flattering.

_____

_____

_____

_____

Review these words and reflect on how they might influence you as you seek to accomplish your mission statement. What changes do you need to make? What will work best for you and your personality? You were created uniquely by God. How can you best accomplish your mission statement?

_____

_____

_____

_____

_____

_____

CHAPTER 16

God in the Foreground

Clarity → Movement → Alignment → FOCUS

Jamie really doesn't think she should be complaining. She thinks she is basically happy.

Thinks?

How can you *think* you're happy? Don't you *know* when you're happy?

"Well," Jamie responds hesitatingly, "most of the areas of my life are good. I have three good kids. My husband and I have a good relationship. And I guess I'm one of the few people out there who really likes my job."

That sounds good to us. So why do you *think* you are happy?

The South Carolina drawl is noticeable as she responds. "Something is missing in my life. I am a Christian. I was raised in a Christian home. And Jeremy and I still attend church almost every week with the kids. But . . ."

Nervousness laced her pause. "But I know I'm not living for God. I'm not a big moral failure; it's just that I don't have a strong relationship with Him. God is just kind of in the background in my life."

We asked her if she could elaborate.

"Before I had kids, I spent regular time in prayer. Now it seems like my prayer life is an occasional, 'Help me, Lord.' I just feel like I'm going through the motions at church. I find myself looking at my watch while my pastor is preaching, and he's really a good preacher. I just have so many things on my mind that I find myself thinking about all the things I have to do."

What would you like most if you could live a simple life?

"Oh, now that's an easy question. If I could really live a simple life, I would enjoy spending more time with God. Praying more. Reading the Bible more. Going on mission trips. Getting more involved in church. Getting into a women's Bible study."

So we asked the obvious question: What's stopping you?

"Let me see," she said, this time with a smile. "Three kids, ages ten, twelve, and fifteen, who have to be transported a thousand different places. A job that requires more than forty hours a week with commute time. A house that is never clean. Trying to keep up with some church activities. Helping the kids with their homework. Going to school functions. You get the picture?"

We got the picture.

So now we asked a leading question. Is there anything that you do that is more important than your relationship with God?

She knew where we were headed.

"If you guys are trying to put me on a guilt trip, you're doing a good job," Jamie said sternly. "I know I need to give God more time. I just don't know where to begin. I don't know what I would eliminate."

Jamie nailed it. She said precisely what we heard throughout this research process. The simple life is elusive because elimination is too difficult for most people. We call this issue *focus*.

When God Is in the Background: The Failure to Focus

A plethora of charts and graphs are not necessary for this chapter. Sixty-nine percent of the respondents wish they had more time for church and other spiritual matters. And few of these respondents would argue that God shouldn't be the top of their priority list. But somehow He still gets pushed to the background, even among well-intending believers.

Jamie has a job that requires her presence. She has three children who must be transported a plethora of places. And she has other responsibilities that she worries are the victims of neglect.

How can Jamie focus on those things that really matter? How can she eliminate just a few items, when they all seem to be "must do"? A journey back two thousand years ago can give us some perspective.

The Not-So-Simple Life Two Thousand Years Ago

We have heard many churchgoers say that they wish the church today could be just like the early church in the book of

Acts. And while we understand the longing and the sentiment, things were not always perfect in Jerusalem. For example, in Acts 6, the church was faced with murmuring and dissension because some widows in the church were getting meals while others were not: "In those days, as the number of disciples was multiplying, there arose a complaint by the Hellenistic Jews against the Hebraic Jews that their widows were being overlooked in the daily distribution" (Acts 6:1).

It would appear that the twelve apostles were expected to take care of most of the ministry needs in the Jerusalem church. But the church was growing at such a rapid pace that the men were unable to keep up with the demands that were placed upon them. So the complaining and murmuring began.

Who has not felt tugged in multiple directions at some point? And most of us attempt to do many things poorly instead of a few things well. And, if most of us were honest with ourselves, our relationship with God is often neglected as we yield to the demands of many voices.

The twelve apostles were focused. Among those tasks they felt compelled to do, prayer and preaching were at the top. But if they were to give time to God in those tasks, they couldn't do everything else, even something as worthy as taking meals to the widows.

The apostles did not mince words: "Then the Twelve summoned the whole company of the disciples and said, 'It would not be right for us to give up preaching about God to wait on tables'" (Acts 6:2).

You can almost anticipate the reaction of the congregation. Who will take care of these widows? Don't you care about these women? Why won't you help them?

But the apostles had a plan. They knew they couldn't do it all, so they selected seven godly men to take care of the neglected widows. And the twelve leaders kept their focus: "But we will devote ourselves to prayer and to the preaching ministry" (Acts 6:4).

Note the incredible response in Acts 6:7 when the apostles remained focused. First, the preaching ministry grew more powerful ("the preaching about God flourished"). Second, more people became followers of Christ ("the number of disciples in Jerusalem multiplied greatly"). And third, some of the hardest to reach became Christians ("and a large group of priests became obedient to the faith").

This text, providing us a fascinating glimpse into life in the early church, shows us how the simple life was a challenge for these Christian leaders. We can only imagine the demands placed upon their lives as they were expected to lead and care for this thriving congregation. But the leaders saw clearly the need to focus, and in these seven short verses of Scripture, we learn five key principles of focus for us today.

They dealt realistically with the messy world in which they lived. How many times have we postponed the simple life because we were certain that, when life's circumstances change, we will have all the time in the world? "When I finish my education, then I can simplify my life." "When the kids are grown, I can have a normal life." "When this major crunch at work has passed, then I can do some things that really matter."

In fact, both of us sometimes didn't practice what we are teaching in this book. We would often tell each other that life will become simple when we are done writing *Simple Life.*

Look at the example of the leaders of the early church. They dealt with the reality of the messiness of life straight on. A significant group in the church were complaining and murmuring. The gospel focus of the early church was in danger of being lost. The widows of Greek origin were being neglected in the church's provision of food.

The leaders didn't say they would forego the matters of utmost importance to deal with the tyranny of the urgent. They didn't say that they would ignore the matter either. They acknowledged the messiness of life and dealt with it

They were brutally honest with themselves and others. Look at Acts 6:2 closely: "Then the Twelve summoned the whole company of the disciples and said, 'It would not be right for us to give up preaching about God to wait on tables.'" Sometimes, the first step is the toughest, because it means that we can't fool ourselves any more. And if God is in the background in our lives, it clearly means that we have lost our focus on the simple life that really matters.

Note that the Twelve told everyone ("the whole company") about the challenge. And they made it clear that they would lose focus on their main calling ("preaching about God") if they took a detour to get involved in yet another activity ("wait on tables"). They not only admitted to themselves they couldn't get it done; the leaders told everyone else.

They acknowledged that something good had to go. One of the most important ministries of the Jerusalem church was taking care of the widows. The biblical mandate to care for widows is evident throughout Scripture. The apostle Paul said in 1 Timothy 5:3, "Support widows who are genuinely widows." And James notes in James 1:27, "Pure and undefiled religion before our God and Father is this: to look after the orphans and widows in their distress and to keep oneself unstained by the world."

Taking care of the widows was important. In fact, it was mandated. But the leaders of the church couldn't do it all. They had to let something go, even if it was something good.

They were creative in discovering alternatives. Sometimes we are too busy, even too busy for God, because we have our own mini-messianic complex. We just don't believe it will be done unless we do it ourselves. The leaders of the early church knew that the ministry to widows was important. They just didn't believe that everything depended on them.

So the Twelve looked for an alternative plan, a plan that would let them continue to focus on their primary calling. It was simple. They found seven others who were fully qualified, in both spiritual depth and physical ability, to carry out the task. And in Acts 6:5, the men are named. The first name on the list is Stephen, who would soon become the first Christian martyr (Acts 7).

They kept their focus. The temptation must have been great for the early church leaders to take on the task themselves. They must have felt the pressure to abandon what really mattered to handle the most vocal issue of the moment. But they didn't. They kept their focus: "But we will devote ourselves to prayer and to the preaching ministry" (Acts 6:4).

Focus. Not easy. But it's a must for the simple life.

The Need to Eliminate

The two of us wrote a book a few years ago called *Raising Dad*. The book was Art's perspective on fatherhood as he observed the life of his own dad, Thom. The pattern of each chapter was the same. Art would give his perspective on Thom's parenting skills (or lack thereof), and Thom would respond.

One of the chapters was called "When a Father Is Like the Father." Art begins by giving a fairly positive view of Thom as a spiritual role model. Thom responds with a perspective that is not quite so glowing.

Consistency in reading and meditating on God's Word? Just so-so.

Prayer life? Okay unless he was too busy.

Pause there for a moment. I (Thom) evaluated my own prayer life as okay as long as I was not too busy. Let's look at the words I wrote:

One would think that I would be wise enough
to see how prayer powerfully impacted my sons,
that I would be a model of a praying man to them.
Now, don't get me wrong. I am a man who believes
in the power of prayer. I have preached, taught, and
exhorted people on the need to have a personal
prayer time with God.

It's just that I have not always been the model of
consistency in prayer. Sometimes I just get too busy
to pray. Writing that previous sentence sends chills
of conviction through me. Did you hear what I said?
Sometimes I don't have time for God. It's ridiculous,
isn't it?

I've read the stories of John Hyde, David Brainerd,
and David Mueller. I've seen the passion of prayer
warriors in the churches I served. Sometimes I seem
to get it; other times I don't.

We can't escape the fact that nothing else really matters in life if our relationship with God is not what it should be. That's why I recognized the absurdity of my comment that I was too busy for God. If we are too busy for God, we are just too busy.

In *Simple Church*, Thom and Eric shared the story of pack rats. Pack rats are a type of rat that continually collects and transports junk. People who collect and hoard meaningless items are also called pack rats.

If you have ever been in a pack rat's home, you were likely shocked at the piles of magazines, newspapers, dishes, and random items. You found it difficult to make your way through the home. You may have volunteered to clean up, but the person insisted that all the stuff is needed.

According to the research we cited, pack rats most likely suffered a brain lesion that damaged the part of the brain that keeps pack-ratting behavior in check. A study done at the University of Iowa showed that all of eighty-six pack rats had some type of brain injury. In other words, eliminating things is neurologically challenging for a pack rat.

Many of us have clutter that we just don't eliminate. We insist that everything we are doing, all of the activities we are involved in, and every minute consumed is nonnegotiable. We just can't eliminate anything.

Except time with God.

Ouch.

This is a spiritual issue because it's a matter of stewardship. Eliminating the nonessentials, even if they are good things, is vital because God says it's important.

Note Ephesians 5:15–16: "Pay careful attention, then, to how you walk—not as unwise people but as wise—making the most of the time because the days are evil."

The apostle Paul had two words in the Greek he could have used for "time" in this verse: *chronos* and *kairos*. *Chronos* refers to time in general. It is clock time and the root word for *chronological*. *Kairos* refers to a predetermined, specific amount of time. It is measured, allocated, and fixed.

Paul used *kairos*.

His word choice is huge. He was saying, in essence, that you have a specific amount of time here in this world. That is it. It is already set. It is fixed. The clock is ticking. Your time is running out. Even now.

So make the most of it. Don't just spend it. Invest it. Be wise with the time God has given you. Eliminating activities, as God leads, is choosing to be wise stewards of the time and resources He has given.

In our survey of 1,077 persons, responders came from a variety of places. They represent all major ethnic and racial groups in our nation. They also represent all adult age groups. They were nearly equally divided between males and females.

But they had common concerns. They wanted a simpler life.

Most of them wanted to get better control of their time. Most of them wanted simpler and healthier relationships. Most of them wanted a simpler life financially. And most of them wanted a life that was closer to God.

The group included a few atheists who didn't believe in God, and therefore a relationship with Him was a moot point. But most of those surveyed said otherwise. They knew that they wanted a closer relationship with God, but in their busyness of life, the one Person who was most important to them just got left out.

It doesn't make sense, but that's the reality of the problem.

Larry, for example, lives near Allentown, Pennsylvania. Even though he and his wife are empty nesters, Larry still has trouble finding time for God. "I made a commitment. I'm not sure if it was to God or just to me," he told us, "but I did make a commitment to become more faithful in my church attendance and to take time each day to pray."

Larry reflected for a moment. "I was sure that, once the kids got on their own, I would have all the time in the world. I had these great plans to start teaching a small group at church and to spend an hour a day in prayer. I was really fooling myself. Activities with the kids have just been replaced with other activities. God is still hardly a part of my schedule."

At one point in 2008, gas prices really took a sharp upward turn. Consumers were faced with increased costs like they had never seen before. Most of the responses were anger, frustration, and fear. But we heard of some families who saw this new reality as an opportunity to get their busy lives back in order.

James and Jan of Fort Myers, Florida, were hit hard by the rising gas prices. Their tight budget couldn't take any more expenses. Most of their discretionary income, what little they had, went for activities for their four children, ages four to eleven.

"We had our four kids in ten activities and sports," Jan said. "Their activities cost us over $400 a month. Then we got clobbered with the high gas prices. We couldn't afford to keep gas in the minivan with all the places we were going. We were at a crisis point."

James and Jan gathered the children together and explained the predicament in a straightforward and simple way. "They all understood what was going on," James said with a degree of amazement. "Even the youngest seemed to grasp the situation.

"We told them they had to choose just one activity or sport," James continued. "We thought they would pitch a fit. But not only did they handle it well; I think they were relieved. It made me wonder how much of their junk was our doing and not theirs. Jan and I would have told you earlier that all this stuff we were doing was important, that we couldn't find anything to eliminate. We were wrong."

So the family went from ten activities with the children to four. They ate at home more as a family to save money and because they had more time together. They even started going to some places on bicycles.

"We started the bike thing to save gas money," Jan told us. "But the more we did it, the more the kids got excited about it. Because we live in Southwest Florida, we are able to ride bikes almost every day."

How have the changes transformed the family?

"Gosh, I really don't know where to begin," Jan said with enthusiasm. "This all started as an expense reduction plan. And sure, we're saving money. We can really tell it each month. But the best benefit has been that our lives are simpler, and we are spending more time together. I think the kids will look back on these times and remember them as some of the best times of their lives.

"But, you know, the greatest benefit of all of this has been spiritual. Now that we have all of us together for some period every day, we take fifteen or twenty minutes to have a family devotional. We've never done that before. There's nothing complicated about what we do. One of us reads a few verses from the Bible. We ask the kids to share what the verses mean to them. Then all six of us say a brief prayer.

"It's really brought us closer together. More important, it's really brought us closer to God."

If there was a common theme about eliminating activities, it was that it is difficult. When Eric and Thom wrote *Simple Church*, they heard from churches across the world that expressed the difficulty of letting go. "This program is vital to the life of the church!" "We will make too many stakeholders mad if we do away with this." "This ministry is a part of the heritage and history of our church. We can't just let it go."

One of our favorites was sent to Thom in an e-mail: "We have one particular ministry that has been a part of our church for nearly thirty years. It has dwindled to only a handful of participants, and it seems to have no benefit to the church or the community anymore. But it represents who we are at this church, so we can't eliminate it."

And we found in this research that people have trouble letting go just like churches have trouble letting go. But elimination is vital to having focus. And focus is indispensable to the simple life and a closer relationship to God.

Fortunately we did hear of several success stories in our research. We heard from people who now spend more time with God because they have been successful at eliminating activities. Here are a few:

- "I watched television an average of fifteen hours a week. All I did was make a commitment to cut my television time to ten hours a week. I gave the other five hours to prayer and Bible study. I now have about forty-five minutes for prayer and Bible study each day that I didn't have before."

- "I spend eight or nine hours commuting to work each week. I decided to eliminate the time I listen to the radio in the car. Instead, I listen to the Bible on CD and spend time in prayer. I also have a lot less road rage now!"

- "My ritual included reading the local paper for forty-five minutes each morning. I limit myself to thirty minutes now and use the other fifteen minutes each day for prayer."

- "It floored me when I decided to measure my time on the Internet for one week. Twenty hours! I couldn't believe it. I cut that time in half immediately and began studying books of the Bible."

- "I run about forty-five minutes each day. I love listening to music and interesting speakers on my iPod. Now I listen to downloaded sermons and Bible readings at least three or four of the days I run each week."

- "My husband and I tried an experiment. We asked our two daughters if they were involved in anything they would like to stop doing. We were shocked when the oldest said she wanted to stop two things, and the youngest named one. Between those three activities, counting commute time, we are saving seven hours a week. So now we have eliminated seven hours and added thirty minutes a day for family devotionals. We still have more than three hours net free time."

The simple life may require some tough choices. It probably will require the elimination of some things you are doing now. But it will free you to do those things that are really important. And seven out of ten we surveyed said they need more time with God. That, we believe, is what really matters.

Limit Adding

Perhaps we are stating the obvious at this point. Focus is necessary for the simple life. Focus often requires elimination. But elimination would not have to take place if we were willing to say no more often.

As we found by listening to more than one thousand people, the problem with many is that they have trouble just saying no. They feel that they will let someone down if they don't agree to help them with some activity. They feel compelled to get their kids in the latest activity or sport. They have to start watching the newly advertised and touted television show. They have to go to that meeting. When the school calls, they must say yes to help.

The list goes on and on. We say yes to more, and something suffers. That something is often Someone.

God is moved to the background. He gets left out of our lives.

Sounds crazy, doesn't it? But you know it's true.

Stop adding so much to your life. You're busy enough. In fact, you told us clearly in our research. Some of you are just too busy for God. And that is being too busy for your own good.

The Simple Life: Moving Closer to God

We began this book articulating the quest for the simple life. And, according to our surveys and research, the need was for help in four major areas: time, relationships, money, and God.

But the vast majority of the respondents told us clearly: the first of the "big four" had to be God.

So we have taken you through a simple process for getting closer to God in the simple life. Let's review.

Clarity. Devise a brief mission statement for a highly intentional plan to have a closer relationship with God. We mean it. Write it down. And make certain that the mission statement is a process you can actually do, not some wordy and unattainable prose.

Just as a sample and reminder, we will take you back to the mission statement of Jack from Tennessee:

> *I will move closer to God by beginning to read the Bible at least fifteen minutes a day, by taking my family to church each week, and by talking about spiritual matters with my family at least once a week.*

Notice the simplicity of the statement. Notice how attainable the goals are. Notice how the mission statement is also a process or plan.

If you haven't yet written it, write your mission statement. Take only a minute or two. You have to begin somewhere, even if it's a small beginning.

Movement. Conceptually, movement is easy. It's getting rid of the congestion and obstacles that hinder the progress of your mission statement. Focus is getting rid of the good stuff, but movement is getting rid of the bad stuff. You know what that bad stuff is. And you, with God's help, can begin to clear the congestion.

Alignment. This step requires an honest look in the mirror. It means that we accomplish the mission statement by aligning our mission statement with our personality, demeanor, gifts, and abilities. Thom, for example, has trouble being still physically, so he often prays while he walks.

Focus. So we're back to the topic of this chapter. Focusing on what really matters means that we often have to eliminate some things from our lives, even if those things are good things. It is a sin to be good if God has called us to be great.

God longs for a deeper relationship with us. But we often let stuff get in the way. The Bible is clear on this relationship in James 4:8: "Draw near to God, and He will draw near to you. Cleanse your hands, sinners, and purify your hearts, double-minded people."

The simple life is not a double-minded life but a single-minded and focused life walking with God. And that's the foundation upon which everything else is built.

The simple life will simply not work without God.

APPLICATION
SIMPLE LIFE: FOCUS
SEVEN HOURS FOR GOD

Take a simple challenge. Pretend that you are in a life-or-death situation. The only way you can live is to free up seven hours a week. You can't cut back on your sleep, so you have to find the time elsewhere.

Look carefully at all options. You only need to find one hour per day on the average. What are you presently doing that you can stop doing or start doing less?

- Cut back on television time?
- Reduce hours on the Internet?
- Find a new route or departure time to work that takes less time?
- Don't talk on the cell phone as much?
- Cut out one of your leisure activities?

You get the point. Now take a few minutes to write some areas that you can eliminate to give more time to God.

Activity   Time Saved

_____

_____

_____

_____

_____

_____

Now, make a decision to focus. Follow through on some of the activities you have thought about eliminating, and give that time to God.

Conclusion

This book had a strange beginning. In fact, before we ever wrote the first word, the beginning was different. It took place in a cemetery, a large graveyard with countless grave markers and tombstones. For Art the most intriguing part of the cemetery was the dash.

The entirety of this book has been about the dash, that period between birth and death. For Thom, the marker currently reads 1955– . For Art, it is 1982– . You notice the blank spots after the dash. That date is our death. Only God knows that year. For the two of us, indeed for all of us, we can only know the birth date that is past, and the dash.

The dash has much of the past in it as well. For Thom, the dash represents a past of more than half a century; for Art it's nearly three decades.

But the dash has a lot of hope in it because it contains the present. We can make choices right now that will profoundly impact the rest of our lives. Indeed those choices can determine if the dash will represent a life lived to the fullest or a life fully wasted.

The simple life is more than mere simplicity. It's all about focusing on that which really matters, and be willing to discard the rest. It's about the courage to make some tough decisions now because you know you need to do so. Because you know your family needs you to do so. Because you know God wants you to do so.

It's about the dash.

The story of the dash is told in the Bible in Matthew 25:14–30. It's the story of the master and the three servants who were given talents by their master. They each had a "dash" to do something with the talents. Two of the servants were faithful and did well with the talents. But one was fearful and lazy. The talent was wasted.

The dash was wasted.

Simple Life has been the story of making much of the dash, not wasting the one life God has given us. It's the story of faithfulness that means we will hear God's words when the dash is done and the second date is written: "Well done, good and faithful servant."

Thank you for your time. We have both prayed for you, even though we don't know you by name. Our prayer has been that God uses this book to move His people to be more like Him in all that we are, all that we say, and all that we do. And that is our prayer for you.

And I pray this: that your love will keep on growing in knowledge and every kind of discernment, so that you can determine what really matters and can be pure and blameless in the day of Christ, filled with the fruit of righteousness that comes through Jesus Christ, to the glory and praise of God (Phil. 1:9–11).

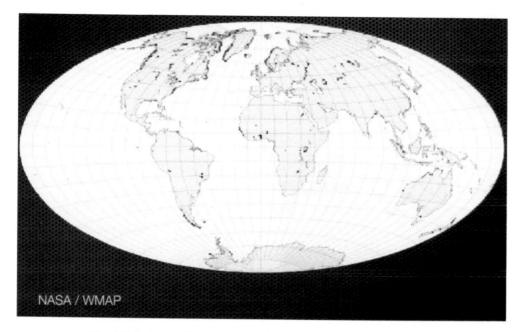

Fig. 9.7(a). A two-dimensional map representation of Earth.
(Image from NASA/WMAP Science Team.)

Fig. 9.7(b). A very precise two-dimensional, outward-looking all-sky
map representation of the temperatures of the variation in cosmic
microwave background radiation from space. This is a snapshot of the
oldest light in our universe, from 380,000 years after the big bang. The
yellow represents higher temperature; the red, the highest temperature
variation of +0.0002 degrees Kelvin; and the dark blue, the lowest temperature variation of −0.0002 degrees Kelvin, compared to an average
of about 2.7255 degrees Kelvin (above absolute zero).
(Image from NASA/WMAP Science Team.)

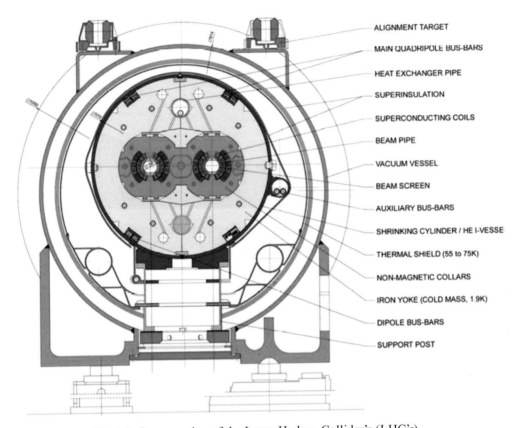

ALIGNMENT TARGET

MAIN QUADRIPOLE BUS-BARS

HEAT EXCHANGER PIPE

SUPERINSULATION

SUPERCONDUCTING COILS

BEAM PIPE

VACUUM VESSEL

BEAM SCREEN

AUXILIARY BUS-BARS

SHRINKING CYLINDER / HE I-VESSE

THERMAL SHIELD (55 to 75K)

NON-MAGNETIC COLLARS

IRON YOKE (COLD MASS, 1.9K)

DIPOLE BUS-BARS

SUPPORT POST

Fig. 9.8. Cross section of the Large Hadron Collider's (LHC's) beam tube and dipole-magnet assembly. The "eyes," shown white at the center, are the beam tubes, and the nearly surrounding collection of sectors contains the superconducting magnet windings, shown in brown. The remaining structure provides mechanical support, cooling, and thermal isolation so that the windings can operate at just 1.9 degrees Kelvin (above absolute zero). (Image from *Wikipedia* Creative Commons; file: The 2-in-1 Structure of the LHC dipole magnets.jpg; authors E. M. Henley and S. D. Ellis. Licensed under CC BY-SA 3.0.)

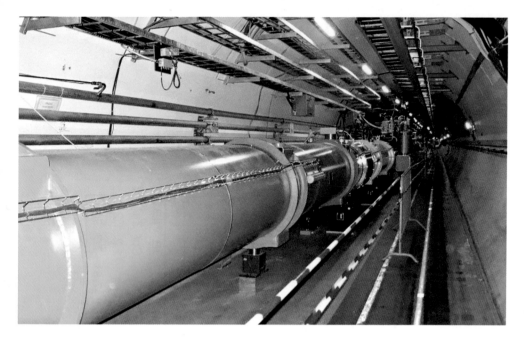

Fig. 9.9. View of the Large Hadron Collider (LHC) beam tube and magnet assemblies of the collider ring inside the ring tunnel. (Image from *Wikipedia* Creative Commons; file: CERN LHC Tunnel1.jpg; author: Julian Herzog; website: http://julianherzog.com. Licensed under CC BY-SA 3.0.)

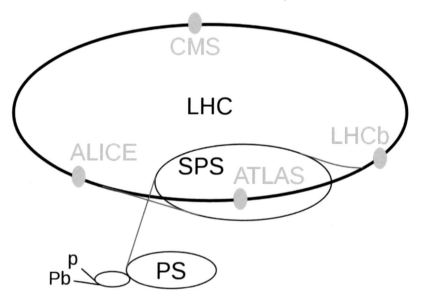

Fig. 9.10. Angled-view sketch of the circular rings of the Proton Synchrotron (PS) and Super Proton Synchrotron pre-accelerators to the Large Hadron Collider (LHC), with its experiment test stations shown in green. The path of the protons (and ions) begins at linear accelerators (marked *p* and *Pb*, respectively). They continue into the booster (the small, unmarked circle), then to the PS and the SPS. Red lines indicate how particles are fed in opposite directions into the two beam tubes of the LHS. (Image from *Wikipedia* Creative Commons; file: LHC .svg; drawn by Arpad Horvath with Inkscape. Licensed under CC BY-SA 2.5.)

Table D.1. Outer Electron Energies* and Relative Sizes of Atoms and Filled Valence Subshell Ions of Some of the Elements.

(*The negative of measured ionization energies.) Note that atoms and ions are unrealistically shown as solid spheres and dashed circles. (In part from Fine and Beall, reference E, Table 16.3, p. 554, with permission from Dr. Leonard W. Fine.)

Group

| IA | IIA | B-Groups | IIIA | IVA | VA | VIA | VIIA | VIIIA | | Row |

E, the Outer Electron Energy (shown in green and given in electron volts, eV) is the energy of the highest-energy (= least negative energy) occupied state of the neutral atom. Atomic/ionic radii (labeled and shown in gray) are in units of one-tenth of one-millionth of a millimeter (where the thickness of a dime is about one millimeter).

Row 6

Atom/Ion: Cs/Cs^+ — Radius 2.35/1.67 — E in (eV) −3.89

Rn/ — −10.75

Row 5

Atom/Ion: Rb/Rb^+ — Radius 2.11/1.48 — E in (eV) −4.18

Xe/ — −12.13

I/I^- 1.33/2.16

Row #4 Transition Metals

Group	IIIB	IVB	VB	VIB	VIIB	VIIIB			IB	IIB
Atom/Ion	Sc/	Ti/	V/	Cr/	Mn/	Fe/	Co/	Ni/	Cu/	Zn/
Radius	1.4	1.3	1.2	1.2	1.2	1.1	1.1	1.1	1.2	1.2
E in (eV)	−6.5	−6.8	−6.7	−6.8	−7.4	−7.9	−7.9	−7.6	−7.7	−9.4

	Atom/Ion Radius	E in (eV)	Atom/Ion Radius	E in (eV)		Atom/Ion Radius	E in (eV)	Atom/Ion Radius	E in (eV)	Atom/Ion Radius	E in (eV)	Atom/Ion Radius	E in (eV)	Atom/Ion Radius	E in (eV)	Atom/Ion Radius	E in (eV)
4	K/K^+ 1.96/1.33	-4.34	$Ca/$ 1.71	-6.11	Row #4 Transition Metals	$Ga/$ 1.22	-5.93	$Ge/$ 1.19	-7.83	$As/$ 1.15	-9.72	$Se/$ 1.12	-9.68	Br/Br^- 1.14/1.95	-11.74	$Kr/$	-14.00
3	Na/Na^+ 1.54/0.98	-5.14	Mg/Mg^{2+} 1.30/0.65	-7.64		Al/Al^{3+} 1.25/0.45	-5.97	Si 1.17	-8.15	P/P^{3-} 1.10/2.12	-10.9	S/S^{2-} 1.04/1.84	-10.4	Cl/Cl^- 0.99/1.81	-12.9	$Ar/$	-15.76
2	Li/Li^+ 1.23/0.68	-5.39	Be/Be^{2+} 0.89/0.31	-9.32		B/B^{3+} 0.80/0.20	-8.3	C 0.77	-11.26	N/N^{3-} 0.74/1.71	-14.54	O/O^{2-} 0.74/1.45	-13.61	F/F^- 0.72/1.33	-17.42	$Ne/$	-21.56
1	H 0.37	-13.6														$He/$	-24.6

The Particle Landscape

All of particle physics rests on a theory known as the Standard Model, which lays out the fundamental particles that exist in nature, as well as the forces that govern them. The Standard Model includes two main families of particles: fermions, which include all the constituents of matter, and bosons, which include all the known force-carrying particles. Fermions come in three generations of progressively greater mass.

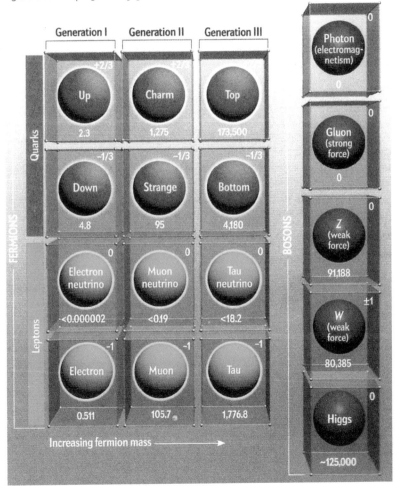

Fig. 9.11. The fundamental particles of the Standard Model.

Appendix A

THE NATURE AND SPECTRUM OF ELECTROMAGNETIC WAVES

Note: It takes a little effort to accurately conceptualize what constitutes a light wave, but when you've done it you understand all electromagnetic radiation, and the subject is rather fascinating. Wavelengths were defined for water in Figure 2.2, but light is a different animal. What I provide here is a relatively simple and accurate classical description that serves much of our discussion and is the basis for our consideration of the quantum nature of light starting in Chapter 2. In particular, following the step-by-step construction in Figure A.1 will require a bit of concentration but will be well worth the effort.

If, however, you'd like a shortcut, a glance at Figure A.1(c) will give you a "picture" of the wave (albeit without full understanding) sufficient to consider the spectrum of electromagnetic wavelengths shown in Figure A.2. That figure has additional information in the rightmost column relevant to Chapter 9.

INTRODUCTION TO FIELDS AND ELECTROMAGNETIC WAVES

In 1865, the Scottish mathematical physicist James Clerk Maxwell developed a theory of electromagnetism suggesting that waves of alternating electric and magnetic fields would propagate through space at the speed of light. He concluded from this that light was itself an electromagnetic wave. This led to the prediction of other electromagnetic waves, among them radio waves.

What Maxwell theorized and what Thomas Young earlier demonstrated (in 1801, as described early in Chapter 2) is that light "looks" and behaves like a wave. It is Maxwell's broader understanding of the nature of light, in this "classical" context, that we present here. Note, however,

that light also exhibits quantum, particlelike properties, suggesting that the energy of light is delivered as photons, discrete packages of energy, and a wave-particle duality as described later in Chapter 2. (The photon is described as the purveyor of the electrostatic force, such as the force on the electron as described in Chapter 9, Part IV (C).)

Although we can see light, we can't see the electric (**E**) and magnetic (**B**) fields of which light is comprised. Even so, we are all familiar with the magnetic field. It causes magnets to attract or repel each other, latch onto refrigerator doors, and attract the needle of a compass to point toward the North Pole. The electric field is less familiar, but most of us have seen the consequences of a strong electric field: in lightning or in the zapped discharge of the buildup of electrons as we walk across the right type of carpeting.

Note that both **E** and **B** are boldface to indicate that they are vectors, that is, they have magnitude but also act or flow in a particular direction. The **E** field is a measure of how strongly voltage changes across space, how strongly other electric charges push or pull on electrons, and whether the electrostatic discharges described above are likely to occur. Suppose that you have walked across the kind of carpet that lets electrons in some way scrape off and charge you up to some voltage level. And then suppose you step forward to shake hands with a friend who hasn't been on the carpet or isn't wearing the kind of shoes that scrape off electrons. (That is, for this illustration, your friend doesn't carry a charge.) Suppose you are charged to 800 volts, and suppose your hands are one inch apart. Then, ignoring some of the effects of the geometry of your hands and some other factors, there is between the two of you an electric field of **E** = (800 volts)/(1 inch) = 800 volts per inch. (These are not the usual units for **E**, but that doesn't matter for our illustration.) Eight hundred volts is not enough to cause a spark through air.

Now suppose your hands come closer, so that they are separated by a tenth of an inch. The voltage changes more rapidly across the much smaller space between your hands. **E** = (800 volts)/(1/10 inch) = 8,000 volts per inch. Still, nothing happens. Suppose your hands become separated by one hundredth of an inch. Then **E** = (800 volts)/(1/100 inch) = 80,000 volts per inch, and your friend gets ZAPPED. There is a flash, because electrons leaving your body under the acceleration of the **E** field break loose electrons from the atoms in the molecules of the air (ionizes them), and then they and those additional electrons are accelerated (in opposite directions under the influence of the **E** field) and some recombine to form atoms, releasing light in the process. You have finally exceeded the approximately 75,000-volts-per-inch breakdown voltage for air at the pressures found near the earth's surface.

The difference between the carpet-caused zap and lightning is in the number of electrons in the discharge, the size of the gap, and the reduced air pressure high up in the sky, which actually makes the discharge easier. The prominence and shape

of objects can also serve to intensify the electric field. Lightning is, of course, a great deal more complicated than is described here, but you have the basic idea.

So, the E field can be a driver of electrons. It exerts a force on them along the direction of the field.

Note that an electron, if it were to travel undisturbed from a place at 800 volts to a place with zero volts, would acquire an energy of 800 electron volts, 800 eV. This compares to the −13.8 eV of the electron in the ground state of the hydrogen atom, as described in Chapter 10. And realize, 13.8 eV is roughly comparable to the ionization energies of most of the elements, as described in Appendix D. So, the electrons released at 800 volts in our thought experiment have much more than enough energy to ionize the atoms of the elements.

THE PLANE-POLARIZED ELECTROMAGNETIC WAVE

We visualize what an idealized light wave might look like through several steps, as shown in Figure A.I. First, in (a) we consider three directions in space, three axes: the x axis, which runs from left to right; the y axis, which runs toward us; and the z axis, which runs vertically upward. The axes cross at a point called the origin. (We define distance along x to have positive values to the right and negative values to the left of the origin; distance along y to have positive values toward us and negative values away from us past the origin; and distance along z to have positive values upward and negative values downward from the origin.)

In (b) we visualize (within short dashed lines) a rectangular block of space roughly centered over and running lengthwise along the x axis. Think of this block as sliced up like a loaf of bread, where the cut surface of each slice is a rectangle that lies in a plane oriented perpendicular to the x axis. (The rectangle defines a limited region within the flat surface of the plane of the cut, but the plane containing the cut surface extends to infinity in the positive and negative of both the y and z directions.)

In (c) we represent an electromagnetic wave. Here's how we construct the concept of it: We start with an identical set of axes to those in (a) and (b), but without the sliced "loaf" that is in (b). At each point where the plane of one of the slices from (b) would cut across the x axis in (c),

we indicate by an up or down arrow (vector) the direction and particular strength of the electric field, E, that is present *throughout the entire plane of that slice, that is, to infinity in the plus and minus y and z directions.*

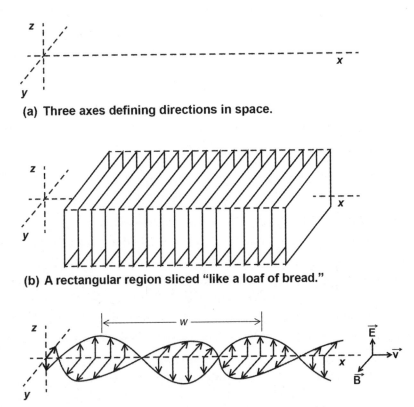

(a) Three axes defining directions in space.

(b) A rectangular region sliced "like a loaf of bread."

(c) "Snapshot" of a plane-polarized electromagnetic wave.

Fig. A.1. Plane-polarized electromagnetic wave. (a) Three axes define directions in space. (b) A rectangular region of space "sliced like a loaf of bread." (c) A "snapshot" of the wave. Each arrow (i.e., vector) shows the magnitude and direction of the electric field, **E**, or magnetic field, **B**, throughout an entire plane in space (beyond the loaf) at the x position where the plane is located. Arrow tips trace out sine waves with crest-to-crest wavelength, w. Each local field (arrow) at each x position alternately increases and then decreases with time, following the rise or fall of the field (arrow) to its left, so that the wave propagates forward in the x direction with velocity **v** (having a magnitude c = the speed of light). (Image (c) modified from *Wikipedia* Creative Commons; file: Onde electro-magnetique.svg; author: SuperManu. Licensed under CC BY-SA 3.0.)

Consider now the E field in the plane of just one of the slices. The longer the arrow E for that plane, the stronger the E field *throughout that plane*. Think of the E field in this plane as being represented by an infinite number of arrows of this same length and direction everywhere in that plane. We choose to show only one arrow to represent all of these arrows, and we start this one arrow from the x axis so that we can compare its length with the length of other arrows that similarly represent the E fields that are present throughout other planes.

Now, if we were to cut our loaf into more and more and thinner and thinner slices, the tips of the resulting more closely spaced vectors would trace out an alternating positive to negative (in the z direction) *sine* wave as shown. The length of the **B** vector is in direct proportion to the length of the E vector at each point along x, so the **B** vectors similarly trace out a sine wave, but running positive to negative in the y direction, and the **B** sine wave is exactly in phase with the E sine wave (both crossing from positive to negative at the same points along the x axis). The peak value of either sine wave is called its *amplitude*.[1] Because our E vectors for this description point only up or down (in the z positive or negative directions) we say that the wave thus produced is *polarized* in the z direction. And because E for each slice is the same everywhere in the *plane* of the slice, we say that the wave is *plane- polarized*.

WAVE PROPAGATION

Now realize that each vector (*representing the field throughout its plane*) changes with time, at first increasing in length, going to the peak positive level of the sine wave, and then decreasing, going negative, and then increasing again. And each vector is slightly out of phase with respect to its neighbor. The vectors successively reach a peak value, one after the other, before dropping down again. This successive peaking of each vector one after the other *propagates* the waves forward in the x direction, in analogy to what occurs when sports fans in successive seating sections of a stadium create a human wave (by successively raising then lowering their arms) that propagates the wave around the stadium. Such prop-

agation is also similar to the propagation of waves in water described in Figure 2.2, except that the human wave circles the stadium while the waves in water move left to right until they hit the breakwater. The plane electromagnetic wave that we have described propagates forward in a straight line in the *x* direction at a velocity **v**, in this case inducing new **E** and **B** vectors in the space just ahead (visualized in new slices and planes). Note: people, molecules of water, or **E** and **B** fields in slices rise and fall or move in and out, but do not actually move in the direction of wave propagation.

The vector **v** shows the propagation of our electromagnetic wave from left to right along the *x* axis. For all electromagnetic waves, as determined by Maxwell and verified by experiments ever since, **v** will always have the same magnitude in empty space: the speed of light, approximately $c = 300,000,000$ meters per second; recall, in scientific notation we write this as 3×10^8 m/sec. (When electromagnetic waves propagate through media, especially for dense media, such as through glass in the case of light, the speed of propagation can be slowed somewhat.)

THE ELECTROMAGNETIC SPECTRUM

As noted earlier, the distance from positive crest to the next positive crest is the same for both the E field and the B field sine waves shown in Figure A.1 and is defined as the wavelength of the electromagnetic wave. I represent this *wavelength* by the letter *w* in Figure A.1(c). Were we to count the number of positive crests passing by per second as the wave propagates past us, we would measure the *frequency* of their passing. We represent this frequency by the letter *f*.

Note that the frequency, *f*, and the wavelength, *w*, are simply related. Because the frequency of the passage of crests times the length between crests is equal to the speed of the propagation *c* (in a vacuum always *c*, and very nearly so otherwise), we can write a formula for the relationship between *f* and *w*. In scientific shorthand: $fw = c$. So, if we know the frequency of a wave and wish to know its wavelength, then by dividing both sides of this equation by *f* we get the formula for *w*: $w = c/f$. Similarly, if we know the wavelength of a wave and wish to know its frequency, then by dividing both sides of this equation by *w* we get the formula for *f*: $f = c/w$.

The entire electromagnetic spectrum—from long-wavelength radio waves through microwaves, infrared (IR) light, visible light, ultraviolet (UV) light, x-rays to very-short-wavelength, high-frequency gamma rays—is defined in terms of wavelength as shown along the left side of Figure A.2.

Amplitude modulation, or AM, radios operate at frequencies in the range of one million cycles per second (one megahertz) with wavelengths about the length of a football field. Frequency modulation, or FM, radio waves in the range of 100 megacycles per second (100 megahertz) have wavelengths on the order of one meter. Microwaves have wavelengths an order of magnitude or two shorter, in the range of inches. Light spans a narrow range of wavelength of hundreds of nanometers (where one nanometer equals a billionth of a meter), while x-rays have wavelengths of tenths of nanometers, on the scale of the sizes of atoms. The presence of electromagnetic waves at frequencies in the microwave range and beyond is often referred to as *radiation*, and this term is even sometimes used to describe the broadcast of radio waves.

LASER LIGHT AND WHITE LIGHT

For any particular quantum of electromagnetic radiation, **B** vectors are always perpendicular to the **E** vectors, and both of these vectors are always perpendicular to the axis of wave propagation, in the manner shown in Figure A.1(c). But subject to these requirements, **E** (and **B**) can be at any orientation in a plane perpendicular to the axis of propagation. A collection of electromagnetic quanta needn't have a collective alignment or predominant polarization.

Multiple quanta can be produced, however, that all have sine waves of the same wavelength (and corresponding frequency), polarization, and phase (that is, having the crests of their waves all line up "in sync"). This synchronization, called *coherence*, has been produced in lasers with billions of quanta of light, with powerful and special effects, as described in Chapters 4 and 20.

While light resulting from the transition of electrons from and to specific states in specific elements may produce monochromatic light (of a spe-

cific polarization and wavelength and associated color), the light emitted from our sun and from hot bodies in general tends to conform pretty much to a (so-called) *blackbody* continuous spectrum of randomly polarized light. It was Planck's study of this blackbody radiation that kicked off the quantum revolution, as described at the beginning of Chapter 2.

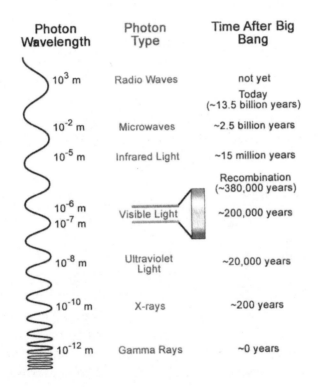

Photon Wavelength	Photon Type	Time After Big Bang
10^3 m	Radio Waves	not yet
		Today (~13.5 billion years)
10^{-2} m	Microwaves	~2.5 billion years
10^{-5} m	Infrared Light	~15 million years
		Recombination (~380,000 years)
10^{-6} m 10^{-7} m	Visible Light	~200,000 years
10^{-8} m	Ultraviolet Light	~20,000 years
10^{-10} m	X-rays	~200 years
10^{-12} m	Gamma Rays	~0 years

Fig. A.2. Electromagnetic radiation is delivered in quanta of energy called *photons*. The left column shows photon crest-to-crest wavelengths increasing (from the bottom to the top of the figure) a million million times, from high-energy gamma rays (at a wavelength of 10^{-12} meters) to the long-wavelength photons of FM radio waves (at a wavelength of about 1 meter). Gamma-ray photons present at the time of the big bang have had their wavelengths stretched by the expansion of space itself (see Chapter 9, Section II) to the point that today, 13.7 billion years after the big bang, we see these photons as a cosmic microwave background radiation with wavelengths in the microwave range, on the order of centimeters or inches. (Figure 12.7 of *Big Bang, Black Holes, No Math*, by David Toback. Copyright © 2013 by David Toback. Reprinted by permission of Kendall Hunt Publishing Company.)

Appendix B

EMPIRICAL DEVELOPMENT OF THE PERIODIC TABLE OF THE ELEMENTS

HISTORY

Consider the situation in 1789. There really was no concept of the atom, other than to postulate that there was such a thing, the smallest unit of an elemental substance. No thought or concept of *its* constituent particles—electron, proton, or neutron. No concept of a nucleus.

Many chemists still clung to the idea that all elements were composed of numbers of hydrogen atoms, a holdover from the days of alchemy when some believed that elements could be transformed one into another,[1] for example, from lead into gold. The noble gases were still unknown and would not begin to be discovered until over a hundred years later, in 1894. Since they were all gases and at that time were found in combination with nothing, they simply did not exist as far as anyone knew.

The nineteenth century was a period of great progress for quantitative research and the systematization of information. By the middle of the century, science had transformed from the quest of well-off hobbyists to the funded operation of dedicated researchers. Laboratories were set up not only to allow for research but also to serve as schools for instruction under the guidance of the leading researchers of the times. And the students in these laboratories then set up such laboratories of their own.

Beginning in 1817, scientists began to notice that certain groups of elements had similar chemical properties. For example, they observed similarities in lithium, sodium, and potassium. These of course are elements of a group whose atoms we now know to have one electron beyond a closed shell of electrons. They also observed, for example, similarities in chlorine and bromine, two of the elements with one fewer electron than fills a shell.

Researchers eventually began listing the elements in order of their relative *atomic weights*, which by then they were able to calculate from measurements of the weights of substances that combined with each other. If the atomic weight of hydrogen, the lightest element, was defined to have an arbitrary unit weight "one," and it combined with approximately eight times its weight of oxygen, then the atomic weight of oxygen would be surmised to be eight, unless of course (as had also been suggested by that time) each atom of oxygen had combined with two atoms of hydrogen, in which case the atomic weight of oxygen would be correctly deduced to be approximately 16. (For all but the lightest elements, approximately half of this weight would come from the protons and the other half from the neutrons, particles of both types composing the atomic nucleus.)

The listing of elements in order of increasing atomic weight turned out to be approximately the same as listing them according to increasing *atomic number* (but they didn't even know of atomic number at the time). As researchers counted through the elements, they would *periodically* come to elements that had chemical properties similar to the properties of previously counted elements, that is, elements of the same group. As early as 1843, they began to arrange the elements in tables, *periodic tables*, that placed the elements in order of their atomic weights but also grouped them in rows or columns according to their chemical properties.[2] For example, if the elements were listed by increasing atomic weight in rows, then the tables would be arranged so that the periodically similar groups of elements appeared in columns.

In all, there were at least six substantial contributors to the evolution of the periodic table. The best-known of the early tables is one published by chemist Dmitri Mendeleev in 1869. It is similar to one put together at about the same time by Oskar Lothar Meyer. In all, Mendeleev published some thirty tables and produced about thirty more that remained unpublished. These appeared in various forms, with the elements listed in order of increasing atomic weights down columns, or across rows, or even in what is labeled as a "spiral" form. While the type of arrangement doesn't change the basic information of the elements, it can indicate in somewhat different ways the underlying chemistry and physics of those elements.

One *long form* table that Mendeleev published in 1879 placed the

sixty-one then-known elements in order of atomic weights within rows, and it grouped those elements having similar chemical properties one above the other in columns.[3] Since the number of elements between like elements varies, this meant that the successive rows thus created would not contain the same number of elements. And the table had many blank spaces where Mendeleev believed that yet-undiscovered elements should be located. But with all of its blanks and unevenness, each row would contain one complete cycle of properties (one *period*).

Table B.1 is a redrawn version of just the first five rows of Mendeleev's 1879 table, retaining all of the columns with their Roman-numeral group headings, but otherwise altered in several ways. First, I've "flipped" the table upside down (starting the first row of elements with hydrogen at the bottom center) to more easily show a connection to the physics of the hydrogen atom that we describe in Chapter 13. Though I've retained the chemical symbol for each element, I've added each element's atomic number (which wasn't known at the time) and its full name. And, finally, I've darkly shaded the regions of the table occupied by the nonmetals, left without shading the regions of the table occupied by metals, and lightly shaded the regions in between that are occupied by the semiconductors. (The inert elements that would occupy a rightmost column had yet to be discovered at the time that this table was constructed.)

Mendeleev (or Scerri?)[4] labels the first seven columns of like elements (groups) in Table A.1 successively with Roman numerals I through VII and then the next three columns together as Group VIII. (All of these labels are shown at the top of each column.) Then he shows some ambiguity as to how to arrange the table, indicating a similarity to the properties of the first columns by starting again with the Roman numerals I, II, and so on, to label the last seven columns. So the elements with properties that we now know all follow from those of hydrogen appear in two columns, and both of these columns are labeled as Group I.

Table B.1. "Flipped" First Rows of

I	II	III	IV	V	VI	VII	VIII

37 Rubidium Rb							
19 Potassium K	20 Calcium Ca	—	22 Titanium Ti	23 Vanadium V	24 Chromium Cr	25 Manganese Mn	26 Iron Fe	27 Cobalt Co

Metals

Metalloids =
Semiconductors

Nonmetals

Mendeleev's Periodic Table of 1879 (Redrawn).

VIII	I	II	III	IV	V	VI	VII	Row
								5
28 Nickel Ni	29 Copper Cu	30 Zinc Zn	31 Gallium Ga	—	—	—	—	4
	11 Sodium Na	12 Magnesium Mg	13 Aluminum Al	14 Silicon Si	15 Phosphorus P	16 Sulfur S	17 Chlorine Cl	3
	3 Lithium Li	4 Beryllium Be	5 Boron B	6 Carbon C	7 Nitrogen N	8 Oxygen O	9 Fluorine F	2
	1 Hydrogen H							1

PREDICTIVE CHUTZPAH

The *key to* being able to start constructing *the periodic table* was in the realization that the nature and strength of the chemical interactions of each element should be examined in relation to its atomic weight, a physical property. Mendeleev was not alone in this realization, although his may have been a more profound understanding.[5] What set him apart was his conviction in the patterns revealed by the table, and this led him to boldly (and famously) predict the existence, chemical properties, and approximate atomic weights of substances that had not even yet been found. (He indicated these by including blank spaces in his tables.)

Among the first four of Mendeleev's predictions (that were made in a ninety-six-page article published in German in 1871) were what he called "eka-aluminum" and "eka-silicon" (*eka* is Sanskrit for "beyond"), with chemical properties expected to be similar to those of the named already-known lighter elements preceding them in the second Group III and IV columns of his 1869 table. The predicted properties of these predicted new elements are compared as follows to the properties of two later-discovered elements that now fill two of the gaps in his tables: gallium, which was discovered in 1875 (and is present in his 1879 table); and germanium, which was isolated in 1886. As you can see, Mendeleev's predictions were very good!

Element	Atomic Weight (relative)	Density (grams/cm³)	Melting Point (degrees F)
Eka-aluminum (predicted 1871)	**68**	**6.0**	**Low**
Gallium (discovered 1875)	69.72	5.904	85.6*
Eka-silicon (predicted 1871)	**72**	**5.5**	**high**
Germanium (isolated 1886)	72.61	5.35	1,737

*Low enough to melt on a hot day

But that's not all. Gallium was discovered by Paul Emile François Lecoq de Boisbaudran, a Frenchman (obviously) who named the element using the Latin (*Gallis*) for the ancient name of his country (Gaul). As Kean

tells it, in his bestselling book *The Disappearing Spoon*,[6] Mendeleev sought to steal some of Lecoq's thunder by claiming that he, Mendeleev, was really responsible for the discovery of gallium, having predicted its existence. Lecoq fought back, claiming that another Frenchman had developed the periodic table much earlier. Mendeleev pointed out that Lecoq's measurements of the properties of gallium had to be in error because they didn't agree with Mendeleev's predictions. (That was really a lot of gall for a Russian!) Lecoq eventually found that Mendeleev was right, withdrew his original data, and published results that did, indeed, agree with Mendeleev's predictions. As Kean phrased it, "The scientific world was astounded to note that Mendeleev, the theorist, had seen the properties of a new element more clearly than the chemist who had discovered it."[7]

It is from the properties of gallium that Kean gets the title of his book, *The Disappearing Spoon*. He relates how chemists would play practical jokes by crafting a spoon of the silvery metal and then serving hot tea by pouring hot water into a cup with the spoon in it. The melting point of gallium is so low that the metal transforms from solid to liquid in hot water. So the spoon would "disappear" before the guest's eyes as it melted into the bottom of the cup.

Fig. B.1. Dmitri Mendeleev at middle age. (Image from AIP Emilio Segre Visual Archives.)

Mendeleev—Teacher, Scientist, Maverick, Showman

We get a sense of the science and society of the times by examining the life of Dmitri Mendeleev, who shaped not only science but also thought and policy in tsarist Russia. He was a promoter intent on improving Russia, and, in the process, in elevating his position within the autocracy of the tsarist state. He entered into Russian society in 1861, the same year that the serfs were emancipated under the beginning of Tsar Alexander II's "Great Reforms." And Mendeleev soon became a powerful figure with close ties to several government ministers and access to the tsar.

Though a political conservative, Mendeleev sought to modernize Russian institutions and Russian science, and he spent as much of his time trying to improve the Russian state as he did working in the sciences. He sought methods for organizing industry and human resources, helped to create the protectionist tariff of 1891, published critiques in the arts, and sat in séances as part of an ongoing personal effort to debunk a widespread spiritualism. He consulted throughout his life in practical technical areas ranging from cheese manufacturing to production in iron, coal, and oil; set the standards for alcohol content in vodka; initiated the first "big science" projects and introduced the metric system in Russia; promoted meteorology through his own balloon ascents; and was the foremost contributor to the development of the periodic table of the chemical elements.

Despite being honored around the world, Mendeleev did not receive the Nobel Prize. The prize had been established in 1901, and he was put forward as a candidate in 1906, but an old grudge from an earlier scientific dispute interfered. There is no doubt that his work was of Nobel Prize caliber. (Had he lived long enough, it would surely eventually have been awarded to him, but, as I've mentioned before, it is awarded only to living scientists.) To quote Scerri: "He is the leading discoverer of the (periodic) system. . . . His version is the one that created the biggest impact on the scientific community at the time. . . . His name is invariably and justifiably connected with the periodic system, to the same extent as Darwin's name is synonymous with the theory of evolution and Einstein's [is] with the theory of relativity."[8] One of the craters on the moon, as well as element number 101, the radioactive mendelevium, are named in his honor.

MUCH OF CHEMISTRY ON A SINGLE PAGE

For later reference, I show in Table B.2 one commonly used modern long-form periodic table of 103 of the 118 elements. For reasons that will become apparent, I display this table "flipped" upside down, as I had done with Mendeleev's 1879 table (Table B.1 above).

I have incorporated Mendeleev's table almost as it is shown into Table B.2, just shifting the block of elements H, Li, and Na, and Be and Mg from the right Groups I and II columns to the left Groups I and II columns. Otherwise, to complete this periodic table, I have filled in Mendeleev's blanks, completed the labeling of the groups, added three more rows of elements, and added a rightmost Group VIII-A column for the noble gases discovered after 1879.

For now, we just note Scerri's general comment: "The periodic table of the elements is one of the most powerful icons in science: a single document that captures the essence of chemistry in an *elegant pattern*. Indeed nothing quite like it exists in biology or physics, or any other branch of science for that matter."[9]

Table B.2. A Modern Arrangement of the Periodic

** Actinide Series
(Insert the entire row after
Ac, Z = 89 below)

90 Thorium Th	91 Protactinium Pa	92 Uranium U	93 Neptunium Np	94 Plutonium Pu	95 Americium Am

** Lanthanide Series
(Insert the entire row after
La, Z = 57 below)

58 Cerium Ce	59 Praseodymiu Pr	60 Neodymium Nd	61 Promethium Pm	62 Samarium Sm	63 Europium Eu

IA	IIA	Group	IIIB	IVB	VB	VIB	VIIB	┌----- VIIIB

87 Francium Fr	88 Radium Ra		89 Actinium Ac**					
55 Cesium Cs	56 Barium Ba		57 Lanthanum La*	72 Hafnium Hf	73 Tantalum Ta	74 Tungsten W	75 Rhenium Re	76 Osmium Os	77 Iridium Ir
37 Rubidium Rb	38 Strontium Sr		39 Ytterbium Y	40 Zirconium Zr	41 Niobium Nb	42 Molybdenum Mo	43 Technetium Tc	44 Ruthenium Ru	45 Rhodium Rh
19 Potassium K	20 Calcium Ca		21 Scandium Sc	22 Titanium Ti	23 Vanadium V	24 Chromium Cr	25 Manganese Mn	26 Iron Fe	27 Cobalt Co
11 Sodium Na	12 Magnesium Mg							
3 Lithium Li	4 Beryllium Be							
1 Hydrogen H								

Metals □

Metalloids = Semiconductors ▨

Table of 103 Elements (Same as Table IV).

Row

96 Curium Cm	97 Berkelium Bk	98 Californium Cf	99 Einsteinium Es	100 Fermium Fm	101 Mendelevium Md	102 Nobelium No	103 Lawrencium Lr	7
64 Gadolinium Gd	65 Terbium Tb	66 Dysprosium Dy	67 Holmium Ho	68 Erbium Er	69 Thulium Tm	70 Ytterbium Yb	71 Lutetium Lu	6

- - - - -| IB   IIB   IIIA   IVA   VA   VIA   VIIA   VIIIA

7

78 Platinum Pt	79 Gold Au	80 Mercury Hg		81 Thallium Tl	82 Lead Pb	83 Bismuth Bi	84 Polonium Po	85 Astatine At	86 Radon Rn	6
46 Palladium Pd	47 Silver Ag	48 Cadmium Cd		49 Indium In	50 Tin Sn	51 Antimony Sb	52 Tellurium Te	53 Iodine I	54 Xenon Xe	5
28 Nickel Ni	29 Copper Cu	30 Zinc Zn		31 Gallium Ga	32 Germanium Ge	33 Arsenic As	34 Selenium Se	35 Bromine Br	36 Krypton Kr	4
				13 Aluminum Al	14 Silicon Si	15 Phosphorous P	16 Sulfur S	17 Chlorine Cl	18 Argon Ar	3
				5 Boron B	6 Carbon C	7 Nitrogen N	8 Oxygen O	9 Fluorine F	10 Neon Ne	2
									2 Helium He	1

Nonmetals

Appendix C

QUANTUM COMPUTER DEVELOPMENT

My intent here is to give you a feel for what physically constitutes qubits and what the state of the art might be in quantum computer development.

In writing Appendix C, I use terms and concepts that may become more understandable after reading about the foundations of chemistry and materials science in Part Four and the nature of various superconductor and semiconductor devices in Part Five of this book. But this appendix is in support of the preview provided in Chapter 8, and so I leap ahead. If you find some of this material hard to understand, please just push on, realizing that more background appears in later chapters. Or, if you find too much detail, just skim through it.

As noted in Chapter 8, John Gribbin, author of *Computing with Quantum Cats*, describes a half dozen approaches being explored for the construction of qubits, tracing the progress of their development and their use in computers until 2014.[1] I briefly summarize these approaches and developments in the following numbered indented sections, noting additional or more recent achievements as appropriate. As you will come to understand, quantum computing is still an application in the infancy of its development, but it is one that holds great promise.

1. *The Ion Trap*: An ion within a small vacuum chamber or a hollow built into a microchip is held in place by electric fields and prevented from thermally induced oscillations by laser beams (optical cooling) "like a big ship being held in place by tugs nudging it from all sides."[2] The outer electrons of the ion can be made to switch from one stable state to another using pulses of laser light (the two states thus actualizing a binary qubit). The ion can also oscillate in its position at either of two distinctly different and attainable resonant frequencies

(providing a second qubit within the same physical element). And rows of ions can be entangled and work in concert. An advantage of this approach is that the states of the ions can be readily accessed, controlled, and read. This approach is where experimentation with qubits started. Experimental work on a small-scale quantum information processor was reported in late 2013.[3]

2. *Nuclear Magnetic Resonance (NMR):*[4] Molecules in a liquid are *excited* (caused to switch) from one nuclear-spin state to another, using high-frequency radio waves. (The z component of nuclear spins, like electron spins, will take on either a parallel or anti-parallel [binary] orientation with respect to an applied magnetic field.) Multiple qubits can be produced within the same molecule. Nuclear spins do not interact strongly with thermal vibrations, and so an advantage for NMR is operation at ambient temperature. But reading the results tends to be difficult. Even so, this was the first approach that actually achieved quantum factoring, in 2001 deriving the prime-number factors of 15 using seven spin-½ nuclei in single molecules within a very large liquid sample.[5] And in November 2011, liquid-crystal NMR was used to factor the number 143 using a quantum algorithm believed to be more suited (than the classical algorithm) to the factoring problem.[6]

3. *Quantum Dots:* Nanoscale[7] local peaks (on the surface of a solid) in the attraction of electrons to the positive charges of the nuclei of atoms, particularly at the interfaces of deposited semiconductor materials, tend to provide small traps where an extra electron may reside. The movement of the electron from one to another of a pair of such traps, or residing in between, provides a switching of (binary) states and the superposition requisite of a qubit. Switching between two quantum-dot electron-spin states is also being explored, and, as of about 2012, a significant spin-coherence time of about 200 microseconds had been achieved. This approach is most amenable to standard semiconductor-manufacturing methods, with the further advantage that operation can occur at ambient temperature, without the complications of thermal isolation and refrigeration required in some of the other

approaches. Recent presentations by Michelle Simmons of the University of New South Wales provide a summary of progress overall in quantum dots, a detailed description of the construction and characterization specifically of chemically implanted phosphorous ion dots in silicon,[8] and the extent to which this approach has progressed using largely standard silicon-based manufacturing technology.[9] The latter presentation describes the construction of a two-qubit device and projects 20 qubit integrated circuits in five to ten years.[10]

4. *Isotopic Nuclear Spins*: The common isotopes of silicon and carbon have no net nuclear spin. So the rare presence of other isotopes with net spin in otherwise-pure solid materials can create qubits that switch from one nuclear-spin state to another (say, "up spin" to "down spin"). One variant of this that involves nitrogen-vacancy (NV) centers is described in greater detail in the indented section below.

5. *Quantum Photonics*: The binary states of photons (single particles of light), such as vertical and horizontal polarization,[11] allow photons to behave as mobile qubits. The CNOT gate operation[12] described in Chapter 8 has been demonstrated not only at a large scale on optical lab benches using this approach, but also (in 2008) by creating hundreds of CNOT gates in silica (glass) on silicon chips of dimensions 70 mm long × 3 mm wide × 1 mm thick (about three inches by 1/8 by 1/32 of an inch). The chips are fabricated using industrial processes. To quote Gribbin: "In the pioneering Bristol (UK) device, four photons are guided into the network and are put into a superposition of all possible four-bit inputs; the calculation performed by gates inside the network creates an entangled output, which is collapsed by measuring the output states of the appropriate pair of photons. In this way the Bristol team used Shor's algorithm to determine the factors of 15, proudly finding the answer 3 and 5. All done at room temperature in a device superficially similar to a common computer chip."[13] By 2012, the Bristol group was projecting in three years the availability of single-purpose "computers" of this type (needing only a couple of pairs of entangled particles) for such things as cryptography.

6. *Superconducting Quantum Interference Devices (SQUIDs):*[14] This last but apparently most advanced of all approaches so far includes developments at IBM and a company called D-Wave. Both companies use the SQUID approach and superconducting technology described briefly in Chapter 19. As of September 2011, researchers at IBM were experimenting with two superconducting junction quantum-coupled qubits.[15] They cited major challenges but suggested that enough might be learned in the span of five years to turn their attention toward the development of computers.

More recently, D-wave reported the development of a 1,000-qubit processor (announced in June 2015).[16] (Some caution here: the actual *quantum* computing capabilities of this processor may still need to be demonstrated.) Small circuits containing superconductor-semiconductor-superconductor Josephson junctions operate at extremely low temperatures.[17] They can be switched between binary quantized states of electrical current. The processor contains 128,000 Josephson junctions on a single chip that is fabricated using standard semiconductor-device-manufacturing techniques. D-Wave, its manufacturer, claims to be the world's first quantum-computer company.

An article published in September 2014, titled "Google's First Quantum Computer," describes the D-wave computers as "quantum annealing computers," only able to solve "optimization" problems, as distinct from more general problems requiring computers using a "universal gated mode blueprint."[18] Google will be working to both develop a more universal model and to help D-Wave to improve the functioning of its machines.

Entangled NV Centers—One Example of Approach No. 4, Isotopic Nuclear Spin

To illustrate the sophistication of materials technology and the considerations under which qubits may be made to work, I summarize and simplify here from one recent (October 2014) review article on NV centers.[19] The article also describes the potential of these centers for the measurement of various properties on a submicroscopic scale. The NV approach is intended to bridge the gap between the readily controllable and readable qubits of the ion trap and the more readily manufactured devices using established semiconductor-chip-construction processes. In the NV center of this example, a nitrogen ion is implanted using an ion gun into a highly pure dia-

mond-structure lattice of carbon atoms. One method of creating the diamond is to grow it by depositing the carbon atoms in perfect array, one atomic layer at a time, using a process called *chemical vapor deposition*.

The ion is coupled with a vacancy, a place in the lattice that is missing a carbon atom, as a result in this case of the impact of the ion. This ion-vacancy pair, this NV center, acts very much like the single ion in an ion trap. An electron at the NV site has ground and excited electron spatial states that are each split into three states through interaction with the magnetic moment of its electron spin. The split states are labeled as $m_s = 0$, $m_s = 1$, and $m_s = -1$, where the $m_s = 0$ state is slightly lower in energy than are the other two states, which are equal in energy.

A small alternating magnetic field applied at microwave frequencies can be used to set which spin state is occupied by the electron initially. Transitions from the excited $m_s = 0$ state emit a red light that is clearly brighter than transitions from the other excited states, so there is an easy mechanism for reading which state the center is in. Furthermore, the transition from state to state occurs within one microsecond (one millionth of a second), so that this readout can take place within a very small fraction of the duration (coherence time) of an entangled state. All of these aspects of the NV have been studied and confirmed experimentally.

The duration of the NV center's spin state is only about a millisecond (one thousandth of a second, 1,000 microseconds) at ambient (room) temperature, which is too short a storage time for the NV center to be practical as a qubit. This coherence time can be extended to an acceptable full second if the NV chip is cooled to the temperature of liquid nitrogen, 77 Kelvin degrees, almost three quarters of the way from room temperature (about 300 Kelvin degrees) to the absolute zero of temperature at 0 Kelvin degrees. But a more exciting alternative for storage is suggested as follows.

The dominant mechanism for interaction with the NV center's quantum states is from the spin of the nuclei of impurity 13C isotopes in the host diamond lattice, composed mainly of the 12C isotope, which has no net nuclear spin. Because the states of the 13C nuclear spins have coherence times of hours, information might be stored in the spins of these 13C isotopes and set (initialized) and accessed (read out) through the interaction of these spins with the nuclear and electronic spins of a nearby NV center. An NV center can thus be thought of as a hybrid spin register, in which the electronic spin serves as an access point to prepare and detect the multiple entangled qubits of proximal nuclear spins. In particular, each proximal nuclear spin can serve to allow (or not allow) a transition in the state of the electron at a laser light "flipping" frequency that effectively marks the carbon nuclear spin, so that the nuclear spin and the electron together operate as a CNOT gate (which is described in Chapter 8).

Only a limited number of nuclear spins can surround one NV center and be entangled in this way, but NV centers can be entangled one to another over distances of a dozen nanometers. The suggestion is further made that "the optical photon is a natural 'flying qubit'" capable of linking quantum registers nearby or far from each other, in the latter case possibly "to create a network akin to a quantum internet."[20]

(Aside from computers, the article goes on to suggest that nanoscale diamond particles containing NV centers may be used as sensors that are embedded in molecules or biological systems or placed in nanoscale proximity to surfaces. The NV

electron energy levels are influenced by the local chemical environment or molecular jostling [i.e., temperature], with attendant shifts in the wavelength of light emitted from these centers. Further shifts in the wavelengths of light through the application of magnetic fields can be used to precisely sense the location from which the light is emitted to image internal or surface properties with a high degree of resolution, in analogy to what is done with MRI [refer to Chapter19], but with much higher resolution.) So these could be used as minithermometers or chemical sensors.

As noted in Chapter 8 and elaborated a bit here, much is underway toward the development of practical quantum-computer systems. Because of the rapid growth in this field, even by the time that this book is published, it is likely that much more will have been accomplished.

Appendix D

THE ATOMIC SIZES AND
CHEMISTRIES OF THE ELEMENTS

IONIZATION ENERGIES

The sizes of the atoms and the chemical properties of the elements depend largely on how strongly the outer electrons in their atoms are bound to their nuclei. As a way of getting a sense of the strength of this binding, measurements have been made of the *ionization energies* that are required to break the outer electrons free from their atoms.

Measurements are typically tabulated in several series, each for the removal of one, two, or more electrons, respectively. The energies are obtained either by using electrical methods or through calculations on spectroscopic data using the quantum relationship between the energy of a photon and its wavelength (as discussed initially in Chapter 2). The ionization energies determined by either method agree quite well. Of the two methods, the spectroscopic method is the more accurate, and the data presented here were obtained mainly by that method.[1]

The ionization energy needed to free a single outermost electron from its ground-state atom[2] is just the energy needed to boost the outermost electron from the negative energy of its bound outer-electron state to the zero of energy that makes it a free particle. (Refer back to Chapter 11 for a discussion of energy and "bound state" energies.) So the negative of this positive ionization energy is just a measure for each element of the depth of the negative energy that holds the electron trapped in its bound state, *precisely what we have been describing throughout this book as the negative energy level of the outermost occupied electron state*. The measurement of ionization energy thus gives us a bird's-eye view into this

energy level for the more complex many-electron atoms for which energies are difficult to calculate or approximate. It also gives us a view into the differences in these highest occupied energy levels as we compare the atom of one element to that of another. Through this we explain bonding. I consider specific bonds in Chapter 15, but here I introduce the subject generally. I show what the energy levels of these outermost states tell us about the propensity to bond.

OUTER-ELECTRON ENERGIES AND THE SIZES OF ATOMS

Table D.1 (located second from last in the photo insert) is a partial periodic table showing the outer-electron energies and sizes of the atoms of 41 of the elements. (Note that this table is to be read looking from the right side of the two pages that it is spread across.) The table becomes simple and easily understandable if we define its features. The symbol for each element appears below a shaded sphere (where there is one, showing relative atomic size) in a ratio-like arrangement along with the superscripted symbol for its valence-subshell ion (to be defined further on in this chapter). For example, we have Mg/Mg^{2+}. Below those symbols is a ratio giving the approximate radius of the atom and the radius of its valence-subshell ion (also to be defined further on), both in units of one-tenth of a millionth of a millimeter (where a millimeter is about the thickness of a dime). The outer-electron energies (the negative of the measured ionization energies) are shown in green as the lowest item below the spheres and symbols.

The elements are divided into the A-type and B-type Groups (types marked by the letters A or B after the Roman numeral that labels the Group, those elements in each column), as defined in Chapter 13. The Groups (columns) correspond to those in our periodic tables IV and B.2. (Note: I have placed the same periodic table in two places, labeled as Table IV in Chapter 13 and Table B.2 in Appendix B, to make examining the periodic table easier in relation to the discussion in the nearby text.)

The inset rectangular box in Table D.1 provides information on ten elements of the B-type groups, the transition metals. The surrounding

rest of the table describes the properties of the atoms of each of 31 (main) A-type group elements at positions corresponding to the locations of those same elements as they are represented in the leftmost and right-most two columns or first (bottom) several rows of the two periodic tables mentioned above. It is easiest to consider one group and one property at a time, and we start by examining the properties of the A-type groups of elements, starting with atomic size.

The first thing we notice in scanning across Table D.1 is a nearly con-tinuous decrease in the sizes of the spheres in each row from left to right. These spheres represent the approximate overall sizes of the atoms of each of the elements.[3] (They are essentially the sizes of the probability clouds of the outermost states occupied by the electrons in each atom. But, remember, all electron states are to be thought of as somewhat diffuse and cloudlike [as shown, for example, in Fig. 3.8], not like the hard spheres drawn in Table D.1. Only the electrons in the outer s states of the elements in the first two columns at the far left or in the completely filled shells of atoms in the last column at the far right are expected to actually have a spherical symmetry, and all of these "spheres" would appear "fuzzy" and diffuse.)

Note that sizes are not shown for the atoms of the noble gases, which are listed without spheres in Column VIIIA at the far right of each row. The atoms of these elements can be surmised to be just a bit smaller than the sizes of the atoms shown in the same row in the preceding column, Column VIIA (since the sizes of atoms are seen to change only gradually left to right across the last elements in each row toward Column VIIIA).

With a few exceptions, to be noted last, the outer-electron ener-gies become steadily more negative (showing greater binding) as we scan through the elements left to right across each row of the table, and down each column. The size of each atom (conversely) generally decreases element to element across the rows (left to right), and this decrease is in rough correspondence with the more negative outer-elec-tron energy, reflecting the stronger binding of the electron that more negative energy produces. And the size of each atom generally decreases element to element down the columns, and this decrease is in rough cor-respondence with the more negative outer-electron energies down each column, reflecting the greater binding of the electron.

Look at the steadily more negative outer-electron energy as we consider successively the elements in the last three columns of each row of the table. This more and more negative energy shows particularly well the general trend of the greater binding of the outermost electrons as we consider each successive element left to right in each row; that is, as we consider elements with successively more and more electrons. Each additional p-state electron in the atoms of these elements is apparently only partially shielded by its fellow electrons from the attraction of the nucleus, while the additional proton in that atom creates a greater attraction and binding of all of the electrons, as reflected in the more and more negative energy of the outermost electron.

Note that the outer-electron energy in each row of the table reaches a minimum (is most negative) for the Group VIIIA element at the end of each row, that is, for those elements completing the occupation of a full shell of electrons. The atoms of these elements hold onto their electrons so strongly that they tend not to have any stripped away in reaction with other elements. Nor do their atoms tend to gain an electron, since the outer-electron energy (as a measure of the tendency to attract and bind) of the state that the added Group VIIIA element's electron would go into is less negative in energy (and less binding) even than the relatively small outer-electron energy of the element starting the next row of the table. That is because the ion that would be formed by addition of an electron to the atom of the Group VIIIA element—though otherwise resembling the atom of the next higher-Z element starting the next row—would have one fewer proton in its nucleus than the atom of that higher-Z element. So the added outermost electron that it would acquire would be less tightly bound and less strongly attracted to the nucleus than the equivalent electron in the atom of the next higher-Z element. Thus an electron in another element would simply not be attracted to the atom of the noble gas, Group VIIIA, element. The lack of any tendency to lose an electron, and the lack of any tendency to gain one, together explain why the Group VIII elements do not tend to react to form an *ionic bond*. Nor do they tend to interact by sharing an electron to form a covalent type of bond. They thus tend to be noninteracting, aloof—and hence the name, "noble gases."

Now, note the less strongly negative outer-state energy of the oxygen atom, represented by the symbol (O) in Row 2, and of that for sulfur, represented by (S) in Row 3 of Column VIA, relative to the outer electron state energies of the atoms of nitrogen (N) and phosphorous (P), respectively, in Column VA. These (O) and (S) less strongly negative energies interrupt the otherwise steady decrease in the outer occupied state energies of the atoms of elements from left to right. These singular energy increases in (O) and (S) (as one scans left to right) occur because oxygen and sulfur are the first elements in their rows to have electrons of opposite spin in their outer p subshell, that is, two electrons occupying the same p spatial state. And that, as mentioned in Chapters 13 and 14, causes a relatively large mutual repulsion of the two electrons in that state, making the energies of these outer electrons less negative so that they are less tightly bound and the ionization energy needed to remove either of them is correspondingly smaller.

THE PROPENSITY TO BOND

In nature, everything tends toward the lowest overall energy state. Atoms will tend to share or transfer electrons one to another as long as the sum of the energies of all of the electrons in both atoms (or ions, if they are formed) after the transfer is less than the sum of these energies beforehand. So, what determines an atom's (element's) propensity to gain or lose or share an electron (react chemically to bond) is the energy level of its last occupied state and that of the state just above it relative to those of the atoms of the other elements that it may bond with. Let me explain.

Consider: if the energy of the next state up (i.e., the first unoccupied state) in an atom of one element is relatively low compared to (i.e., more negative than) the energy of the last occupied state of the atom of a second element, then the first atom will tend to be reactive in trying to acquire the outermost electron of the second. That is because in transferring from the second atom to the first, the electron "drops down" to a lower energy, and nature loves an overall lower-energy state. This type of reactivity for acquisition is typical of atoms of the *nonmetals*, which are represented at the lower right in Table D.1 and darkly shaded and

represented to the lower right in our periodic tables IV and B.2. (That is, typical with the exception of the noble gas elements in the last column, which I describe further on from here.) One such atom, for example, the fluorine atom, is so acquisitive as a constituent of hydrofluoric acid that it will rip silicon from its (SiO_2) bond with oxygen to etch glass.

Conversely, if the energy of an atom's present outermost occupied state is relatively high (less negative) compared to the (unoccupied) next higher-energy state of the atom of another element, the first atom will tend to be reactive in letting its outermost electron "drop to a lower energy" and go to the second atom. This type of reactivity is more and more typical of the *metals* as one looks more and more to the upper left in Table D.1 and the upper left in the two periodic tables mentioned above. For example, the single outer 1s electron of the sodium atom has such a small negative energy that, if a chunk of this metal is dropped in water, oxygen atoms, which are very acquisitive with much-more-negative energy states available, will shove aside their previously bonded hydrogen atoms to latch onto that higher energy (less negative energy) sodium electron. The event produces hydrogen gas, which can combine to burn with the oxygen in the air, releasing heat and light (and, if sufficient quantities are involved, explosion).

If the electron is transferred completely from one atom to another in either of the above cases, then the atom that acquires the electron acquires a net negative charge and thus becomes an *anion*. The atom that loses the electron is left with a net positive charge and thus becomes a *cation*. The two oppositely charged ions attract each other electrostatically and tend to stick together in what is called an *ionic bond*. For example, sodium and chlorine form an ionic bond, making NaCl, common table salt.

If the outer states and next higher-energy unoccupied states of two atoms tend to be comparable in acquisitiveness, they may still lower the overall energy of their electrons by sharing their outer electrons (in a way that distorts the states of both atoms to lower energy) in what is call a *covalent bond*. In this bond, the energy of the overall molecule is lower than that of the two atoms separately. Note that all bonds are some combination of ionic and covalent bonds. (Specific bonds and bond types are described a bit more in Chapter 15.)

Atoms whose outermost electrons occupy states of completely filled shells (therefore states of relatively low energy) tend *not* to have that electron stripped away. And if their next higher in energy (unoccupied) state is not very strongly negative in energy, they won't tend to acquire an electron into that state either. They simply tend not react with other atoms either to lose or to gain an electron. These are the "aloof" Group VIIIA *noble gas* elements, represented in the rightmost column of Table D.1 and our periodic tables IV and B.2. Note: another way to describe the propensity to bond is to say that the atom of each element tends to gain or lose electrons so as to more closely approach the just-filled occupancy of a shell displayed by the atom of the nearest (in atomic number) noble gas element.

MORE ABOUT THE SIZES OF ATOMS AND IONS

The decrease in atomic size from left to right in Table D.1 is counterintuitive. As we move from left to right in the table, we successively consider elements whose atoms have more and more electrons, that is, atoms of higher and higher atomic number. And wouldn't we expect that more electrons make for larger (rather than smaller) atoms?

From the physics described in Chapter 14 and earlier in this appendix, we know that the answer is no. More electrons surrounding the nucleus means an equally greater number of positively charged protons in the nucleus. This results in a greater attraction of each electron to all of the protons, mitigated to some extent by the screening of the protons by the negative charges of the other electrons that surround the nucleus. The net effect is that (as we consider atoms having more and more electrons across a given row of the table) every additional electron (except for those in column/Group VIA, as noted earlier) sees a greater attraction to the nucleus, with a corresponding reduction in the size of all of the electron states, that is, a smaller atom with more electrons. But this works only within each row until the last p state for that row, that approximate energy level, is filled.

The atoms of elements in Column IA have one electron more than

completely fills a shell (except, of course, for hydrogen, which has only one electron). And (except for hydrogen) this one electron occupies a higher (less negative) energy s state (as compared to the energy of the states in the preceding completely filled shell of states). In every case, the lone outer electron is largely screened from all but one positive unit of charge in the nucleus because of the tightly bound, spherically symmetric, completely filled shells of the rest of the electrons within. And so this last electron is not strongly attracted to the nucleus, and its s state is substantially larger than the states of the filled shell of electrons in the atom of the noble gas in the row before. It's really a little bit like having that electron in a higher-n (less negative energy) state of hydrogen—one electron around a core that has (as seen by the outer electron) a screened net approximately single positive charge, as it would appear in an atom with $Z = 1$ (hydrogen). Thus atoms of each successive element up column/ Group IA is larger in size and less negative in binding energy. Each of these atoms, followed by atoms successively having one more electron than the atom of its predecessor element, starts the progression across a row again toward smaller-size, completely filled, compact shells, and finally the leap to a still larger, less tightly bound s state for the atom of the element listed first in the following row.

The largest atom shown in Table D.1 is the cesium atom—symbol Cs, atomic number $Z = 55$, at the top-left of the table. It has a diameter of nearly one-half of one-millionth of a millimeter. That is, $2 \times$ (Cs radius of 2.35 units) $\times$ (one unit = 0.1 $\times$ one-millionth of a millimeter) = 0.470 millionths of a millimeter. And, since one millimeter is about the thickness of a dime, and atoms of higher atomic number don't get to be much larger, we can say that the spatial extent of most atoms is less than half of one-millionth of the thickness of a dime.

Note that the radius of the cesium atom, atomic number 55 with just two more electrons than the iodine atom, is nearly 1.6 times the radius of the iodine atom. This illustrates the huge jump in size that takes place as electrons are added beyond a completely filled (or nearly completely filled) shell into the next, much-larger-in-size, s state. And the radius of the iodine atom with its 53 electrons is only 3.6 times the radius of the one-electron hydrogen atom, illustrating the degree to which the filled

inner shells and nearly filled outer shell of states in the iodine atom are drawn down to a relatively small size.

Note also the relatively large drop in the sizes of the atoms of the elements in Column IIA as compared to the sizes of the atoms of elements in their same row in Column IA. This can be explained by the unusually large decrease in the outer occupied state energies (reflecting the correspondingly tighter binding of the outer electrons) that results from the just filling of the s-state subshells in the atoms of the elements in Column IIA. (Refer to the corresponding s-block subshell of states shown in Table III, which shows only the atomic number, Z, identifying each element. (Those atoms with just completed subshells feel a bit of the kind of tight binding that comes with having electrons that just complete the population of a full shell.)

VALENCE-SUBSHELL IONS

Remember that an *ion* is created when an atom either is stripped of one or more of its electrons, or acquires one or more extra electrons. (Ions may also consist of combined atoms that collectively are either stripped of or acquire electrons, as for example the hydroxide ion which is created when water, H_2O, is dissociated into a hydroxide ion, OH^-, and a hydrogen ion, H^+, stripping an electron from H as it is acquired by OH.) And remember that the number of electrons that an atom of an element tends to gain or lose is called its *valence*. When electrons are stripped away, (+) valence *cations* are produced, because there are more protons than electrons and a net positive charge. When electrons are acquired, (−) valence *anions* are produced, because there are then more electrons than protons and a net negative charge. The valences of the ions explain much of the way that atoms of the elements toward the upper left and lower right of Table D.1 (and our two periodic tables) tend to combine to form compounds; plus-valence atoms (of elements to the upper left) tend to lose electrons in combination with minus-valence atoms (of elements to the lower right) that tend to acquire them.

(+) valence-subshell ions are produced when the outermost elec-

trons of an atom are all stripped away, leaving only the completely filled 1s state valence subshell in Row 2 or a completely filled p state valence subshell in subsequent rows, with any inner subshells also entirely filled. (–) valence-subshell ions are produced when enough extra outer electrons are acquired by an atom to form the next completely filled valence subshell of states.

Dashed circles within the spheres in Table D.1 show the relative measured sizes of the valence-subshell cations that are produced when one, two, or three electrons are *removed* from atoms, respectively symbolized by the superscript (+), (2+), or (3+). Note for example, lithium, Li, and its valence-subshell cation, Li^+, shown respectively by the sphere and the dashed circle in the second row on the far left in Column IA after hydrogen. (Note also that there is no dashed circle for the hydrogen ion. When the hydrogen atom loses its one electron, all that is left is the lone proton, ten thousand times smaller than the sphere shown for the hydrogen atom and not visible at the scale shown in Table D.1.) Dashed circles surrounding the spheres show the relative sizes of the valence-subshell anions that are created when one, two, or three extra electrons are *acquired* by atoms, situations respectively symbolized by the superscript (–), (2–), or (3–). Note, for example, nitrogen, N, and its valence-subshell anion, N^{3-}, shown as N/N^{3-} in the second row of Column VA.

ELEMENTS OF THE TRANSITION METAL B-TYPE GROUPS AND THEIR PROPERTIES

We next consider the properties of the "B" group transition metal elements, the fifty-nine B-type elements across the middle and top of the periodic tables IV in Chapter 13 and B.2 in Appendix B, those elements whose atomic numbers mark their place in the d block of Table III in Chapter 13.[4] The properties of ten of these transition metals, those found in the first transition metal series in the middle of the fourth row of Tables III and IV, are shown inset as a block in Table D.1. Note the relatively small variation in both atom size and outer-electron energy across most of the set of ten elements. And yet these elements have different

chemical and physical properties. Atomic size and outer-electron ener-gies serve to explain the gross features of the atoms of the elements and consequently the tables, and the smaller differences in energies should help to explain other less dramatic variations in properties.

The transition metals include some of the most commonly known elements, including some of the first of the elements to be found or iso-lated in their pure elemental form. With reference also to Tables IV and B.2, I note particularly now some of the more familiar of these elements (*in italics below*). For the elements in the first transition metal series of the fourth row, starting with scandium, atomic number Z = 21, followed by titanium, vanadium, chromium, and manganese, we have *iron*, cobalt, *nickel*, *copper*, and *zinc*. And, below the last three of these, in the fifth row (second transition metal series) we have palladium, *silver*, and cadmium; while in the sixth row (third series), we have *platinum*, *gold*, and *mercury*.

What holds metals together as solids, what produces their electrical properties, and what accounts for their magnetic properties, is presented briefly, along with a similarly brief description of some aspects of their practical use and related inventions, in Chapter 16. We'll not go into detail here regarding their chemical properties. To dig deeper, I would recommend that you read a good text, like Fine and Beall, *Chemistry for Engineers and Scientists*, Reference E, or Housecroft and Sharpe, *Inorganic Chemistry*, Reference H.

THE RARE EARTH AND HEAVIER ELEMENTS (NOT SHOWN IN TABLE D.1)

In contrast to the d states, the f states have little influence on an element's properties. And so it is that the filling of the 4f states in the rare earth 4f block of elements, atomic numbers Z = 58 through Z= 71, causes little change in element properties from those displayed by their predecessor lanthanum, atomic number Z = 57. That is why these elements are often referred to as the *lanthanide* (or *lanthanoid*) *series*. Similarly, the filling of the 5f states of the 5f block of elements, atomic numbers Z = 91 through Z = 103, causes little change in element properties from those displayed

by their predecessor actinium, atomic number $Z = 89$. And so these elements are often referred to as the *actinide* (or *actinoid*) *series*. The filling of d states in atoms of the elements following the lanthanide series, starting with atoms of the element hafnium, atomic number $Z = 72$, is once again accompanied by significant differences in properties element to successive element, except, as already noted, in regard to atomic size.

Appendix E

THE PRODUCTION OF X-RAYS

With reference to the discussion in Chapter 14, the extremely low energy levels for the inner-electron states in the atoms of some of the transition metals is demonstrated dramatically in the production of x-rays. Note that the two electrons in the innermost, 1s, shell of an atom of any of the elements (except hydrogen and helium, that is) are located almost entirely inside of the clouds of the rest of the electrons, relatively unscreened from the total charge in the nucleus. An electron in this innermost state is mainly screened only by its fellow 1s electron and thus sees all but a fraction of one of the proton charges of the protons in the nucleus. For the atoms of elements of higher atomic number, this inner electron thus has a negative energy nearly like that of the one-electron ions examined in Chapter 14, roughly in proportion to the number of protons in the nucleus squared (that is, in proportion to the atomic number Z squared). The higher-atomic-number elements thus have very, very highly negative (very low) inner state energies. If one of these inner electrons is knocked into a higher energy state or even out of the atom, another electron may transition into the removed electron's lowest energy state. That requires that this other electron lose energy (to go to the lower, more negative, energy state), and it does so by sending off a very, very high-energy penetrating photon called an *x-ray*. (X-rays have been used, of course, for many applications, including medical diagnostic imaging and the detection of flaws in the welds of metals and alloys.)

X-rays are typically created by bombarding a metal with electrons that have been accelerated to energies of tens of thousands of electron volts, energies high enough to knock an inner electron completely free of its atom. The metal (held at high positive voltage to attract the bombardment of electrons) and the bombarding electron source (typically a heated tungsten filament) are usually enclosed in an evacuated tube.

Once the inner electron is knocked free, the transition described above can take place, in the process radiating an x-ray photon. Of course, the bombardment of a metal involves billions of electrons in billions of atoms, and billions of x-ray photons are emitted.

Two metallic elements commonly used to create x-rays are copper (Z = 29) and tungsten (Z = 74). If one assumes a complete lack of screening (which is not actually the case, but we're approximating here), the energy levels of the inner, $n = 1$, lowest energy states can be *calculated* from Schrödinger's formula just as were the energies of the electrons in ions as described in Section (A) of Chapter 14 and displayed in Figure 14.1. For $n = 1$, in our formula from that chapter,

$$E = (-13.60 \text{ eV}) \times (Z)^2/(n)^2,$$

we get, respectively for copper and tungsten, −11,438 eV and −74,474 eV. The highest *measured* energies of x-rays emitted from these elements (for transitions from the outermost electrons to these inner, $n = 1$, electron levels) suggest inner state energy levels of −8,990 eV and −69,550 eV, which are in relatively good agreement with the theoretical values just calculated, considering the complexity of these atoms and that some screening of each inner electron from charge of nucleus is expected from the other inner electron and the partial penetration of the outer electrons. By their very appearance at specific energies these x-rays confirm once again the validity of quantum mechanics in describing the atom. Classical theory would not predict a specific energy at all.

NOTES

FOREWORD

1. Carl Sagan, "Why We Need to Understand Science," *Skeptical Inquirer* 14, no. 3 (Spring 1990).

PREFACE

1. Rosenblum and Kuttner, Reference X, p. 5.
2. Ibid., preface, p. 5, p. 116.
3. In a letter to Max Born on March 3, 1947, Einstein wrote: "physics should represent reality in time and space, free from spooky action at a distance." This is quoted from Max Born, *The Born–Einstein Letters 1916–1955: Friendship, Politics and Physics in Uncertain Times*, by Manjit Kumar (New York: Macmillan, 2005), p. 155, in Kumar, Reference K, p. 312.

CHAPTER 1: INTRODUCTION TO PARTS ONE AND TWO

1. McEvoy and Zarate, Reference A, p. 3.
2. Scerri, Reference D, p. 229.
3. Gribbin, Reference Z, photo insert, caption for the identical photo shown in *Quantum Fuzz*, Figure 1.1.
4. Kumar, Reference K.
5. Bortz, Reference B, pp. 212–27. A similar listing (also in order by the year in which the award is presented, and also starting from 1901when the first award was given) can be found in *Wikipedia*, s.v. "List of Nobel Laureates in Physics," https://en.wikipedia.org/wiki/List_of_Nobel_laureates_in_Physics (last accessed September 22, 2016).

CHAPTER 2: PLANCK, EINSTEIN, BOHR

1. Andrew Robinson, *The Last Man Who Knew Everything* (New York: Pi, 2006), p. 96.
2. Kumar, Reference K, p. 56.
3. A listing of all Nobel Prize winners in Physics and the rationale for the award, from the first in 1901 through 2000, is provided in Bortz, Reference B, pages 212–27. An updated list may be found in *Wikipedia*, s.v. "List of Nobel Laureates in Physics," https://en.wikipedia.org/wiki/List_of_Nobel_laureates_in_Physics (last accessed September 22, 2016). As mentioned in the preface, all subsequent quotes showing the rationales for the awards are from these sources.
4. Einstein initially did well in his entrance exams in math and physics, but he failed in history and languages. As a result, he was encouraged to finish high school in a small town near Zurich, where he boarded with the family of the school director, had a great time socially, became a gregarious freethinker, and graduated at the head of his class.
5. Kean, Reference R, p. 43.

CHAPTER 3: HEISENBERG, DIRAC, SCHRÖDINGER

1. Bortz, Reference B, p. 55.
2. Kumar, Reference K, p. 150.
3. Moore, Reference M, p. 272.

CHAPTER 5: THE ESSENTIAL FEATURES OF QUANTUM MECHANICS

1. I modify the format and terminology put forward by Chad Orzel in Reference L, p. 59, to recognize that each state may be represented by a wavefunction, and that these wavefunctions for the states may be components of an overall wavefunction.

CHAPTER 6: CLASH OF TITANS

1. Bohr made a distinction between the macroscopic world, for which classical physics would apply, and the submicroscopic world for which quantum theory would apply. But, as you will come to see, ours is a quantum world, micro or macro, and complementarity, a key principle of quantum theory, may apply critically in explaining the nature of even so massive a body as a black hole (see Chapter 9).

2. From Alice Calaprice, *The New Quotable Einstein* (Princeton: Princeton University Press, 2005), p. 89, as quoted by Kumar, Reference K, p. 278.

3. Kumar, Reference K, p. 256.

4. Ibid., p. 271.

5. Ibid., p. 316.

6. Ibid.

7. Ibid., p. 295.

8. Ibid., p. 338.

9. Orzel, Reference L, p. 149.

10. But the researchers did not report their results in percentages, so we must translate. Orzel, Reference L, reports on page 159: "Physicists like to deal with numbers, and for the specific configuration they used, a local hidden variables treatment predicts that their results should boil down to a number between –1 and 0. When they did the experiment, they measured a value of 0.126, with an uncertainty of plus or minus 0.014.'" (*This uncertainty is based on the accuracy of their measuring apparatus, and having nothing to do with Heisenberg's uncertainty principle.) Orzel goes on: "The difference between the maximum LHV value and their measurement is nine times larger than the uncertainty in the measurement, meaning that there's a one in 10^{36} probability of this happening by chance. 10^{36} is a billion billion billion billion, a number so large that it might have made even Carl 'Billions and Billions' Sagan blink." To see how this relates to the percentages of Bell's inequality described earlier, realize that having LHV "boil down to a number between –1 and 0," corresponds to having a scale with 100 percent at –1 and 33 percent at 0. On this scale, the 25 percent minimum probability (for a filter misorientation of 60 degrees) would be exactly +0.125, very close to the +0.126 that they measured and well within the uncertainty of the measurement.

11. Ibid., p. 162.

12. Kumar, Reference K, p. 354.

13. *Wikipedia*, s.v. "Interpretations of Quantum Mechanics," https://en.wikipedia.org/wiki/Interpretations_of_quantum_mechanics (accessed August 9, 2016).

14. *Wikipedia*, s.v. "Many Worlds Interpretation," https://en.wikipedia.org/wiki/Many-worlds_interpretation (accessed August 9, 2016).

15. Kumar, Reference K, p. 358.

16. *Wikipedia*, s.v. "Interpretations of Quantum Mechanics," https://en.wikipedia.org/wiki/Interpretations_of_quantum_mechanics (accessed August 9, 2016).

17. Orzel, Reference L, p. 89.

18. Ibid., p. 101.

19. Greene, Reference C, p. 212; and Greene, Reference AA, p. 224.

CHAPTER 7: WHAT DOES IT ALL MEAN?

1. Galileo Galilei, *Il Saggiatore* (in Italian) (Rome, 1623); Galilei, *The Assayer*, translated by Stillman Drake, in *Discoveries and Opinions of Galileo* (Garden City, NY: Doubleday Anchor Books,1957), pp. 237–38.

2. S. Chandrasekhar, *Newton's Principia for the Common Reader* (Oxford: Clarendon, 1995), p. 43.

3. Moore, Reference M, p. 196.

4. McEvoy, Reference A, p. 3.

5. As a practical matter for large objects, where a grain of sand is very large, this doesn't make a difference—it doesn't matter. Suppose that you watched a batter hit a baseball. The classical physicist or engineer would say: "If you tell me the exact position of the baseball relative to the bat and the trajectory of the incoming ball and the swinging bat and the rotation on the ball and the wind and the resistance of the air, I will calculate the exact velocity and trajectory of the ball after it is hit." (After all, through such calculations we put rockets around the moon.) And they would be right. But in principle, to know the underpinnings of our universe, we need to pay attention. The quantum physicist would say: "No, you *can't know exactly* both the position and velocity of the ball, or its rotation or the movement of the bat in the first place, and so you cannot calculate the exact outgoing trajectory." And the quantum physicist or engineer would be right! Consider the Heisenberg uncertainty principle described in Chapter 8. The spread-out probability clouds for the location of the electron in the states of the hydrogen atom are just one manifestation of this uncertainty and lack of determinism. And the uncertainty principle *does* also apply to large objects: we cannot know with *absolute* certainty both the location and the motion of an object.

6. *The Structure of Scientific Revolutions*, by Thomas S. Kuhn, Reference T.

7. Because the product of the uncertainty in an object's position multiplied by the uncertainty in its momentum (mass times velocity) is always equal to or greater than a constant (Planck's constant, as discussed in Chapter 8), knowing an object's position exactly would mean that you can't accurately know its velocity, or vice versa. But Planck's constant is very small in relation to the size and momentum of large objects, so uncertainties in size and velocity can be pretty small compared to their actual size and velocity. If, hypothetically (referring to the earlier endnote), we were to measure the position of a baseball at any instant of time to within about a thousandth of the thickness of a human hair, then we can calculate that the minimum uncertainty for the velocity of the baseball would be about a trillionth of a trillionth of one mile per hour. Even at many many times this minimum, the uncertainty in the speed of the baseball would be an extremely small percentage of the velocity of a baseball moving at maybe ninety miles per hour. And at a thousandth of the thickness of a human hair, we know the baseball's position to within a very, very small fraction of a percent of its size. So the uncertainties in position and velocity, though they are there, are of no *practical* consequence for the baseball, the batter, or the classical engineer.

CHAPTER 8: APPLICATIONS

1. "Krysta Svore on Quantum Computing," YouTube video, 28:34, originally presented by Microsoft Research Luminaries, posted by Larry Larson on October 28, 2014, https://youtu.be/kK_pbb66ss (October 5, 2016)

2. I remember the objective of the game as determining the identity of physical objects, but he apparently remembers it as identifying a particular word.

3. In December 2007, ASCII was incorporated into a more advanced UTF-8 coding system.

4. Gribbin, Reference Z, p. 34.

5. Steven Rich and Barton Gellman, "NSA Seeks to Build Quantum Computer That Could Crack Most Types of Encryption," *Washington Post*, January 2, 2014.

6. "Krysta Svore on Quantum Computing."

7. The Bell states are the four binary combinations of the qubit states, representing respectively the binary digit combinations: "0, 0," "0, 1," "1, 0," and "1, 1."

8. Gribbin, Reference Z, pp. 168 and 169.

9. Ibid., pp. 159–68.

10. Ibid., p. 180.

11. Ibid., p. 190.

12. Ibid., p. 188.

13. Jeffrey Kluger, "Teleportation Is Real and Here's Why It Matters," *Time*, May 30, 2014.

14. Orzel, Reference L, p. 184.

15. *Wikipedia*, s.v. "Quantum Cryptography," *September 13, 2016* (accessed October 4, 2016).

CHAPTER 9: GALAXIES, BLACK HOLES, GRAVITY WAVES, MATTER, THE FORCES OF NATURE, THE HIGGS BOSON, DARK MATTER, DARK ENERGY, AND STRING THEORY

1. Parker, Reference CC, particularly Chapter 4.

2. Bojowald. Reference FF, p. 19.

3. Toback, Reference U, p. 56.

4. Bojowald, Reference FF.

5. Greene, Reference AA, p. 19.

6. Ibid., p. 11.

7. Ibid., p. 20.

8. Michael S. Turner, "Origin of the Universe," in Reference DD, p. 38.

9. Toback, Reference U, p. 122.

10. Greene, Reference AA, p. 22.

11. Toback, Reference U, p. 206.

12. Greene, Reference AA, p. 23.

13. Ibid., p. 21, p. 22.

14. Coles, Reference GG, p. 57.

15. Ibid., p. 58.

16. Ibid.

17. Ibid.

18. Ibid., p. 57.

19. *Wikipedia*, s.v. "Universe," last modified September 11, 2016, https://en.wikipedia.org/wiki/Universe (accessed October 14, 2016).

20. Toback, Reference U, p. 125.

21. Ibid., p. 170.

22. Calculated as the distance in miles of the 13.2 billion light-years of the light's travel from the oldest stars that we have seen. Light-years given by David Toback in Reference U, p. 170.

23. *Wikipedia*, "Universe."

24. Toback, Reference U, p. 211.

25. Ibid., p. 231.

26. The sizes of objects were mainly taken from Toback in Reference U, Chapters 2 and 3. The time frame in which they appeared is taken from the timeline of Turner's article "Origin of the Universe," in Reference DD, pages 40 and 41.

27. Turner, in Reference DD, p. 40.

28. Ibid.

29. Richard P. Feynman, Robert B. Leighton, Matthew L. Sands, *The Feynman Lectures on Physics*, vol. 1 (Reading, MA: Addison-Wesley, 1963), pp. 52–11.

30. Turner, in Reference DD, p. 40.

31. Ibid.

32. Toback, Reference U, p. 211.

33. Ibid., p. 165.

34. Once again, for a good, readable description of gravity and four-dimensional space-time, I suggest that you read Chapter 4 of Barry Parker's book *Einstein's Brainchild—Relativity Made Relatively Easy* (Reference CC).

35. Toback, Reference U, pp. 170 and 236.

36. Ibid., p. 164.

37. Ibid., p. 188.

38. Ibid., p. 183.

39. John Gribbin, e-mail correspondence with the publisher regarding *Quantum Fuzz*, September 26, 2016.

40. Gribbin, Reference LL, p. 83.

41. In ibid., Gribbin writes:

An atomic nucleus can exist in what is known as its ground state, with minimum energy, or it can absorb certain precise amounts of energy (quantised, like everything else in the subatomic world) which raise it to different energy levels. Once "excited" in this way, it will, sooner or later, get rid of the extra energy, probably in the form of a gamma ray, and fall back to its ground state. The energy levels are like steps on a staircase, with nuclei jumping from one step to another (first up, then down) if suitably excited (like an excited child). Hoyle's insight was that an excited nucleus of carbon-12 could form from the collision of a helium-4 nucleus with a beryllium-8 nucleus, if (and only if) there was a step on the carbon-12 energy staircase corresponding to the combined energy of a beryllium-8 nucleus and the incoming helium-4 nucleus. It would be like tossing a ball from the bottom of a staircase with just the right speed for it to come to rest on a high step without bouncing; then, it could gently roll back down the stairs. This was the 7.65 MeV resonance that Hoyle predicted. If the resonance existed, the beryllium-helium interaction could manufacture carbon nuclei in the excited state, which could then radiate the excess energy away and settle into the ground state. But if the resonance did not exist, there would be no carbon, and since we are a carbon-based life form, we would not be here.

42. Toback, Reference U, p. 164.

43. Ibid., p. 187.

44. Ibid., p. 188.

45. Ibid., p. 160.

46. Ibid., p. 176.

47. Ibid., p. 189.

48. Parker, Reference CC, pp. 104 and 141.

49. Bortz, Reference B, p. 84.

50. Susskind, Reference BB, p. 118.

51. Hawking, Reference W, p. 87.

52. Toback, Reference U, p. 196.

53. Ibid., p. 4.

54. Ibid., p. 4.

55. Emily Conover, "Gravitational Waves Caught in the Act," APS News 25, no. 3, March 2016, p. 4. https://www.aps.org/publications/apsnews/201603/waves.cfm (accessed October 14, 2016).

56. Ibid.

57. Hawking, Reference W, p. 105.

58. Ibid., p. 106.

59. Ibid., p. 10.

60. "The Swift Gamma-Ray Burst Mission," NASA, July 6, 2016, http://swift.gsfc. nasa.gov/ (accessed October 14, 2016).

61. Susskind, Reference BB, p. 21.

62. I say that this was a "quiet" bombshell because, according to Susskind, it was only Hawking, Susskind, and Gerard 't Hooft who realized the significance of what Hawking was saying. ('t Hooft would in 1999 share the Nobel Prize in Physics with his thesis advisor Martinus J. G. Veltman *"for elucidating the quantum structure of the electroweak interactions."* Those are to be described briefly later in this chapter.)

63. Susskind, Reference BB, p. 91.

64. *Wikipedia*, s.v. "Holographic Principle," last modified October 8, 2016, https://en.wikipedia.org/wiki/Holographic_principle (accessed October 14, 2016). This entry reads as follows: "The holographic principle is a property of string theories and a supposed property of quantum gravity that states that the description of a volume of space can be thought of as encoded on a boundary to the region—preferably a light-like boundary like a gravitational horizon. First proposed by Gerard 't Hooft, it was given precise string-theory interpretation by Leonard Susskind. . . ."

65. BEC Crew, "Stephen Hawking Just Published a New Solution to the Black Hole Information Paradox: How Black Holes Can Erase Information, But Also Retain It," *Science Alert*, January 11, 2016, http://www.sciencealert.com/stephen-hawking-just-published-new-solution-to-the-black-hole-information-paradox (accessed October 14, 2016). Dennis Overbye, "No Escape from Black Holes? Stephen Hawking Points to a Possible Exit," *New York Times*, June 6, 2016, http://www.nytimes.com/2016/06/07/science/stephen-hawking-black-holes.html?_r=0 (accessed October 17, 2016).

66. Coles, Reference GG, p. 59.

67. Ibid., p. 60.

68. Ibid., p. 62.

69. Toback, Reference U, p. 156.

70. Ibid., p. 136, n. 2.

71. Ibid., p. 206.

72. Ibid., p. 211.

73. Turner, in Reference DD, p. 40.

74. Barnett et al., Reference HH, p. 214.

75. Toback, Reference U, p. 59.

76. Ibid., p. 61.

77. *Wikipedia*, s.v. "Gravitational Lens," last modified October 12, 2016, https://en.wikipedia.org/wiki/Gravitational_lens (accessed October 14, 2016).

78. Ibid.

79. Toback, Reference U, p. 168.

80. Ibid., p. 225.

81. Ibid., p. 210.

82. Ibid., p. 211.

83. *Wikipedia*, s.v. "Supernova Cosmology Project," last modified July 25, 2016, https://en.wikipedia.org/wiki/Supernova_Cosmology_Project (accessed October 14, 2016).

84. Turner, in Reference DD, p. 40.

85. Fred Bortz provides a very nice short summary of the development of these machines and the sequence of discovery achieved with them in his book for young readers (which I find to be a quick, informative read well suited to adults) *Understanding the Large Hadron Collider*, which is part of his series Exploring the Subatomic World (Reference EE).

86. Barnett et al., Reference HH, p. 134.

87. Ibid., p. 124.

88. Bortz, Reference EE, p. 53, mentions these planned circular colliders and the International Linear Collider to be constructed in Japan and presently in design.

89. Except where noted otherwise, this data is taken from *Wikipedia*, s.v. "Colliders," last modified October 1, 2016, https://en.wikipedia.org/wiki/Collider (accessed October 14, 2016).

90. Bortz, Reference EE, p. 53. This collider is described as a Chinese "Higgs factory."

91. Ibid. The "Very" Large Hadron Collider is just in the early stages of discussion.

92. *Wikipedia*, s.v. "Large Hadron Collider," last modified October 12, 2016, https://en.wikipedia.org/wiki/Large_Hadron_Collider (accessed October 14, 2016).

93. Barnett et al., Reference HH, p. 226.

94. Ibid.

95. Michael Riordan, Guido Tonelli, and Sau Lan Wu, "The Higgs at Last," in Reference DD, p. 4.

96. Barnett et al., Reference HH, p. 215.

97. Ibid., p. 212.

98. Many particles of the Standard Model, including quarks, neutrinos, and the Higgs boson, are separately described in a very interesting, readable, and well-illustrated series of books for young people: *Exploring the Subatomic World*, by Fred Bortz (Reference EE).

99. Bose was known for early work in the 1920s on quantum mechanics. He suggested a "Bose-Einstein condensate" that we now know explains superconductivity, as described in Chapter 19.

100. *Wikipedia*, s.v. "Elementary Particle," last modified October 11, 2016, https://en.wikipedia.org/wiki/Elementary_particle (accessed October 12, 2016).

101. Lincoln, "The Inner Life of Quarks," in Reference DD, p. 15.

102. Ibid., p. 15.

103. Bortz, Reference B, p. 62.

104. Ibid., p. 143.

105. Ibid., p. 62.

106. Ibid., p. 72.

107. Martin Hirsch, Heinrich Päs, and Werner Porod, "Ghostly Beacons of New Physics," in Reference DD, p. 25.

108. Bortz, Reference B, p. 147.

109. Barnett, et al., Reference HH, p. 212.

110. Bortz, Reference B, p. 145.

111. Barnett et al., Reference HH, p. 212.

112. Ibid.

113. Bortz, Reference B, p. 92–95.

114. Feynman gave a series of lectures to the general public in which he described this method and some of these diagrams. These lectures have been simplified and re-presented in his book *QED—The Strange Theory of Light and Matter* (Reference Q).

115. Bortz, Reference B, p. 148.

116. Ibid.

117. K. C. Cole, "The Strange Second Life of String Theory," *Quanta Magazine*, September 15, 2016, https://www.quantamagazine.org/20160915-string-theorys-strange -second-life/ (accessed October 17, 2016).

CHAPTER 10: INTRODUCTION TO PART FOUR

1. I mean "simple" in the sense that one central concept of the atom explains everything around us.

2. According to *Wikipedia*, s.v. "Eric Scerri," last modified September 27, 2016 (accessed October 15, 2016), Scerri is a lecturer at the University of California, Los Angeles, the founder and editor in chief of *Foundations of Chemistry* (an international peer -reviewed journal), and a world authority on the history and philosophy of the periodic table. In his book *The Periodic Table*, Reference D, p. 247, Scerri writes: "The aim of this chapter has not been to decide whether or not the periodic system is explained by quantum mechanics *tout court*, since the situation is more subtle," essentially defining "reduction" in this context with his words "the periodic system is explained by quantum mechanics *tout court*." He goes on to say, "It is more a question of the extent of reduction or extent of explanation that has been provided by quantum mechanics. Whereas most chemists and educators seem to believe that the reduction is complete, perhaps there is some benefit in pursuing the question of how much is strictly explained from the theory. After all, it is hardly surprising that quantum mechanics cannot yet fully deduce the details of the periodic table, which gathers together a host of empirical data from a level far removed from the microscopic world of quantum mechanics."

3. Wikipedia, "Chemical Element", last modified October 13, 2016, accessed October 15,2016.

4. Reference D, starting on pp. 183, and p. 205.

CHAPTER 11: ENERGY, MOMENTUM, AND THE SPATIAL STATES
OF THE ELECTRON IN THE HYDROGEN ATOM

1. Actually, it is the *square* of the angular momentum, the angular momentum times itself, that is quantized, and this produces the quantum numbers l that we discuss here. The square of the angular momentum $= l\,(l+1)\,(h/2\pi)^2$. There it is: Planck's constant again!

2. The z component of angular moment is $mh/2\pi$, and "m" is confined to the range $-l$ to $+l$ because the vector for m is only that part of the vector for l that lies in the direction of a magnetic field. Since it is only part of the vector for l, m must always be equal to or smaller in magnitude than l. This range for m also results directly from the solutions to Schrödinger's equation: there simply are no solutions which have m outside of this range.

CHAPTER 12: SPIN AND MAGNETISM

1. This is described in Leighton, Reference F, p. 668, as "one of the greatest successes of theoretical physics."

2. In the same work, Dirac also predicted the existence of the *positron*, which is like the electron but with positive rather than negative charge. The positron was subsequently discovered. It was the first manifestation of what has come to be called "antimatter," so called because an electron contacted by a positron would annihilate both of them with the release of great energy. Richard Feynman jokingly carried the idea of antimatter to an extreme, as described in the subsection on antimatter in Chapter 9.

3. And there it is again: Planck's constant; independently the result of the Dirac's calculations!

4. For a more complete description of spin and magnetic moments, see Leighton, Reference F, p. 185.

CHAPTER 13: EXCLUSION AND THE PERIODIC TABLE

1. Leighton, Reference F, Figure 7-5, p. 251.

2. This is further explained in Chapter 14. *To the left* because the fewer the number of electrons beyond a completed p block subshell, the less tightly each electron is held and the more easily it is lost in reaction. *Farther up* because, for each atom, exclusion prevents the electrons from occupying the more tightly binding lower energy states, and because the outer, higher energy states (those available particularly to electrons in the heavier atoms farther up the column) are not very tightly binding. That is because the

outermost electrons in these left-side atoms are largely screened (by completely filled inner shells of electrons) from the attraction of the protons in the nucleus. The converse applies to the atoms of those elements to the right in the table, whose atoms become more acquisitive in trying to completely fill an energy shell the closer the shell is to being filled, that is for elements further *to the right*. In this case, the outermost electrons in the lighter atoms have available to them lower and more tightly binding energy states that are closer to the nucleus, and so the atoms are more acquisitive and more reactive for elements located *farther down* in these right-side columns of the table. These arguments do not apply to the atoms of the inert elements in the rightmost column of the table.

CHAPTER 15: A FEW TYPES OF CHEMICAL BONDS, FOR EXAMPLE

1. The importance of quantum mechanics in providing an understanding of the electronic structure for chemistry is underscored in some modern general chemistry texts, such as Reference H. This text begins its first chapter with a description of Schrödinger's equation and its solutions for the hydrogen atom, which are further utilized to understand the electron structure of the rest of the elements and the formation of molecules.

2. The electronic structure of the isolated carbon atom consists of two occupied spatial 1s states (one with an electron having plus spin and one with an electron having minus spin), two occupied spatial 2s states, and two different half occupied spatial 2p states. But the energies of the 2s and 2p states are so close to each other that these states will sometimes combine, that is, *hybridize*, to lower overall energies in bonding with other atoms. When they do this, they form the same total number of total states, but some of the spatial states are differently shaped and oriented at different angles than were the spatial states from which they were formed.

3. Pauling, Reference P, p. 111.

4. Private communication with L. Howard Holley, with reference to Martin Chaplin, "Water Structure and Science," *London South Bank University*, June 22, 2016, http://www1.lsbu.ac.uk/water/ (accessed October 16, 2016).

5. This hybridization is somewhat similar to that which occurs in the carbon atom, as described above.

CHAPTER 17: INSULATORS AND ELECTRICAL CONDUCTION IN NORMAL METALS AND SEMICONDUCTORS

1. Kittel, Reference V, p. 159. The resistance in a wire or circuit is measured in ohms, which is defined as the volts applied to a wire or circuit divided by the current,

as measured in amperes, that flows as a result. The intrinsic resistance to the flow of electrical current in a metal, insulator, or semiconductor is usually measured in ohm-cm, which when multiplied by the length of the material and divided by the area of its cross section provides a measure of the resistance of an actual piece of material.

2. Schrödinger's solution for free electrons is well presented in Chapter 6 of Kittel, Reference V.

3. The number of states occupied up to the Fermi level is directly proportional to the number of atoms in the metallic specimen being considered, literally billions even for a small sample. The bigger the specimen, the smaller the energy difference between the successive energy levels, and the more states available up to any energy level. But at the same time, the number of atoms and electrons is increased, so that the states are occupied by additional electrons to the same Fermi level. Thus the same Fermi level and related physical properties are produced, independent of the size of the metallic specimen.

4. Chapter 7 of Kittel, Reference V.

5. See Ibid., p. 128.

CHAPTER 18: NANOTECHNOLOGY AND INTRODUCTION TO PART FIVE

1. In Rosenblum, Reference X, p. 116.

2. Katherine Bourzac, "Nano-Architecture," *MIT Technology Review* 118, no. 2 (March/April): 35.

3. Julie Shapiro, "Breakthrough: 'A Metal That's (Almost) Lighter Than Air,'" *Time*, November 2, 2015, p. 25.

CHAPTER 19: SUPERCONDUCTORS I

1. This was John Bardeen's second Nobel Prize. His first is noted in Chapter 23. An avid golfer, he was said to have remarked, as noted in Bortz, Reference B, p. 130: "Well, perhaps two Nobels are worth more than one hole in one." You may wish to browse further through this excellent history for additional short biographies of many of the physicists mentioned in *Quantum Fuzz*.

2. "High-temperature" is a relative term. More recently developed "high-temperature" superconductors operate superconducting to temperatures as high as 138 degrees Kelvin, high enough to be cooled in liquid nitrogen, which boils at 77 Kelvin, and much higher than those of the superconductors presently used in MRI magnet systems. But as discussed in part in Chapter 24, the issue is whether they can be produced in

practical forms, and at what cost. (*Wikipedia*, s.v. "High-Temperature Superconductivity," last modified October 20, 2016, https://en.wikipedia.org/wiki/High-temperature _superconductivity (accessed October 22, 2016).

 3. Another interesting and somewhat-similar quantum phenomenon, but one of no practical importance at least for now, is superfluidity. Liquid helium, at temperatures just 4 Fahrenheit degrees [2 Celsius degrees] above the absolute zero, transitions into a state that exhibits a loss of viscosity and a much increased ability to conduct heat, in analogy with the ability of superconductors to conduct electricity without resistance. This so-called *superfluid* helium is marked by a strange quiescence. It boils without producing any bubbles, and it will climb over the walls of its container to reach lower levels, providing only that all surfaces are maintained at sufficiently low temperatures.

 4. *"Go Ahead for Japanese Maglev,"* Maglev, May 16, 2011, http://www.maglev.net/ news/go-ahead-for-japanese-maglev (accessed October 24, 2016).

 5. Rosenblum and Kuttner, Reference X, p. 126.

 6. MRI was originally called "Nuclear Magnetic Resonance (NMR)" because it is the resonance of radio waves of just the right frequency (radio-wave photon energy) that (when transmitted through the body) produces transitions of spins in the nuclei of atoms (e.g., phosphorous atoms) in the body to higher-energy spin states. (Because some patients associated the word "nuclear" with radioactivity, the manufacturers choose to call the devices "MRI machines.") When these spins then transition back down to lower-energy spin states, they emit radio waves whose frequencies contain information on the type and health of the tissues from which they are emitted. Since the central frequency of these waves depends on the magnetic field that the body is in, by setting the main superconducting background field and then varying it in x, y, and z directions using smaller magnets, the location of these transmitted bits of information can be "tagged" (by small frequency shifts) as to their x, y, and z locations. When this information is assembled using computers, it can be used to provide images showing the location of various tissues and their state of health. The pulsing of these x, y, and z magnets on and off causes sudden forces when they are attracted to the high magnetic field of the superconducting magnet, and one hears the sudden mechanical impacts of these forces as loud staccato bursts or clicks, a more spaced-out series of clicks, or a short, coarse, rumble.

 7. A sense of the magnitude of magnetic fields will be provided in Chapter 21.

 8. This is not one of the louder types of sounds of the sort described above, which come from the magnets of the machine itself.

 9. SQUIDs use the quantum condition that the flux⁺ of a magnetic field within a superconducting ring is quantized. (⁺Flux is the magnetic field strength times the area that the field passes through.) As each quantum of magnetic flux enters the ring, the ring produces an electrical voltage signal, so that the number of these quanta or even fractions of these quanta can be counted as a measure of the strength of the field. One can detect about two-millionths of a billionth of one tesla ($2 \times 10-15$ T). For comparison, as noted before, a common approximate field used in MRI magnets and the maximum

field achieved with ferromagnetic materials in motors and generators is about 2T, common refrigerator magnets produce about 0.2 T, and the earth's magnetic field is about 5 hundred-thousandths of a tesla ($5 \times 10{-}5$ T).

10. Stefania Della Penna, Vittorio Pizzella, and Gian Luca Romani, "Impact of Superconducting Devices on Imaging in Neuroscience," *Superconductivity News Forum Global Edition* (October 29, 2013), http://snf.ieeecsc.org/abstracts/cr36-impact-superconducting-devices-imaging-neuroscience (accessed September 15, 2016); and S. Della Penna, V. Pizzella, and G. L. Romani, "Impact of Superconducting Devices on Imaging in Neuroscience" (presentation of pre-published plenary paper CR36), *Superconductivity News Forum Global Edition* (January 17, 2014), http://snf.ieeecsc.org/abstracts/crp39-impact-superconducting-devices-imaging-neuroscience-0 (accessed September 15, 2016).

11. Leyna P. De Haro et al.," Magnetic Relaxometry as Applied to Sensitive Cancer Detection and Localization," *Superconductivity News Forum Global Edition* (July 2016), http://snf.ieeecsc.org/abstracts/st518-magnetic-relaxometry-applied-sensitive-cancer-detection-and-localization (accessed October 24, 2016).

12. Carl H. Rosner, Chairman and CEO of Cardiomag, private discussion with the author, September 16. 2016.

13. *IEEE/CSC & ESAS European Superconductivity News Forum*, no. 3 (January 2008).

14. Intelligence Advanced Research Projects Agency, "IARPA Launches Program to Develop a Superconducting Computer," IARPA press release, December 3, 2014, through *Superconductivity News Forum Global Edition*, http://snf.ieeecsc.org/sites/ieeecsc.org/files/HE93_The%20C3%20IARPA%20Program_finally%20announcedfinal%20link.pdf (accessed October 24, 2016).

15. Oleg A. Mukhanov, "Recent Progress in Digital Superconducting Electronics," *Superconductivity News Forum Global Edition* (July 2015), http://snf.ieeecsc.org/abstracts/crp54-recent-progress-digital-superconducting-electronics (accessed October 24, 2016).

CHAPTER 20: FUSION FOR ELECTRICAL POWER, AND LASERS ALSO FOR DEFENSE

1. Reported by Marin Lamonica in the magazine of the Institute for Electrical and Electronic Engineers, *IEEE Spectrum* (North America), April 2015, p. 12, and by Kevin Bulis, *MIT Technology Review* 118, no. 3 (May/June 2015): 13.

2. Lev Grossman, "A Star Is Born," *Time*, November 2, 2015, p. 30.

3. David Kramer, "ITER Cost and Schedule Still Not Pinned Down," *Physics Today*, January 2016, p. 30.

4. Thomas Rummel, Beate Kemnitz, Thomas Klinger, and Isabella Milch, "First Plasma in the Superconducting Fusion Device Wendelstein 7-X," *Superconductivity*

News Forum Global Edition (January 2016), http://snf.ieeecsc.org/sites/ieeecsc.org/files/documents/snf/abstracts/HP104_RummelTh_First%20plasma%20in%20W7-X_012016.pdf, and references therein (accessed October 24, 2016).

5. Grossman, "Star Is Born."

6. Ibid.

7. Rachel Courtland, "Laser Fusion's Brightest Hope: The National Ignition Facility Houses the World's Most Powerful Laser. Is It Enough to Ignite a Fusion Revolution?" *IEEE Spectrum*, March 27, 2013, http://spectrum.ieee.org/energy/nuclear/laser-fusions-brightest-hope (accessed October 24, 2016).

8. This is about one thousand times as much power as the United States consumes, on average, at any moment. But, again, remember that power is the rate of delivery of energy, and the energy of these lasers is delivered in just four-billionths of a second. Were their energies delivered much more slowly, say, in one second, the power would still be substantial—about two megawatts—enough, if delivered at this rate continuously, to light a couple of thousand average homes.

9. *Wikipedia*, s.v. "National Ignition Facility," last modified September 14, 2016, https://en.wikipedia.org/wiki/National_Ignition_Facility (accessed November 4, 2016).

CHAPTER 21: MAGNETISM, MAGNETS, MAGNETIC MATERIALS, AND THEIR APPLICATIONS

1. Diamagnetic substances are repelled from a place of high field to places of lower field, and the strength of the repulsion depends on how much the field changes with change in distance, what is called the field "gradient."

2. The tesla is a Standard International, SI, mks (meter kilogram second), unit of what is called "magnetic induction," what is commonly referred to as "magnetic field." One tesla is equivalent to 10,000 gauss, where the gauss is a cgs (centimeter, gram, second) unit of this field.

3. *Wikipedia*, s.v. "Francis Bitter," last modified July 14, 2016, https://en.wikipedia.org/wiki/Francis_Bitter (accessed October 21, 2016).

4. Solenoids are typically wound as contiguous turns of wire around a structural tube, with additional layers similarly wound back and forth over the first layer.

CHAPTER 22: GRAPHENE, NANOTUBES, AND ONE "DREAM" APPLICATION

1. *Wikipedia*, s.v. "Graphene," last modified October 15, 2016, https://en.wikipedia.org/wiki/Graphene (accessed October 21, 2016).

2. Ibid.

3. Ibid.

4. Warner et al., Reference JJ.

5. Andre K. Geim, "*Atomic Scale Legos*," *Scientific American* 311 (November 18, 2014): 50–51.

6. "Introducing the Micro-Super-Capacitor: Laser Etched Graphene Brings Moore's Law to Energy Storage," *IEEE Spectrum*, October 2015, pp. 41–45.

7. Katherine Bourzac, "*Bend by Design*," *Scientific American* 311 (November 18, 2014): 19.

8. John Pavlus, "*The Search for a New Machine*," *Scientific American* 312 (April 14, 2015): 58–63.

9. *Wikipedia*, s.v. "Graphite," last modified October 21, 2016, https://en.wikipedia.org/wiki/*Graphite (accessed October 21, 2016)*.

10. *Wikipedia*, s.v. "Fullerene," *Wikipedia*, last modified October 21, 2016, https://en.wikipedia.org/wiki/*Fullerene (accessed October 21, 2016)*.

11. *Wikipedia*, s.v. "*Carbon Nanotube*," last modified October 19, 2016, https://en.wikipedia.org/wiki/Carbon_nanotube *(accessed October 21, 2016)*.

12. Ibid.

13. Ibid.

14. Ibid.

15. "Konstantin E. Tsiolkovsky," Aeronautics Learning Laboratory for Science Technology, and Research (ALLSTAR) Network, March 12, 2004 (retrieved June 10, 2015).

16. Bob Hirschfeld, "Space Elevator Gets Lift," *TechTV*, G4 Media, January 31, 2002, https://web.archive.org/web/20050608080057/http:/www.g4tv.com/techtvvault/features/35657/Space_Elevator_Gets_Lift.html (archived from the original on June 8, 2005; retrieved September 13, 2007): "The concept was first described in 1895 by Russian author K. E. Tsiolkovsky in his 'Speculations about Earth and Sky and on Vesta.'"

17. *Wikipedia*, s.v. "Space Elevator," last modified October 11, 2016, https://en.wikipedia.org/wiki/Space_elevator (accessed October 21, 2016).

18. *Wikipedia*, s.v. "Carbon-Fiber-Reinforced Polymer," *Wikipedia*, June 23, 2016, https://en.wikipedia.org/wiki/*Carbon-fiber-reinforced_ polymer last modified October 20, 2016(accessed October 21, 2016)*.

19. *Wikipedia*, s.v. "*Boeing 787 Dreamliner*," last modified October 20, 2016, https://en.wikipedia.org/wiki/Boeing_787_Dreamliner *(accessed October 21, 2016)*.

20. Boeing used a new design of lithium-ion battery in its planes, with the result that it overheated and threatened to cause fires. The plane was grounded for a time. Boeing redesigned the battery and overcame the problem. The lithium-ion battery is an excellent example of innovation in chemistry and materials science. It effectively uses that element with the highest per unit weight concentration of electrons outside of a filled valence shell to make a light and powerful accessory for electrical and electronic devices, including electric and hybrid electric vehicles, and now the Dreamliner.

21. Originally available at the IMAX's of the National Air and Space Museum in Washington, DC, and the Henry Ford Museum in the Detroit area (among others); this movie is now available on 3-D Blu-ray and DVD. A trailer for the movie can be viewed on the internet at *http://www.youtube.com/watch?v=dpoxMVwIEM4*.

22. *Wikipedia,* "Boeing 787 Dreamliner." *Wikipedia,* s.v. "Airbus A350 XWB," last modified October 21, 2016, https://en.wikipedia.org/wiki/Airbus_A350_XWB (accessed October 21, 2016).

CHAPTER 23: SEMICONDUCTORS AND
ELECTRONIC APPLICATIONS

1. There are many different types of transistors, and they operate using various physical mechanisms. I have described just one type, but they all have this characteristic of having the input to one terminal control the flow of current through the other terminals.

2. Reference X, p. 119.

3. Charles Q. Choi, "Nitrogen Supercharges Super-Capacitors," *IEEE Spectrum* (North America), February 2016, p. 14.

4. Ibid., p. 9.

5. Ibid., p. 12.

6. "Survival in the Battery Business," *MIT Technology Review* 118, no. 4, July/August 2015, p. 35.

7. "SolarCity's ($750 million) Gigafactory," *MIT Technology Review* 119, no. 2, March 2016, p. 54.

8. IEEE Spectrum (North America), September 2016, p. 9.

CHAPTER 24: SUPERCONDUCTORS II

1. Liquid nitrogen is available as a by-product of the commercial separation of oxygen from the air by liquefaction. It costs about as much as tomato juice. The boiling point of liquid nitrogen is 77 Kelvin, fully a quarter of the way from absolute zero toward normal room temperatures at around 300 Kelvin.

2. René L. Flukiger, "Advances in MgB2 Conductors," Superconductivity News Forum Global Edition, October 2014, http://snf.ieeecsc.org/abstracts/crp46-advances-mgb2-conductors-annotated-plenary-slide-presentation (accessed October 24, 2016), on MgB2 wires and the short review of applications therein.

3. Measuring in megavolt-amperes (MVA) is a way of taking into account both resistive and reactive components in the flow of power. Resistive power is like that used

to operate incandescent light bulbs or toasters in our homes. Note that one MVA is one megawatt only for resistive power. Reactive power usually involves energy transferred in and out of electric or magnetic fields, and the latter occurs particularly in motors and transformers. One MVA is the time-averaged approximate power needed for about one thousand average American homes.

4. A 10 MVA generator was subsequently built and tested at GE, and other generators have been built and tested variously around the world, most notably in Japan where 70 MVA and then 200 MVA generators were constructed and tested in the 1980s. These machines are of a commercial size for efficient power generation and begin to approach the size of the largest generators in commercial operation, typically on the order of 1000 MVA. But the power industry has yet to install one of these machines for commercial use. For context refer to the section "A Comment on Energy Resources and Global Warming," which follows this chapter.

5. Mark Stemmle, Frank Schmidt, Frank Merschel, and Matthias Noe, "Ampacity Project—Update on World's First Superconducting Cable and Fault Current Limiter Installation in a German City Center," *Superconductivity News Forum Global Edition*, October 2015, http://snf.ieeecsc.org/abstracts/stp475-ampacity-project-%E2%80%93-update-world%E2%80%99s-first-superconducting-cable-and-fault-current (accessed October 24, 2016).

6. For example, faults caused by tree branches (or unlucky squirrels) that short across power lines (making an electrical connection phase-to-phase or phase-to-ground). These faults often cause lights to blink or go out until the fault is cleared.

7. Electrical power is the rate at which electrical energy is generated, transmitted, or utilized. At any instant it is just the phase-to-phase (or, in the home, phase-to-neutral) voltage times the phase-to-phase (or phase-to-neutral) current flow. Because power lines would need to be unreasonably thick and heavy to carry the currents required by tens of thousands of homes at the 110-volt home level, transformers are used to first step up the voltages (from generators) to very high levels (hundreds of thousands of volts) so that only small currents and small-diameter, lightweight lines are needed to carry the same power, tower to tower, across the country. Then large very high voltage transformers, and subsequently, many medium-power transformers are used to step the voltage back down at substations for the distribution to neighborhoods. And then there are many more even smaller, and then smaller yet pole-mounted, transformers to successively step down the voltage to the level that we use in our homes.

8. As for preceding ASC conferences, those papers presented are reviewed and published in the *IEEE Transactions on Applied Superconductivity*. For example, those for the 2012 conference, which was held in Portland, Oregon, are in vol. 23, no. 3 of these transactions.

APPENDIX A

1. The distance from positive crest to the next positive crest is the same for both the E field and **B** field sine waves shown in Figure A.1(c), and this distance is defined as the wavelength, w, of the electromagnetic wave. In the classical view of the electromagnetic wave, the crest value (the amplitude) can have any value down to zero, and the energy of the wave can correspondingly have any value down to zero. But, actually, electromagnetic energy comes in indivisible chunks called *quanta*. And the energy of each quantum is related to the wavelength of the wave (or its equivalent frequency).

APPENDIX B

1. We now know that the forming of elements from one or more others can happen by nuclear fission or fusion, not by chemical processes. (This is discussed in Chapter 20.)

2. In this book I will often be referring to material written by Eric R. Scerri. Professor Scerri teaches chemistry as well as history and philosophy of science at UCLA. He is the editor in chief of the journal *Foundations of Chemistry*. Here I cite from his book *The Periodic Table* (Reference D, p. 45).

3. Ibid., p. 112.

4. The table in Scerri, Reference D, p. 112, has already been redrawn. It's not clear whether the Roman numerals are from Mendeleev or Scerri.

5. Ibid., starting at the bottom of page 112.

6. Kean, Reference R, p. 49.

7. Ibid., p. 50.

8. Scerri, Reference D, p. 101.

9. Ibid., p. xiii.

APPENDIX C

1. Reference Z, p. 159–68.

2. Ibid., p. 161.

3. Philip Schindler et al., "*A Quantum Information Processor with Trapped Ions*," *New Journal of Physics*15 (August 14, 2013): 123012, http://arxiv.org/abs/1308.3096 (accessed October 24, 2016).

4. Nuclear magnetic resonance is the key physical process utilized in the medical diagnostic tool MRI (magnetic resonance imaging). "Nuclear" was considered to be too frightful a word for the naming of this device, the construction and operation of which is described in Chapter 19.

5. Lieven M. K. Vandersypen et al., "*Experimental Realization of Shor's Quantum*

Factoring Algorithm Using Nuclear Magnetic Resonance," *Nature* 414, no. 6866 (December 20–27, 2001): 883–87.

6. Nanyang Xu et al., "*Quantum Factorization of 143 on a Dipolar-Coupling NMR System,*" *Cornell University Library*, arXiv:1111.3726 (November 16, 2011).

7. Referring to dimensions on the order of one nanometer = 10^{-9} meters = one millionth of the thickness of a dime, on the scale of the sizes of atoms.

8. Michelle Simmons, "Quantum Computing in Silicon and the Limits of Silicon Miniaturization—Michelle Simmons," YouTube video, 43:27, from part of discussion meeting on advances in graphene, Majorana fermions, and quantum computation, presented at the International Centre for Theoretical Sciences at the Tat Institute of Fundamental Research, posted by International Centre for Theoretical Sciences, May 22, 2013, https://www.youtube.com/watch?v=gDi3Jl6PuVc (accessed September 16, 2016). This presentation was made as a part of a working discussion group between physicists and materials scientists in this field of work. It is highly technical but worth watching not only for the presentation of the history of development but also just to get an idea of the complexity of the physical systems considered and the scientific tools that are required both to make and characterize materials.

9. In one very much nonstandard part of chip fabrication, the electrostatic attraction of the needlepoint tip of a scanning tunneling microscope (STM) is used for the selective removal of just six adjacent atoms from a protective single-atom-thick layer of hydrogen deposited on the silicon surface. Subsequent exposure to phosphine gas and heating then results in the substitution of just one phosphorous atom for one of the silicon atoms that was exposed by the hydrogen removal. This forms a quantum dot.

10. Michelle Simmons, "Practical Quantum Computing Applications" (public presentation given at *Science at the Shine Dome* under the auspices of the Australian Academy of Sciences, session "Atomic-Scale Electronics"), the speech is available at "Atomic-Scale Electronics for Quantum Computing: Prof. Michelle Simmons—Science at the Shine Dome 15," YouTube video, 14:42, posted by the Australian Academy of Science, May 28, 2015, https://www.youtube.com/watch?v=hg2UUdQm26s&index=7&list=PL9DfJTxCPaXIJZgp6kBprILssq_AEAnY8 (accessed September 16, 2016).

11. All photons are electromagnetic in nature and are polarized so that their tiny electric fields alternate in time in one direction in space, as illustrated in Figure A.1(c) of Appendix A, with related discussion. All polarization possibilities can be represented as the combination of any two perpendicular polarization states, for example, vertical and horizontal polarizations.

12. One particular logic gate, the CNOT gate (not possible with classical bits), operates by flipping the state of a target qubit only if (for example) a second control qubit is in a 1 (as opposed to a 0) state. What makes this process special in another way is that the two qubits can become *entangled* in the CNOT operation, linked together to represent any one of their four so-called Bell states, regardless of how far the qubits may later become physically separated from each other.

13. Reference Z, p. 161.

14. SQUIDs have also been used, for example, for the detection of very small magnetic fields as a way of monitoring heart function, as described in Chapter 19.

15. M. Steffan, D. P. DiVincenzo, J. M. Crow, T. N. Theis, and M. B. Ketchen, "Quantum Computing: An IBM Perspective," *IBM Journal of Research and Development* 55, no. 5, paper 13.

16. Press release issued on D-Wave.com by D-Wave: The Quantum Computing Company, "D-Wave Systems Breaks the 1000 Qubit Quantum Computing Barrier," *D-Wave Systems, Inc.,* June 22, 2015, http://www.dwavesys.com/press -releases/d-wave-systems-breaks-1000-qubit-quantum-computing-barrier.

17. Low temperatures are conveniently represented in Celsius-sized units, but on a Kelvin scale between absolute zero (the lowest temperature attainable), zero degrees Kelvin, and the temperature at which ice freezes, 273 degrees Kelvin. These SQUID-based computers typically operate close to one degree Kelvin, that is, one degree above absolute zero.

18. Jeremy Hsu, "Google's First Quantum Computer," posted September 12, 2014, published in *Superconductivity News Global Edition*, September 22, 2014, http://snf.ieeecsc. org/pages/googles-first-quantum-computer (accessed October 24, 2016); and "Progress in Quantum Computer Error Correction," *Superconductivity News Global Edition*, June 2, 2014, http://snf.ieeecsc.org/pages/progress-quantum-computer-error-correction (accessed October 24, 2016).

19. Lillian Childress, Ronald Walsworth, and Mikhail Lukin, "Atom-like Crystal Defects: From Quantum Computers to Biological Sensors," *Physics Today*, October 2014, pp. 38–43.

20. Ibid., p. 41.

APPENDIX D

1. Richtmyer, Reference G, p. 167.

2. Remember that an atom in its ground state is an atom with all of its lowest energy states occupied by electrons, only one electron per combined spin and spatial state, as required by exclusion.

3. One way that the radius of an atom of an element can be determined is by the diffraction of x-rays from a crystal of that element. At certain angles, x-rays are reflected from the crystal with increased intensity in a way that depends on the wavelength of the x-rays and the spacing between the atoms in the crystal.

4. Though sometimes zinc, cadmium, and mercury are not considered transition metals.

GLOSSARY

Note: Part of this glossary has been copied or modified from that of Reference B, *Physics: Decade by Decade*, with the permission of Alfred B. Bortz.

Explanatory words that are defined elsewhere in this glossary are shown in **bold print**.

absolute frame of reference: see **frame of reference**.

absolute temperature: measured from **absolute zero**, usually in degrees **Kelvin**.

absolute zero: the theoretical minimum of **temperature** that can ever be achieved.

acceleration: how rapidly the speed and/or direction of an object's motion is changed.

actinides: the fourteen **element**s of successively higher **atomic number** following actinium, **atomic number** 89.

alchemy: an early pseudoscience that professed to be able to convert one **element** into another (i.e., lead into gold), before the knowledge of nuclear **fusion** and **fission**, which do under special conditions produce transformations from one **element** to another.

algorithm: a self-contained set of logical mathematical operations. By carrying out these operations, a computer can make judgments or perform calculations based on input information.

alkali metals: the **Group** IA metallic **element**s, **atom**s of which are increasingly reactive (from those of lithium through those of francium) in giving up an **electron** in chemical combination with other **element**s.

alkaline earth metals: the **Group** IIA metallic **element**s, **atom**s of which are increasingly reactive (from those of beryllium through those of radium) in giving up two **electron**s in chemical combination with other **element**s.

alloy: two or more **metal**s melted together as a solution and solidified into one or more solid solution **phase**s.

alpha rays (or **alpha particles**): the least penetrating form of **radio-activity**. Alpha particles are helium nuclei, and the process that produces them is often called **alpha decay**.

amorphous: a kind of solid in which the **atoms** lack the orderly arrangement of a **crystal**.

ampere: a **unit** of current. The flow of electrical charge corresponding in magnitude to the passage of approximately six billion billion **electrons** per second.

angular momentum: a measure of the **mass**, radial extent, and rotating speed of an object. Rotating objects have angular momentum and an **inertia** of rotation in the same sense that traveling objects have **momentum** and an **inertia** of linear motion.

anion: see **ion**.

annihilation: an event in which two particles interact and destroy one another, such as the combination of an **electron** and a **hole** in a **semiconductor** or the combination of a particle and its **antiparticle**.

antimatter: a type of **matter** with identical properties to its normal-**matter** counterpart except for carrying an opposite electric **charge** and **parity**.

antiparticle: see **antimatter**.

ASCII (**American Standard Code for Information Interchange**): the representation of all letters, numbers, and other keyboard elements in a seven-**bit** register.

atom: the smallest particle of a substance that can be identified as a chemical **element**.

atomic number: the number of **protons** in the **nucleus** of an **atom** of an **element**, or the equal number of surrounding **electrons**. Its **atomic number** is used to specify an **element**'s position in the **periodic table**.

atomic weight / atomic mass: a number that specifies the **mass** of a **nucleus**, equal to the total number of **protons** and **neutrons** it contains.

band gap: in solids, a "forbidden" zone, a gap in the band of states available to the **electron**.

baryon: a **subatomic** particle at least as heavy as a **proton**, that is composed of three **quarks** and responds to the **strong nuclear force**.

beta rays (or **beta particles**): a form of **radioactivity** that is more penetrating than alpha rays but less penetrating than gamma rays. Beta particles are **electron**s, and the process that produces them in nuclei is often called **beta decay**.

bit: every yes or no answer to a question represents a single "bit" of information. In computers, a **bit** is represented as a 1 or a 0, perhaps being represented physically by a **transistor** having a high or a low current flow.

blackbody radiation: the electromagnetic **energy** emitted by an object as a consequence of its temperature.

black hole: a collapsed star so dense that nothing can escape from it, including **light**.

Bohr theory: an early **quantum theory** of atomic structure assuming discrete energies for classical-looking **electron** orbits of the **atom**.

boson (gauge boson): generally, a **subatomic** particle with integral **spin**; particularly, a **gauge boson** that is exchanged to create a fundamental force, such as **photon**s for the electromagnetic force, **gluon**s for the **strong nuclear force**, and W and Z particles for the **weak nuclear force**.

bound state: see **energy level**.

BTU (British thermal unit): a **unit** of **energy** equivalent to approximately 0.0003 kilowatt-hours (kWh).

byte: a register of eight **bit**s.

cathode ray: a stream of negative electricity emitted from a hot electrode in a vacuum tube, discovered in 1897 to be comprised of **electron**s.

cation: see **ion**.

Celsius: see **temperature scale**.

chain reaction: a sequence of nuclear fissions in which **neutron**s emitted in one **fission** event cause one or more additional nuclei to **fission**, resulting in a rapid and intense release of **energy**.

charge: a fundamental property of the **electron**, designated by the symbol e. See also **ampere** and **electron volt**.

chemical properties: those properties of the **element**s primarily relating to the electronic structure of its **atom**s, or to the electronic structure of molecules composed of **atom**s.

chemistry: the science of substances and the composition of matter.

classical: reference to the physics that described the universe, and particularly the **atom**, before the advent of **quantum theory** and **quantum mechanics. Classical** physics is still valid for large objects, where even a grain of sand is large.

clock: a signal generator internal to the computer that sets the **frequency** with which a processor can perform sets of operations.

cloud: see **probability cloud.**

cloud chamber: a device in which condensation of a vapor reveals a trail of ions such as those produced along the path of a charged **subatomic** particle; cloud chambers were used in early studies of cosmic rays and **subatomic** particles.

coherence: when two or more **photons are** all in **phase** and of the same **frequency** and **wavelength.**

color: (a) the appearance of an object that has absorbed and therefore not reflected **photon**s of particular **wavelength**s in the visible range, or the appearance of **light** consisting of photons of particular **wavelength**s. (b) the property of a **quark** that interacts with the **strong nuclear force**, equivalent to positive or negative **charge** for the electromagnetic force.

compound: a chemical substance made up of a combination of ele-ment**s** in definite proportions.

conduction band: a set of closely spaced **electron energy level**s in a solid in which the **electron**s belong to no particular **atom**s and thus move freely through the material.

continuous spectrum: see **spectrum.**

Copenhagen interpretation: an understanding of physics that assumes that the **spin and spatial-state** solutions of **Schröding-er's equation** for any physical situation can be used to provide the probability for the location of particles or the occurrence of events, and that the realization of any one of these locations or events occurs only upon observation.

correspondence: a region of physics in which two otherwise- conflicting theories may give the same practical results, one as an approximation to the other.

cosmic rays: energetic particles that come to Earth from distant parts

of the universe or result from the interaction of such particles with the upper reaches of Earth's atmosphere.

cosmological constant: a quantity that arose in Einstein's mathematical description of general relativity; its value and algebraic sign determined the rate of change of the expansion or contraction of the universe.

cosmology: the scientific study of the universe as an entity.

covalent bond: a type of chemical bond in which the participating **atoms** share **electrons**.

critical current: the maximum current that a superconductor can carry without significant **resistance**.

critical temperature: the **temperature** below which a material becomes superconducting.

crystal: a solid substance that is characterized by a regularly repeating three-dimensional arrangement of its **atoms**.

cyclotron: a device that accelerates **subatomic** particles to very high energies as they follow a spiraling path in a very large magnetic field.

d: named after the "diffuse" **spectral line**, used as a label for the **angular momentum quantum number** $l = 2$.

dark energy: a form of **energy** suggested as responsible for the accelerated expansion of our universe over the last six billion years.

dark matter: **matter** that cannot be seen directly but is inferred from its influence on **light** and other **matter** in the cosmos.

decoherence time: the time in which an entangled state can be maintained.

defect: an irregularity in the regular stacking of **atoms** or **molecules** in a crystal.

diode: an electronic device that permits an electric current to pass through in only one direction.

discrete: having one of only a subset of specific allowed values within a continuous range of values. See, for example, **spin** and **spatial-state angular momentum**.

domain: a relatively large region within a **ferromagnetic** material, in which the **spin** and/or **spatial-state** magnetic moments of **atoms** spontaneously align with each other.

drift chamber: a device that uses the electrostatic attraction of **ions**

and **electrons** to determine the track of particles created in particle accelerators.

ductility: the ability to draw a substance into wire—usually related to **metals**.

electrical potential: an electrical field of force and **potential energy** that drives the movement of an **electron**. Measured in **volts**. See also **potential energy**.

electrical resistance: a property of **matter** that impedes the flow of electricity through it.

electrolysis: decomposition produced by passing an electric current through a molten or dissolved **compound**, as for example the decomposition of water, H_2O, into hydrogen and oxygen gases.

electromagnetic waves / electromagnetic radiation: quantum packets of alternating electric and magnetic fields that propagate through space at the **speed of light** and within a **frequency** and **wavelength** range from **radio waves** through **microwaves, light, x-rays, and gamma rays; they are** called **photons** primarily in the visible range of frequencies.

electromagnetism: an aspect of nature that includes both electricity and magnetism, the basis for **electromagnetic waves**, including **light**.

electron: a small **subatomic** particle of **charge** $-e$, found to determine an **atom**'s chemical and electrical behavior and to be useful as the basis for electronic technology.

electron volt (eV): the **energy** change caused by the movement of an **electron** (of **charge e**) through a change in **electrical potential** of one **volt**. Also, the **unit** of measure used to describe an **energy, energy** difference, or **energy level**, as related to the **atom** or objects on an atomic or **subatomic** scale.

element: a chemical substance made up of only one kind of **atom**.

energy: (generally) the ability to cause motion (do work) or **heat** something, defined also as **power** (the rate of delivery or change in **energy**) times time. For electrical systems, **energy** is commonly measured in watt-hours or kilowatt-hours (kWh). Physicists define different forms of **energy** as follows: Objects that move around freely have a *positive, kinetic* **energy** of motion depending on how heavy they are and how fast they are moving. In contrast,

a static object under some force of attraction is said to have a *negative* ***potential*** energy. The **potential energy** is made more negative if the object is placed closer to the source of attraction. The static object could be a hypothetical unmoving planet attracted by the **gravity** of the sun or a hypothetical unmoving **electron** attracted by the pull of its negative **charge** toward the positive **charge**s of the **protons** in an atomic **nucleus**. If an object is in some sense moving (i.e., has **kinetic energy**) in the presence of an attraction, then it can break free of the attraction if its positive **kinetic energy** is larger than its negative **potential energy** so that the sum of the two energies is greater than zero. If this sum is less than zero, negative (that is, if the negative **potential energy** of attraction overcomes the positive **kinetic energy** of motion), then the object will be in a *bound* state, perhaps still moving around in some sense but unable to break completely free of the attraction. The more negative this *total* **energy**, the more tightly the object is bound.

energy level: the net **energy** of an **electron** in an **atom**.

entanglement: see **quantum entanglement**.

exclusion: see **Pauli exclusion principle**.

excited state: a **state** of an **atom** occupied by an **electron** while a lower **energy** state or states are unoccupied.

f: named after the "fundamental" **spectral line**, used as a label for the **angular momentum quantum number** $l = 3$.

Fahrenheit: see **temperature scale**.

ferromagnetism: a property of certain types of **matter**, such as iron, in which the **spin** and/or **spatial-state** magnetic moments of its **atoms** spontaneously align with each other in relatively large regions (**domains**) within the material.

fission: a process in which a **nucleus** of the **atom** of a heavier **element** splits into two smaller nuclei and several **neutrons**, usually with the release of a relatively large amount of *atomic* energy.

flavor: a term used to distinguish the different types of **quarks**; a **quark**'s flavor can be *up, down, strange, charm, top,* or *bottom*.

frame of reference: a point of origin and set of directions in space (such as north–south, east–west, up–down) against which the **relative** position and motion of an object can be specified. The **lumi-**

niferous ether was presumed to be an **absolute**, unmoving frame of reference until Einstein's special **theory** of relativity demonstrated that no such frame exists.

frequency: the rate at which an event repeats itself, such as the *frequency* with which the peaks of a wave passes a particular observation point (with respect to **electromagnetic radiation**, see **Planck's constant**).

fullerenes: a family of geometric structures having a monolayer surface of **atom**s (or **molecules**); one of these structures is the **buckyball**, another is the **nanotube**.

fundamental particles: make up all **matter** as we know it; as three generations of **leptons** and quarks plus gauge **bosons**, the latter carrying the action of the forces of nature.

fusion: a process in which the nuclei of the **atoms** of lighter **elements** are joined (usually under extremely high temperatures and pressures) to form the **nucleus** of a heavier **atom**, usually with the release of other particles and a relatively large amount of *thermonuclear* **energy**.

gamma rays (or **gamma radiation**): the most penetrating form of **radioactivity**. Gamma rays are high-**energy photons**.

gate: a set of **transistors** (**bits**) that can operate together to perform some logical function.

generic table of states: one table representing the many different actual tables of states, one each for the **atoms** of every **element**.

glass: an **amorphous** solid or a liquid of such high viscosity that it appears to be a solid.

gluon: the gauge **boson** exchanged between **quarks**, thereby acting as the carrier of the **strong nuclear force**.

grain: a crystalline region of particular orientation within a polycrystalline substance consisting of grains of many different orientations. See also **recrystallization**.

Grand Unification Theory (GUT): a goal of theoretical physicists who are seeking a **theory** to unify all the fundamental forces.

graphene: the basic structural configuration for many forms of carbon, including some **fullerenes**, including **nanotubes**, and the more familiar graphite, charcoal, and soot.

gravity / gravitational field: a basic force of nature that creates an

attraction between any two bodies that have **mass**. The attraction of **gravity** on a **mass** produces a force that we measure as **weight**.

ground state: the situation in an **atom** when its **electrons** all occupy the lowest **energy** states available to them.

groups: sets of **elements** with similar chemical properties, one group per column of our modern **periodic table**.

halogens: **element**s in Group VIIA of the **periodic table**, whose atoms are very aggressive in seeking to gain one **electron** in reaction with other **elements**.

heat: see **temperature**.

hole: a region in a **semiconductor** in which an **electron** is missing and behaves as if it is a mobile positive **charge**.

hybridization: the combination of the states of the **electron** in an **atom** to form a new set of states with energies more favorable to a particular bonding situation.

hypothesis: the yet-to-be-tested suggestion of a **theory** or **law**.

inflation: a **theory** that explains the unexpected uniformity of the cosmic background radiation by a very brief period just after the big bang when the cosmos and **space-time** itself expanded at a rate much faster than the speed of **light**.

inert: in reference to the **noble gases**, the tendency of an **atom** of an **element** not to react or combine with other **atoms** to form **molecules**.

inertia: proportional to **mass**, the tendency for an object in motion to stay in motion or an object at rest to stay at rest.

interference: a phenomenon that occurs when waves overlap; for two **light** waves of the same **wavelength**, this results in a series of bright and dark bands.

ion: an electrically charged **atom** (or combination of **atoms**). An **atom** with positive **charge** through the loss of one or more **electrons** is called a **cation**. An **atom** with negative **charge** through the acquisition of one or more **electrons** is called an **anion**.

ionic bond: a type of chemical bond in which the participating **atoms** exchange **electrons**, thereby becoming oppositely charged **ions** held together by electrical attraction.

ionization: the creation of electrically charged **atoms** (or combinations of **atoms**) called **ions**.

ionization energy: the positive **energy** that must be supplied to lift an **electron** free of its bound, negative **energy**-level state in an **atom** or **ion**. Usually in relation to the outermost, least negative **energy**-level **electron**s.

isotope: one of several nuclei with the same **atomic number** but different atomic **masses**.

Josephson junction: consists of two superconductors coupled by a weak link, which can be either a thin insulator, a short section of a normal **metal**, or a weakened superconductor. It has important application in quantum-mechanical circuits, such as **SQUIDs** and **qubits**.

Kelvin: see **temperature scale**.

key: a string of **bits** used, for example, in the one-time pad to encode and decode a message.

key distribution: the method used to distribute the **key** to one or more receivers of a coded message.

kinetic energy: see **energy**.

l: the **angular momentum quantum number**.

Lamb shift: a slight splitting in the **spectrum** of hydrogen, first observed by Willis Lamb and critical to understanding **quantum electrodynamics**.

lanthanides: the fourteen **elements** of successively higher **atomic number** following lanthanum, **atomic number** 57.

large object: something of a size observable in an optical microscope, or larger.

laser: **light** amplification through the stimulated emission of radiation, in which **photons** released in the **transition** of an **electron** from one higher **energy state** to a specific lower **energy** state in an **atom** stimulate similar **transitions** in other **atoms** to create a pulse or beam of **coherent light**.

law: see **theory**.

lepton: a **light subatomic** particle that does not respond to the **strong nuclear force**; **leptons** include **electrons**, **muons**, taus, and their neutrinos and **antiparticles**.

light: **electromagnetic radiation** in the visible range of **frequency** and **wavelength**.

line spectrum: see **spectral line.**

luminiferous ether: a hypothetical substance once presumed to permeate all space as the carrier of **electromagnetic waves.**

m: the magnetic **quantum number.**

macroscopic: the quality of being directly observable with the human eye.

magnetic moment: for the purposes of this book, something to be visualized as having the properties of a tiny bar magnet.

main groups: the eight **groups** of the **periodic table** whose **elements** have outer **electrons** in the s and p blocks of states.

malleability: a property, usually of **metals** and **alloys,** that allows them to be pressed or hammered into different shapes.

many worlds: the idea that all possible outcomes of an event are represented in separate worlds, each of which includes the observers of the outcome.

mass: a measure of the amount of **matter. Mass** has **inertia,** and in a gravitational field is acted upon by a force that we call **weight.**

matter: any collection of particles.

Maxwell's equations: a set of four formulas that describe the interrelationships between **electricity** and **magnetism** and predict the existence of **electromagnetic waves** that travel at the **speed of light.**

meson: a middle-**weight subatomic** particle that consists of a **quark** and an antiquark; the first usage of the term referred to pions.

metal: an **element** that tends to give up **electrons** in combination with other **elements;** this includes most of the **elements** toward the bottom and left of our **periodic table,** and which become increasingly metallic in that direction. **Metals** conduct electricity, and they tend to exhibit a lustrous appearance and to be **malleable** and **ductile.**

metalloid: also known as a **semiconductor** or **semimetal, this is** an **element** whose **atoms** have properties between those of the **metals** and those of the **nonmetals.**

microscopic: requiring the use of an optical microscope to be seen.

microwaves: see **electromagnetic radiation.**

molecule: a combination of **atoms** making up the smallest particle of a substance that can be identified as a particular **compound.**

momentum: the **mass** of an object times its velocity.

MRI (magnetic resonance imaging): uses the sensitivity to chemical surroundings of the spins of the nuclei of certain **element**s to view the tissues of the body.

muon: a **subatomic** particle that is the second-generation equivalent of the **electron** in the **Standard Model**.

n: the primary **quantum number**.

nanotube: or, more specifically, the *carbon nanotube* has been made as narrow as one nanometer in diameter, the span of about seven carbon **atom**s; these tubes can be made millions of times longer than their diameters.

neutron: a **subatomic** particle with slightly more **mass** than a **proton** but without electric **charge**; **nuclei** are made up of **protons** and **neutrons** bound together by a **strong nuclear force**.

neutron star: a super-dense star in which all its **matter** has been compressed into **neutrons** (see also **pulsar**).

noble gases: those **elements** whose **atoms** tend to be **inert**. They are listed in the **Group VIIIA** column of the modern **periodic table**.

nonmetal: an **element** that tends to acquire **electrons** in combination with other **elements**; most of the **elements** toward the top and extreme right of the **periodic table** are increasingly nonmetallic in that direction.

n-**type semiconductor:** a **semiconductor** with an excess of **electrons** over **holes**.

nucleon: a **proton** or **neutron**; the atomic **mass** of a **nucleus** is the total number of **nucleons** it contains.

nucleus: (plural: **nuclei**) the tiny, positively **charged** central part of an **atom** that contains most of its **mass**; the **nucleus** is composed of **protons** and **neutrons**.

one-time pad: a method of encryption that allows a single **key** (string of **bits**) to be used for coding and decoding a message.

orbital: what we in this book call a "**spatial state**" because the term *orbital*, retained from the early days of developing **quantum theory**, misleadingly connotes a specifically located particle and orbit. See **spatial state**.

p: named after the "principal" **spectral line**, used as a label for the **angular momentum quantum number** $l = 1$.

parity: an inherent left- or right-handedness of a subatomic particle.

Pauli exclusion principle: also called **exclusion**—originally that no two electrons can occupy the same state. More generally, that no two indistinguishable fermions can do so.

periodic table of the elements: an arrangement of the chemical elements in rows and columns that reveals similarities in their physical and chemical properties.

phase: (a) liquid, solid, or gas, or a solid with a particular crystalline stacking of **atoms**; or (b) the relative alignment of waves of the same **wavelength** and **frequency**, as to whether their peaks line up or are shifted somewhat "out of **phase**."

photoelectric effect: a phenomenon in which shining a **light** can cause **electrons** to be emitted from a **metal** surface.

photon: a **quantum** or packet of **light** or electromagnetic **energy**.

Planck's constant: a fundamental ratio in nature that relates the **energy** of a **quantum** to the **frequency** of its corresponding electromagnetic wave.

polarization: either a **photon** having either plus or minus one **unit** of **angular momentum or a molecule** having poles of net plus or minus **charge** concentration.

positron: the **antimatter** counterpart of an **electron**.

potential energy: see **energy**.

power: the rate of delivery or change of **energy** from one form to another. For electrical systems it is usually measured in **watts**. It is the **electric potential** (that drives the flow of **electrons**, usually measured in **volts**) times the flow of the **electrons** (comprising the electrical **current**, usually measured in **amperes**). When the current and voltage are in **phase**, one **volt-ampere** = one watt. For motors, generators, and large electrical delivery systems, **power** is often measured in **megavolt amperes (MVA)**, and that part of the **energy** actually consumed (the in-**phase** voltage and current component) is measured in **megawatts**.

precipitate: the appearance of one **phase** within another **phase**, as in the precipitation of water droplets out of the air or of one solid **phase** of an **alloy** out of another primary solid **phase**.

prime number: an integer that can be divided evenly only by the number 1 and itself.

privatdozent: a lecturer in Germany or Switzerland who was paid

directly by his students and given a place to teach but without a professorial position at the university.

probability cloud: a visual representation for any particular **spatial-state** solution to **Schrödinger's equation** in which the probability of finding an **electron** at any point in space surrounding the **nucleus** of an **atom** is portrayed in the figures and tables of this book as whiteness (in proportion to the probability) against a black background.

processor: that part of a computer that manipulates information, usually according to a set of instructions.

proton: a **subatomic** particle having one **unit** of positive electric **charge** and one **unit** of atomic **mass**; the **nucleus** of normal hydrogen is a single proton.

pulsar: a type of star that produces **light** that pulsates at very regular intervals, now known to be a rapidly rotating **neutron** star.

p-**type semiconductor:** a **semiconductor** with an excess of **holes** over **electrons**.

quantum (plural: **quanta**): a packet of **energy** devised by Planck to explain the shape of blackbody radiation; later generalized to be a packet of any physical entity, such as electric **charge** or a particle's **angular momentum**, that varied in steps rather than continuously.

quantum dots: nanoscale local peaks (on the surface of a solid) in the attraction of **electron**s to the positive **charge**s of the nuclei of **atom**s.

quantum electrodynamics (QED): a subfield of physics that restructures Maxwell's **theory** so that it is consistent with the **quantum** nature of **matter** and **energy**.

quantum entanglement: a phenomenon in which determination of the **quantum** state of one particle immediately affects the **quantum** state of another particle some distance away because a relationship between those states had been established previously; Einstein referred to the phenomenon, when first predicted, as "spooky action at a distance."

quantum mechanics: the formal mathematical formulation of the broader **quantum theory**.

quantum number: a value that describes a physical property that can take on integer multiples of a fundamental value, such as **Planck's constant** (or half-integer values, in the case of **spin**).

quantum states: see **spatial state** and **spin**.

quantum theory: either the early quasi-**classical** ideas used to portray the **atom**, otherwise generally known as the **Bohr theory**, or the overall description of a subfield of physics based on the **quantum** description of **matter** and **energy** as having a dual wave-particle nature, more formally and mathematically characterized as **quantum mechanics**.

quark: a type of **subatomic** particle that is considered the fundamental building block of **baryon**s and **meson**s, that is, particles that interact via the **strong nuclear force**.

qubit: a **quantum bit**; unlike **classical bits**, the qubit can simultaneously represent a 1 and a 0 or combinations of both.

radioactivity: the spontaneous **fission** (splitting apart) of an atomic **nucleus**.

radio waves: see **electromagnetic radiation**.

recrystallization: the growth of new, relatively **defect**-free, **crystalline grain**s from the **defect**-ridden grains within a work-hardened **metal** or **alloy**.

reduction: the argument that the properties of the **elements** and the **periodic table** can be completely derived directly from the underlying physics. (We do not claim that here.)

register: a succession of **bits**.

relative frame of reference: see **frame of reference**.

renormalization: a mathematical technique applied to **quantum electrodynamics** that enables the equation to handle infinities that were problems in previous approaches.

resistance: the resistance to the flow of electrical current in a wire or circuit. In Standard International (SI) **units** it is measured (in *ohms*) as the electrical potential (in *volts*) applied to a wire or circuit divided by the electrical current that then flows through it as a result as measured (in *amperes*).

resistivity: the intrinsic **resistance** to the flow of electrical current in a **metal**, **insulator**, or **semiconductor**. It is usually presented in

ohm-cm **units**, which when multiplied by the length of the material and divided by the area of its cross section provides a measure of the **resistance** of an actual piece of material.

resonance: a phenomenon with a natural **frequency** that occurs in response to stimulation, such as the vibration of a the string or air column of a musical instrument.

s: named after the "sharp" **spectral line**, used as a label for the **angular momentum quantum number** $l = 0$.

salt: an ionic combination of **elements** to make a **molecule** that tends to dissolve in water into constituent **ions** (e.g., common table salt, NaCl).

scattering: a phenomenon in which a stream of particles or **energy** is diverted by interaction with a target. The resulting pattern reveals details of the target, as the scattering of alpha particles revealed the nuclear structure of **atoms**.

Schrödinger's equation: one of several approaches to the mathematical formulation of **quantum mechanics**. The **energy** of a system is expressed in terms of **wavefunctions** which by the **Copenhagen interpretation** can be used to determine the probability of events or the location of particles.

screening: in the many-**electron** atom, the tendency of **electrons** with their negative **charges** to reduce the apparent **charge** of the **nucleus** seen by other **electrons**.

semiconductor: (adj.: semiconducting) a material with electrical properties between that of an **insulator** and a **metal**; the electrical conductivity of a **semiconductor** can be controlled by making small changes to its composition. Also called a **metalloid** or a **semimetal**.

semimetal: see **metalloid** or **semiconductor**.

shell: a set of states corresponding to particular **quantum numbers**. The chemical properties of **elements** show periodic behavior depending on the degree to which the states in particular **shells** are occupied.

small object: something so small as not to be observable in an optical microscope.

solid-state physics: a subfield of physics dealing with the properties

of solid **matter**, later included in the broader category of condensed **matter** physics.

solution: a mixture of substances on an atomic or molecular scale so as to form a homogeneous single **phase**.

sound: the ear's sensing of waves of vibrations of **molecules** in the air or in liquid or solid substances, with the pitch increasing with the **frequency** of the vibrations and the corresponding decrease in **wavelength**.

space-time: a four-dimensional combination of space and time that resulted from Einstein's theory of relativity.

spatial state: one of the possible **quantum states** for the **electron around the nucleus** in an **atom**, as distinct from the **intrinsic spin** state of the **electron** that is present whether or not the **electron** is in an atom. Each **quantum spatial state** has a **discrete energy**, magnitude of **angular momentum**, and **magnetic moment**. In the **Copenhagen interpretation** of Schrödinger's **wave-mechanics**, the **spatial state** is a spread-out and diffuse **wavefunction** with these **discrete** properties that can be used to calculate or estimate the probability (in this book, **clouds**) for the spatial location of an **electron** around the **nucleus** of an **atom**.

spectral line: a measured distinct specific **wavelength** or **frequency** of electromagnetic **radiation** (specifically, a distinct **color** within the visible **light** spectrum), often produced by the emission of **photons** in the **transition** of **electrons** from one **energy level** to another in an **atom**.

spectral-line splitting: a phenomenon in which a single **spectral line** splits into several with the application of an external influence such as an electric or magnetic field.

spectrograph: an optical device that separates the **photons** of **light** (or other **electromagnetic waves**) according to their **wavelengths** where the photons produce markings on a screen.

spectrometer: an optical device that separates the **photons** of **light** (or other **electromagnetic waves**) according to their **wavelengths** and measures the intensity of the **light** (number of photons) at each **wavelength** and corresponding **frequency**.

spectrum: the various **colors** contained in **light**, or more generally the various **wavelength** in any **energy** carrying waves, often displayed as a continuous graph of intensity versus **wavelength** or as a series of lines specifying intensity (number of **photons**) at specific **wavelengths**.

speed of light, c: the speed with which all **electromagnetic radiation** propagates through empty space, approximately three hundred million meters per second.

spin: a fundamental property of an **electron**, represented by a plus or minus **quantum number** that corresponds to its intrinsic **angular momentum** and **magnetism**.

SQUID (superconducting quantum interference device): is built of superconducting lops containing Josephson junctions. It can be used for **quantum** computing, communication, and extremely sensitive measurements of magnetic fields.

Standard Model of particle physics: a description of the fundamental particles that make up all **matter** as we know it as three generations of **leptons** and **quarks** plus gauge **bosons**; the latter are exchanged to create a fundamental force, such as **photons** for the electromagnetic force.

standing wave: a wave or wavelike mathematical function or variation in a physical property, in which a spatially fixed pattern of peaks and valleys oscillates in time from positive to negative values and back continuously.

state: see **excited state**, **spatial state**, and **spin state**.

strangeness: a **quantum** mechanical property that was found to be conserved during transformations of **subatomic** particles under the influence of the **strong nuclear force**, later recognized as the total number of strange **quarks**.

string theory: a mathematical approach devised to unify the fundamental forces and explain fundamental particles as allowed vibrations on a ten-dimensional string.

strong force: the force that binds the **neutrons** and **protons** together in the **nucleus** of **atoms**, overcoming the mutual repulsion of the positively **charged** **photons**.

strong nuclear force: a fundamental force of nature that acts between

quarks and is responsible for binding **protons** and **neutrons** together in **nuclei.**

subatomic: on the scale of the constituents of the **atom: electrons**, the constituents of the atomic **nucleus** and various other particles.

submicroscopic: smaller than what can be seen with an optical microscope.

superconductivity: a **quantum** mechanical property of certain substances that causes them to lose all **resistance** to electric current below a certain **critical temperature.**

superfluidity: a **quantum** mechanical property observed in liquid helium in which it loses all viscosity, or **resistance** to flow below a certain **critical temperature.**

superstring theory: an improvement on **string theory** that adds an eleventh dimension.

temperature: a measure of the **energy** of particles, for example, the degree to which the **atoms** in a solid substance are agitated by heating, with those feeling hot to the touch jostling with greater **energy** than the atoms in the fingers that sense them.

temperature scale: in this book, either of three **temperature** scales: The **Fahrenheit** scale, which observes the melting point of water (at a standard atmospheric pressure) as 32 degrees and the boiling point of water as 212 degrees; the **Celsius** scale, which observes the melting point of water (at a standard atmospheric pressure) as zero degrees and the boiling point of water as 100 degrees; and the **Kelvin** scale, which has the same **units** of **temperature** as the **Celsius** scale but starts from the absolute zero of **temperature** and observes the melting point of water as 273 degrees and the boiling point of water as 373 degrees.

theory: a well-tested and predictive set of ideas, otherwise often called a **law**, as distinct from a **hypothesis**, which is an as-yet-untested suggested **theory** or set of ideas.

tokomak: a device to convert the **energy** of controlled **fusion** into electrical **power**, specifically one that traps a hot **fusion** plasma within a magnetic field that circles on itself in a toroidal (donut-shaped) geometry.

torus: (adj.: toroidal) a donut-like shape.

transistor: an electronic device made of semiconducting material that can function as an amplifier or a controllable switch.

transition: the change in occupancy of **states** of the **electron** in an **atom**, usually caused by the absorption or resulting from the emission of a **photon**.

transition elements / transition metals: the **elements** listed in the center blocks of our **periodic table**, those specifically tending to have the outermost **electrons** of their **atoms** primarily in either **d** or **f** states.

transmutation: the transformation of one **nucleus** into another by a radioactive emission.

transuranic elements: chemical **elements** with **atomic numbers** greater than uranium's 92.

uncertainty principle: a consequence of the **quantum** nature of **matter** and **energy** discovered by Werner Heisenberg, stating the existence of natural limits on the certainty and precision of measurement of the paired quantities **energy** and time or position and momentum.

unit: a standard quantity for projecting by **theory** or measuring, such as the pound or the kilogram for projecting or measuring **weight**, or the **Celsius** degree or the **Fahrenheit** degree for projecting or measuring **temperature**.

valence: a property of an **atom** expressed as a positive or negative number that describes the way that the atom accepts or contributes **electrons** in a chemical reaction.

valence band: a set of closely spaced **electron energy levels** in a solid in which the **electrons** are shared among a few **atoms** and are involved in chemical bonding within the material.

volt: a **unit** of **electrical potential**.

wavefunction: a mathematical representation used in the **Schrödinger equation** that describes the position of an object as a diffuse and spread out or wavelike variation in space rather than as a fixed point.

wavelength: the distance between successive peaks of a wave or wavelike entity.

weak nuclear force: a fundamental force of nature that acts within the **nucleus** and governs the process of beta decay.

weight: see gravity.

x-ray: a **photon** released during the **transition** of an **electron** into one of the inner, most negative **energy states** of one of the heavier **elements**. (See also **electromagnetic** radiation.)

x-ray diffraction: a phenomenon in which the interaction of x-rays with a solid produce a pattern of **interference** that reveals information about the solid's crystal structure.

REFERENCES AND RECOMMENDED READING

A. McEvoy, J. P., and Oscar Zarate. *Introducing Quantum Theory*. Cambridge, UK: Icon Books, 2004.

B. Bortz, Alfred B. *Physics: Decade by Decade*. Twentieth Century Science. New York: Facts on File, 2007.

C. Greene, Brian. *The Fabric of the Cosmos*. New York: Vintage Books, 2004.

D. Scerri, Eric R. *The Periodic Table*. New York: Oxford University Press, 2007.

E. Fine, Leonard W., and Herbert Beall. *Chemistry for Engineers and Scientists*. Orlando, FL: Saunders College Publishing, 1990.

F. Leighton, Robert B. *Principles of Modern Physics*. New York: McGraw-Hill, 1959.

G. Richtmyer, F. K., E. H. Kennard, and T. Lauritsen. *Introduction to Modern Physics*. New York: McGraw-Hill, 1955.

H. Housecroft, Christine E., and Alan G. Sharpe. *Inorganic Chemistry*. 3rd ed. Edinburgh Gate, Harlow, England: Pearson Education, 2008.

I. Sachs, Oliver. *Uncle Tungsten: Memories of a Chemical Boyhood*. New York: Alfred A. Knopf, 2001.

J. Morrish, Allan H. *The Physical Principles of Magnetism*. New York: John Wiley & Sons, 1965.

K. Kumar, Manjit. *Quantum: Einstein, Bohr, and the Great Debate about the Nature of Reality*. New York: Norton, 2010.

L. Orzel, Chad. *How to Teach Physics to Your Dog*. New York: Scribner, 2009.

M. Moore, Walter. *Schrödinger: Life and Thought*. Cambridge, UK, and New York: Cambridge University Press, 1992.

N. Gordin, Michael D. *A Well-Ordered Thing: Demitrii Mendeleev and the Shadow of the Periodic Table*. New York: Basic Books, Perseus Books Group, 2004.

O. Strathern, Paul. *Mendeleyev's Dream: The Quest for the Elements.* London, UK: Penguin Books, 2000.

P. Pauling, Linus. *The Nature of the Chemical Bond.* 3rd ed. Ithaca, NY: Cornell University Press, 1960.

Q. Feynman, Richard. *QED: The Strange Theory of Light and Matter.* Princeton, NJ: Princeton University Press, 1985.

R. Kean, Sam. *The Disappearing Spoon, and Other True Tales of Madness, Love, and the History of the World from the Periodic Table of the Elements.* New York: Little, Brown, 2010.

S. Gribbin, John. *In Search of Schrödinger's Cat: Quantum Physics and Reality.* New York: Bantam Books, 1984.

T. Kuhn, Thomas S. *The Structure of Scientific Revolutions.* 50th anniv. ed. Chicago: University of Chicago Press, 2012.

U. Toback, David. *Big Bang, Black Holes, No Math.* Dubuque, IA: Kendall Hunt, 2013.

V. Kittel, Charles. *Introduction to Solid State Physics.* 6th ed. New York: Wiley & Sons, 1986.

W. Hawking, Stephen. *A Brief History of Time.* New York: Bantam Books, 1988.

X. Rosenblum, Bruce, and Fred Kuttner. *Quantum Enigma: Physics Encounters Consciousness.* New York: Oxford University Press, 2011.

Y. Schumacher, Benjamin. *Quantum Mechanics: The Physics of the Microscopic World.* Chantilly, VA: Great Courses, 2009. DVD.

Z. Gribbin, John. *Computing with Quantum Cats.* Amherst, NY: Prometheus Books, 2014.

AA. Greene, Brian. *The Hidden Reality: Parallel Universes and the Deep Laws of the Cosmos.* New York: Alfred A. Knopf, 2011.

BB. Susskind, Leonard. *The Black Hole War: My Battle with Stephen Hawking to Make the World Safe for Quantum Mechanics.* New York: Back Bay Books, 2008.

CC. Parker, Barry. *Einstein's Brainchild: Relativity Made Relatively Easy.* Amherst, NY: Prometheus Books, 2007.

DD. "Extreme Physics." Special issue, *Scientific American* 22, no. 2 (Summer 2013).

EE. Bortz, Fred. *Exploring the Subatomic World.* 7 vols. New York: Cavendish Square, 2015–2016. Some volumes of this series are coauthored with B. H. Fields.

FF. Bojowald, Martin. *Once Before Time: A Whole Story of the Universe.* New York, Vintage Books, 2010.

GG. Coles, Peter. *Cosmology: A Very Short Introduction.* New York: Oxford University Press, 2001.

HH. Barnett, R. Michael, Henry Muhry, and Helen R. Quinn. *The Charm of Strange Quarks.* New York: Springer-Verlag, 2000.

II. Gubser, Steven S. *The Little Book of String Theory.* Princeton, NJ: Princeton University Press, 2010.

JJ. Warner, Jamie H., Franziska Schaffel, Alicja Bachmatuik, and Mark H. Rummemeli. *Graphene: Fundamentals and Emergent Applications.* New York: Elsevier, 2013.

KK. Wiggins, Arthur W., and Charles M. Wynn. *The Human Side of Science* Amherst, NY: Prometheus Books, 2016.

LL. Gribbon, John. *13.8: The Quest to Find the True Age of the Universe and the Theory of Everything.* New Haven, CT: Yale University Press, 2016.

INDEX

Page numbers in **bold** indicate photos, charts, and tables.

Fig. 9.3. Top and side views of a spiral galaxy, our Milky Way. Stars orbit a miniature elliptical-galaxy-like central bulge with a supermassive black hole at its center. We do not see the dark matter that is also present. The galaxy is like a thin disk, approximately one million billion miles thick, and fifty times as wide. (Image from NASA/JPL-Caltech.)

Fig. 9.4. Example of an elliptical galaxy, the gargantuan NGC 1132, the bright region at the center of the photo. Stars trace out elliptical orbits in all manner of orientations about the center of the galaxy. (Image from NASA, ESA, and the Hubble Heritage [STSeI/AURA]-ESA/Hubble Collaboration; acknowledgment: M. West [ESO, Chile].)

Fig. 9.5. Illustration of a stellar black hole (*at the left*) attracting atoms from a blueish-appearing star (*at the right*). As material falls into the hole, vertical-directed beams of light are released. (Image of x-ray from NASA/CXC/M. Weiss; image of optical from Digitized Sky Survey.)